Gardens *for a* Beautiful America

1895–1935

[*Frontispiece*]   MOUNT VERNON, GEORGE WASHINGTON HOUSE, MOUNT VERNON, VIRGINIA

Privy in Vegetable Garden, 1894

Gardens *for a* Beautiful America

1895–1935

PHOTOGRAPHS BY FRANCES BENJAMIN JOHNSTON

Sam Watters

Preface by C. Ford Peatross

PUBLISHED IN COLLABORATION WITH THE LIBRARY OF CONGRESS

Acanthus Press

NEW YORK : 2012

ACANTHUS PRESS LLC
1133 Broadway, Ste. 1229
New York, New York 10010
212-414-0108
www.acanthuspress.com

FOR THIS EDITION, 50 COPIES HAVE BEEN BOUND
IN HALF LEATHER AND ARE NUMBERED 1 TO 50

No.

This book has been supported by a grant from Furthermore: a program of the J. M. Kaplan Fund
All photographs of and by Frances Benjamin Johnston are courtesy of the Library of Congress
A Classical America Series in Art and Architecture publication

LIBRARY OF CONGRESS CATALOGING-IN-PUBLICATION DATA

Watters, Sam, 1954-
Gardens for a beautiful America 1895-1935 : photographs by Frances
Benjamin Johnston / Sam Watters ; preface by C. Ford Peatross.
p. cm.
Includes bibliographical references and index.
ISBN 978-0-926494-15-2
1. Gardening--United States--Pictorial works. 2. Gardening--United
States--History. 3. Gardens, American--Pictorial works. 4. Gardens,
American--History. 5. Johnston, Frances Benjamin, 1864-1952--Photograph
collections. 6. Women photographers--France--Paris--History--20th century.
I. Title.
SB451.3.W38 2012
635.0973--dc23
2011046568

PRINTED IN CHINA

Contents

Preface

Sumptuous and scholarly, *Gardens for a Beautiful America, 1895–1935, Photographs by Frances Benjamin Johnston,* provides both a time machine and a magic carpet capable of transporting us back to a lost, golden age in the development of the American garden. We can travel from north to south, east to west, and coast to coast, from Bar Harbor to Charleston, Southampton to Santa Barbara, and places in between. We can pass through the gated entrances of the wealthy and privileged to gaze upon gardens of enormous scale and beauty, and then travel to Italy, France, and England to see famous gardens from which Americans drew inspiration. We can observe the gardens of aspiring middle-class Americans and also see gardens intended to bring a better life to city dwellers and factory workers. These American gardens were meant not only to delight the senses but also to serve as vessels of identity and engines of change.

The hand-colored glass-plate lantern slides so faithfully reproduced herein have not been seen in their full glory for more than 70 years, when their seductive imagery and subtle colors were projected before elite audiences fortunate enough to attend one of Frances Benjamin Johnston's garden lectures. An artist as well as a photographer, Johnston carefully conceived and composed her lantern-slide "paintings" and guided their coloring to have the maximum effect, to inform and to educate during this revolution in American garden design. Some of these images are of such beauty that they take your breath away. The eminent designer Frederick Law Olmsted Jr. considered Johnston's lantern slides to be "the finest existing on the subject of American gardens."

Frances Benjamin Johnston was a protean figure—pioneer photographer, photojournalist, and visual artist—who moved with equal ease among presidents and plutocrats, reformers, architects, designers, publishers, and promoters. Johnston was a force of nature who passed through her world like a fresh breeze, bending the stiff backs of convention and clearing the air to allow us to see and understand her subjects in new ways. Those touched by the power of her personality, images, and ideas were rarely left unchanged. Seemingly unforgettable, she nevertheless has almost been forgotten. This publication, with its groundbreaking research, will go far to correct that deficiency and allow us to begin to recognize and evaluate her accomplishments anew.

We thank Sam Watters and Acanthus Press for bringing Johnston and her times back to life so magnificently. Proof of the many sources consulted and the many miles traveled to develop this well-rounded history of garden photography is in the extensive acknowledgments. With a fervent passion for and knowledge of his subject, Sam has painstakingly examined Johnston and her work within the rich and complex artistic, social, and historical context of her time. It was an era in which the American garden came of age, defined and promoted by a flourishing garden club movement that used the garden to serve multiple agendas. Johnston's clients, colleagues, and associates represented a "Who's Who" of the first half of the "American Century" and of the American Renaissance in architecture and landscape design.

Since the 1930s, the Library of Congress has been working to preserve and make available for study and research what became a vast archive of Johnston's photographs and papers. Leicester B. Holland, chief of the Library's Fine Arts Division, chairman of the Committee on the Preservation of Historic Buildings of the American Institute of Architects, and, not incidentally, author of *The Gardening Blue Book: A Manual of the Perennial Garden* (1915), recognized Johnston's talent by providing tangible support. In 1930, he exhibited her Fredericksburg Survey prints and also purchased some of her negatives for "the purpose of creating a national foundation for the study of early American architecture and of garden design."

The digitization of the colored lantern slides used in Johnston's garden lectures represents the culmination of the library's efforts. With the catalog information provided by Sam Watters, these images will now shine forth as a jewel in the crown of Johnston's achievements, representing her incomparable legacy to the American people and to the world. They join the documentary records of the Historic American Landscapes Survey, the early Papers of the American Society of Landscape Architects, the Papers of Frederick Law Olmsted and Olmsted Associates, and many other collections in the Library of Congress. Together these basic tools advance our understanding and appreciation of the varied roles that the garden has occupied in our national life and of the garden's ongoing potential to improve and enrich the daily existence of all Americans. As Thomas Jefferson wrote to Charles Willson Peale in August of 1811: "No occupation is so delightful to me as the culture of the earth, and no culture comparable to that of the garden ... But though an old man, I am but a young gardener."

—C. FORD PEATROSS
THE LIBRARY OF CONGRESS
OCTOBER 2011

Introduction

Miss Johnston is a lady, and whom I personally know & can vouch for; she does good work, and any promise she makes she will keep. —Theodore Roosevelt to Admiral George Dewey, 1899

In 1930 the popular garden chronicler Marion Cran traveled from her home in Kent, England to assess America's gardening achievements. From New England, through the Midwest, out to California, and to the mid-Atlantic, she visited the gardens of businessmen and movie stars. She spoke to gardeners and plantsmen, small-house owners and park superintendents, many of them no doubt unsuspecting the pithy account to follow in her 1932 *Gardens in America*, the early critical view of gardening she wrote from her experiences across the continent.

When Cran arrived in century-old Washington, D.C., which she observed would "soon" be the most beautiful city in the world, she whirled her way through diplomatic receptions and official meetings. She met "other enchanting people such as Frances Benjamin Johnston, whose wonderful photographs are kept in the Library of Congress; she is one of the women one does not forget; joyous and vigorous; difficult and gentle. Her garden pictures are the best I have seen in my life."[1]

Johnston (FBJ) was the only photographer Cran deemed noteworthy for her book, and she was not alone in her regard. The critic Royal Cortissoz thought Johnston's images of European gardens were "striking" and not "forced." Landscape designer and photographer Mary Rutherford Jay wrote that FBJ's work convinced her of "the need of having proper photos of my gardens."[2] By the time Cran reached Washington,

upper-middle-class magazines had published Johnston's photographs for 20 years and garden club members and landscape architects had collected her prints for study and exhibition. These were the images, as well as photographs by Johnston's contemporaries, that had lured Cran to America.

Frances Benjamin Johnston (1864–1952) was born one year before the close of the Civil War and died seven years after the bombing of Nagasaki, Japan. An educated woman needing to make a living, she pragmatically forged a 60-year career. As an American working in a progressive era, she combined advocacy for social change with strategies for paying the rent. She began in the 1880s as a photojournalist and promoted photography as a profession for women. When magazines devoted to the new American home emerged from 1900, she used her professional skills to become a house and garden photographer. From 1910 until the mid-1930s, she photographed gardens for house owners, editors, and landscape architects. With photographs from these commissions, she produced glass slides for lectures she delivered across America to advance the Garden Beautiful movement and to enhance her reputation as an artist, lecturer, and garden authority.

In 1930 Johnston conceived creating "a national foundation for the study of Early American Architecture and of Garden Design" at the Library of Congress, with her manuscript and photograph collections as its archive.[3] She had matured in an era when the farm gave way to the urban factory, leaving a deep sense of loss alleviated by a faith in progress to overcome inequalities in all spheres. FBJ's response to this profound change was her architectural photography, which began with houses and gardens in the 1920s and ended with historic buildings in the 1930s. The library's ultimate acquisition of Johnston's collections from her estate was an apt conclusion to the photographer's career documenting American life.

Johnston was prescient in her intention to secure her archive for future study and recognition. With few exceptions, the fate of garden photographs has been grim. Heirs, public institutions, and photographers themselves dispersed and trashed collections they considered merely illustration. Those photographers who have received attention, including Jessie Tarbox Beals, Mattie Edwards Hewitt, and Loring Underwood, are remembered not because their photographs are necessarily the best or representative, but because their archives, at least in part, survive.

FBJ has been the subject of biographies, articles, and catalogs establishing her role in the history of photography by women.[4] In 2012 the Prints & Photographs Division of the Library of Congress is expanding this legacy by adding to its online catalog the 1,134 color and black-and-white lantern slides produced by Johnston and preserved by the library for more than half a century. They depict city and country gardens, both American and European, from the 1890s through the 1930s; landscape plans; historic garden images from illustrated books; domesticated plants and wildflowers; and buildings of the Old South. Johnston produced these slides for lectures on garden design and architecture that she delivered across America from 1915 until the 1940s. Notes and press releases suggest the library's collection represents an estimated 70 percent of her slide production.

Five years ago, in their uncataloged state, without identifying labels, dates, or discernible order, Johnston's slides appeared idiosyncratic and disparate. In fact, as research revealed, the collection is remarkably coherent. It broadly reflects American garden design in the first two decades of the 20th century and the work of an early commercial photographer who helped define what a garden photograph needed to be in a new era of professional design.[5]

Until today's generation, American landscape architecture and specifically design by women were neglected subjects. As an allied art, garden photography has similarly remained unexamined, a notable lacuna considering that the photograph has been essential to the history of landscape architecture. Our understanding of what America's first professional architects and their wealthy clients intended their gardens to be is to a great extent due to the black-and-white garden images that first appeared in magazines and books from 1900.

This book has been conceived as a companion to the online catalog of FBJ's slide collection and as a case study to advance garden photography scholarship. Three essential questions guided the research. What were the gardens Johnston photographed? Why did she photograph these gardens and present them in lectures? And, finally, how did she photograph and produce slides, both technically and aesthetically?

Remarkably, for someone who led a public life, Johnston remains curiously elusive. Though FBJ herself understood, and resisted, the anonymous status of the commercial photographer in the early 20th century, she ultimately contributed to her own anonymity by leaving a fragmented manuscript archive and uncataloged photograph collections. Like many women of her generation, she remained unreflective in print. What autobiography she left is in publicity and newspaper profiles, remarkably consistent for their inconsistency. A dedicated self-promoter, FBJ mixed fact and fiction to make herself and her photography acceptable to clients who lived by defined manners and the era's "good taste."

Fortunately, FBJ was already an accomplished photographer when the American garden emerged at the turn of the 20th century. Her creative talents and entrepreneurial skills made her an early participant in the period's lively garden book and magazine culture. Consequently, research in the era's periodicals and landscape archives has overcome some of the limitations imposed by Johnston and her peripatetic life.

This book is in three parts: an introduction to Johnston as photographer of gardens and garden advocate, from 1895 to 1935; an explication of her garden photography as it emerged with professional garden design, from 1900; and selections from the five garden-slide collections Johnston assembled. With rare exceptions, the images are of gardens, defined spaces dedicated to ornamental planting, sometimes as part of greater designed landscapes.[6] Introductions to each garden collection are intended as background for the images that follow and guidance for future investigation of Johnston and of garden photography's role in American landscape design. As is the case with disciplines associated with photography, the historical, theoretical, and aesthetic implications of the garden photograph are myriad.

For one of the many press releases she issued to advance her work, FBJ wrote: "In any interview or personal story however brief, the points which seem most important to me are first the background, second the training, third the experience and fourth the study I have given to what may be termed an absolutely unique field of work; that of the photography in both color and monochrome of gardens and flowers, and the use of the material I have myself collected in slides for my lectures."[7]

Here is Frances Benjamin Johnston's story as an artist who became an American garden photographer.

[Fig. 1] Gertrude Käsebier and Frances Benjamin Johnston Dining, Venice, Italy, August, 1905. Photographer unknown. On a summer tour the photographers stopped in the city of lagoons where Baron Adolph de Meyer (1868–1949), the fashion photographer, made his darkroom available. The older woman called the determined Johnston, "Bronco." From here, FBJ traveled north to meet Claude-Antoine Lumière, pioneer of the autochrome color process Johnston used for her early garden photographs.

A Garden Photographer

I know my chief assets were persistence, patience, an instinctive tact about bothering people at the wrong time, a considerable saving sense of humor and not the slightest awe of position or prestige. —1936

Frances Benjamin Johnston was born January 15, 1864, in West Virginia, the only child of Frances Antoinette Benjamin (1837–1920) and Anderson Doniphan Johnston (1828–1906). On her mother's side she was related to American Revolutionary soldiers, and her father descended from 18th-century Southern Baptist preachers. FBJ recounted throughout her career that her uncle sent Ulysses S. Grant to West Point, that her aunt was author Elizabeth Bryant Johnston (circa 1835–1907), and that she was a relative of First Lady Frances Cleveland. FBJ explained to a reporter that because of her relations to well-known figures in the Protestant establishment, she was at ease with the officials and presidents she photographed for magazines and newspapers.[1]

The Johnston family lived in Ohio and Rochester, New York, before moving in the early 1870s to Washington, where FBJ's father worked for the U.S. Treasury Department and her mother was a journalist.[2] After graduating from a two-year academy in Baltimore, Johnston sailed in 1883 to Paris, the city philosopher Walter Benjamin called the "capital of the 19th century."[3] She entered the Académie Julian, founded by painter Rodolphe Julian (1839–1907) in 1868. He accepted women artists, excluded from the state-sponsored École des Beaux-Arts until 1897.[4] Training in classical traditions was a valued credential for aspiring artists in industrial America turning to Old World Europe for cultural guidance.

Cecilia Beaux (1855–1942), a painter of wealthy women; society portraitist John Singer Sargent (1856–1925); and architectural painter Edward Emerson Simmons (1852–1931) attended Julian's school, a fact known to Johnston's wealthy, art-collecting patrons whose houses and gardens she photographed 25 years later.[5]

FBJ returned to Washington after two years in France. Living at home, she joined the capital's art community, which flourished as wealth gravitated to federal power. She pursued further training at Washington's Art Students League, founded in 1884 to expand public art education, but soon realized "how terrible my sketches and drawings were."[6] Determined to make a living despite family support, she became a freelance commercial artist, first as an illustrator and then as a photographer, at the urging of fellow artist and editor Elizabeth L. Sylvester (d. 1939).[7] In technological developments—portable cameras and plates, panchromatic emulsions, and wide-angle lenses expanding photography subjects for magazines proliferating with half-tone printing—Johnston recognized opportunities for creative work.

To burnish her image as a photography maverick, Johnston refashioned the history of her first camera. By her account, she wrote, unsolicited, to George Eastman (1854–1932): "Please send me a camera which will take good pictures for newspapers." Impressed, he in turn mailed the

[Fig. 2a, top] Students at the Académie Julian, Paris, France, circa 1885. Photographer unknown. [Fig. 2b, bottom] Students at the Art Students League, Washington, D.C., circa 1889. With her fellow students pictured here, FBJ learned composition by drawing and painting flowers, portraits, and landscapes. Later she applied academic conventions to garden photography.

young artist a camera.[8] In fact the inventor, a family friend, gave Johnston and her mother's sister Cornelia Johnston Hagan (1839–1927) a Kodak in January 1888, four months before it went into manufacture. For several years Hagan courted Eastman by sending him photographs, but the relationship faded.[9] Hagan did not become a photographer, but Johnston succeeded in two fields open to women and pursued by her mother and her aunt: journalism and photography.

At the turn of the century, Washington, D.C., governed with renewed authority. Americans had turned to the presidency to remedy post–Civil War laissez-faire policies and to compete in a global economy. The subject of Johnston's early published assignments was the new world of reform and federal power. In the 1890s, *Demorest's Family Magazine* and *The Ladies' Home Journal* published her photo essays on coal miners in West Virginia, on The White House interiors, and on the U.S. Bureau of Printing and Engraving. In 1893 she photographed the Chicago Columbian Exposition in association with the Smithsonian's Thomas William Smillie (1843–1917). The institution's first official photographer trained FBJ and other students to bring photography to government work.

Secure as senior clerk at the treasury, Anderson Johnston built his daughter a studio, circa 1895, at the back of the family house on V Street. He had purchased the 10-room villa in 1873 from its builder, treasury colleague and family friend, writer John Burroughs (1837–1921).[10] The nature essayist, biographer of Walt Whitman, and voice for John Muir's preservation of western forests was famous by 1900 as America's "Nature Poet." The new glass-roofed atelier overlooked rose beds planted by Burroughs, a fact that FBJ publicized in newspaper interviews and lectures to establish her gardening bona fides.[11] In 1898 she photographed the backyard in summer bloom, winning second prize in a *The Ladies' Home Journal* amateur photography contest for a "pretty" American garden.[12]

On completion of the addition, Johnston turned to the expanding field of photo portraiture. Children's book author Frances Eliza Hodgson Burnett (1849–1924); Gifford Pinchot (1865–1946), champion of nature

conservation; and Mabel Osgood Wright (1859–1934), founder of the Connecticut Audubon Society and garden book author, were among the officials, artists, and progressives who sat for the enterprising photographer. Her success in photographing presidents and first ladies earned FBJ the title of unofficial "Court Photographer" for four White House administrations, from Benjamin Harrison through Theodore Roosevelt.

Portraiture was transformative for FBJ's career. Not only did it bring her in contact with leading figures of the era who owned houses and gardens she would photograph, but in posing individual sitters both for news and artistic portraits, Johnston learned the power of photography to present constructed scenes as real. The broad public at the turn of the century assumed a scientific correspondence between reality and the photograph image. FBJ used this assumption to picture diplomats and presidents, posed at their desks, as thoughtful world leaders and to portray the progressive benefits of education through tableaux of Washington

[Fig. 3, top left] Anderson Doniphan Johnston House, Washington, D.C., Studio Interior, circa 1898. FBJ's father built his daughter a glass-roofed studio that she considered "more like a painter's workshop than a photographer's room."

[Fig. 4, bottom left] Anderson Doniphan Johnston House, Washington, D.C., Studio Garden, 1898. The Arts and Crafts studio overlooked roses and wisteria planted by renowned nature writer and the house's builder, John Burroughs, a history Johnston recounted to establish her gardening credentials. She won a Ladies' Home Journal *photography prize for this image.*

[Fig. 5 opposite] North View over South Canal, World's Columbian Exposition, Chicago, 1893. Daniel Hudson Burnham, Frederick Law Olmsted and McKim, Mead & White conceived the "White City" as a Renaissance spectacle to inspire a new America, one that looked back to the past for design and to technology for the future. FBJ conformed to their vision, photographing the city as a painting by Canaletto, with revival buildings and streets lighted by electricity. Her ability to interpret the intentions of architects led to success as a garden photographer 20 years later.

high school students and African Americans at the Hampton Normal and Agricultural Institute. In 1899, her skill as an image-maker secured FBJ the commission that made her reputation international. With Theodore Roosevelt's endorsement, she travelled to Italy and photographed Admiral Dewey and his crew onboard the battleship USS Olympia, victorious after their invasion of the Philippines.

Johnston expanded her professional circles in the 1890s by joining Alfred Stieglitz (1864–1936) in claiming for photography fine-art status. Fifty years after its invention, the medium was still considered a science. Endorsing photography as a profession for the new working woman, FBJ became the first female member of Washington's Capital Camera Club, exhibited her photographs at the New York Camera Club in 1898, and was both an exhibitor and juror at the second annual Philadelphia Photograph Society exhibition in 1899. Critics were unimpressed with the staged portraits Johnston produced for gallery exhibitions. Photographer and essayist Carl Sadakichi Hartmann (1867–1944) wrote in 1900 that

her photograph "Cigarette," of a woman in a kimono, smoking, did not evoke the "poetry and mystery" possible through selective attention to detail. "What is the use of making such a picture, if it does not portray a peculiar mood?"[13] Despite critique of her art photography, FBJ was a founder of Stieglitz's *Camera Work* journal in 1902 before turning to full-time commercial work for magazines and newspapers.

Her support of professional women and her success as a published photographer landed Johnston the assignment of delegate to the 1900 Paris Exposition. Bertha Honoré Palmer (1849–1918), honorary commissioner from Illinois to the fair, endorsed her appointment. Johnston organized an exhibition of work by 35 American women photographers and exhibited her own photographs of Washington schools.[14]

FBJ was an established photographer for newspapers and magazines by the time she was 36 in 1900. Since the 1880s, she had succeeded through proficiency, social position, and self-promotion to build a career as a news photographer. Using her academic training to master photo genres in the expanding field of commercial photography, she rode to success, as Verna Posever Curtis writes, the waves of the "new" America: the "New Woman," the "New Education," the "New Negro," and the "New School of American Photography."[15] Her next challenge was the new house and garden.

In the American Garden

Johnston came of age in an era of change. Thomas Jefferson had defined his generation's republic as a land of fields and distant shores. By the time FBJ photographed the Chicago Fair celebrating the fourth centennial of

[Fig. 6] Pennsylvania School of Horticulture for Women, Ambler, Pennsylvania, Demonstration Kitchen and Flower Garden, May 1919. Founded in 1910, the Ambler school was one of the first to train women in landscape architecture, a new profession that brought the Garden Beautiful to private houses and public parks. FBJ lectured here to promote garden photography.

[Fig. 7] Hacienda del Pozo de Verona, Phoebe Apperson Hearst Ranch, Pleasanton, California, Country Life in America, *June, 1904. October, 1903. This article by California booster Charles F. Lummis featured FBJ's first published photographs of a landscaped American country house. Johnston was a leader in photographing West Coast gardens for East Coast magazines.*

puffing, clanking, screeching, smoking for twelve to fourteen hours a day, sometimes going around the clock."[16]

The contrast between the woeful conditions of the American metropolis and the white spectacle of the Chicago fair inspired Americans to consider where their country had been and where it needed to go. Their response was manifested in the national City Beautiful movement. Civic reformers led campaigns to plan, build, and plant urban centers worthy of an international power, while back-to-nature activists took up the causes of forest preservation and the plight of rural communities devastated by flight to cities. Reading Ralph Waldo Emerson (1803–82), Walt Whitman (1819–92), and Henry David Thoreau (1817–62), Johnston's generation of city dwellers experienced nature as a source of spiritual renewal in a mechanical age.

Industrialization profoundly changed the American home. In 1900 more people still lived on farms than in cities. By 1920 the national census revealed that for the first time the reverse was true. Unsettled by physical conditions and immigrants living in crowded tenements, the wealthy at the close of the century moved from city houses to country estates, laying out short-run commuter railroads that brought middle classes to suburban developments in the 1920s.

To design the houses they built on hills overlooking family farms they now owned, the rich turned to graduates from new programs in landscape architecture. Men attended Cornell, Harvard, and MIT and women studied at the Lowthorpe School of Landscape Architecture, Gardening and Horticulture for Women, founded by Judith Eleanor Motley Low (1842–1919) in 1901, and the Pennsylvania School of Horticulture for Women

Christopher Columbus' landing on the continent, America was a country of interconnected industrial cities in a degraded environment. Railroad syndicates had dynamited mountain passes and ripped through bison plains to connect the East to the West and the North to the South. Tree stumps and brush littered sides of the iron rail, and billboards pushing the era's manufactured goods lined trafficked roads. Where wildflowers once grew along riverbanks, there were barren fields and sluggish streams blackened by steel-mill waste. Chicago, Cleveland, and Pittsburgh were noisy, sooty agglomerations of mid-century neighborhoods, immigrant slums, and the brown stone mansions of Mark Twain's Gilded Age elite who managed the banks and businesses building the modern world. Towns and cities, wrote Lewis Mumford (1895–1990), were "dark hives, busily

[Fig. 8] *The Orchard, James Lawrence Breese House, Southampton, New York, McKim, Mead & White, Architects and Landscape Architects, 1898–1907, Conservatory Entrance with Hydrangeas,* Ageratum, *and White Clematis,* The House Beautiful, *June 1913. FBJ's only color magazine cover of a garden secured her reputation as a professional photographer and early association with The Garden Club of America.*

at Ambler, founded by Jane Bowne Haines (1869–1937) in 1910.[17] Their graduates were mostly wives or children of prosperous farmers or white-collar men, who, like FBJ, could pursue independent professional careers because of household servants and manufactured goods.[18]

Capitalizing on the interests of house owners building and planting estates, publishers from the turn of the century introduced new magazines. In 1901 Doubleday, Page & Company launched *Country Life in America.* Its first editor was Liberty Hyde Bailey (1858–1954), Cornell University educator and later chairman of Theodore Roosevelt's 1908 Country Life Commission, formed to study rural life. Mixing nostalgia for a simpler agrarian world with practical advice to the "Home-maker, the Vacation-Seeker, the Gardener, the Farmer, the Nature-teacher, the Naturalist," the large-format magazine pictured country houses.[19] In 1905 Doubleday introduced *The Garden Magazine,* offering horticultural advice. The magazine's editor, Wilhelm Miller (1869–1938), explained that the publication was "the logical working out of the growing interest in the garden, not merely as a means of livelihood … but as a delight and pursuit for busy people."[20] *The House Beautiful* (founded 1896) and *House & Garden* (founded 1901), with newsstand prices lower than *Country Life*'s, broadened the market for garden photography.[21]

These magazines presented FBJ opportunities for continued success. Her experience photographing The White House and Washington mansions for news stories in the 1890s eased her transition from the competitive field of celebrity portraiture into the emerging profession of photography illustrating American design. In June 1904, *Country Life*

in America published her first photographs of a new American country estate.[22] Seven pages, illustrated with black-and-white photographs, introduced readers to Hacienda del Pozo de Verona, the Mission Revival ranch southeast of San Francisco owned by Phoebe Apperson Hearst (1842–1919). FBJ knew the benefactor of colleges and kindergartens from photographing Hearst's Washington, D.C., mansion for *Demorest's*

Family Magazine in 1890. In October 1903, Johnston had photographed the California estate and met the feature's author, Los Angeles booster Charles Fletcher Lummis (1859–1928), a Harvard classmate of Theodore Roosevelt.[23] The Hearst story was an early prestige profile by a magazine that competed with *Town & Country, Vogue, Harper's Bazar,* and *Arts & Decoration* for affluent readers. Self-defined and promoted by FBJ as magazines of "class," they published garden photographs by her and others in her generation working in commercial photography.[24] Leading photographers included Goroku Amemiya (1886–1972), Jessie Tarbox Beals (1870–1942), Arnold Genthe (1869–1942), John Wallace Gillies (1883–1927), and Samuel Herman Gottscho (1875–1971) in New York; Alice Boughton (1886–1943) and Charles Peter Gabriel Moulin (1872–1945) in California; Mary Harrod Northend (1850–1925) and Antoinette Rehmann Perret (1880–1952) in Massachusetts; and Ella Maud Boult (1865–1951) in Connecticut.[25]

In 1909 FBJ moved from Washington to New York after winning a commission to photograph Carrère & Hastings' New Theater. As the center of architectural photography, the city offered the aspiring photographer potential for new commissions. Her widely published images of the Beaux-Arts theater led to assignments from McKim, Mead & White, Bertram Grosvenor Goodhue (1869–1924), and John Russell Pope (1874–1937) to photograph city houses and country estates they were designing for newly rich industrialists.

Johnston worked with Mattie Edwards Hewitt (1869–1956), a photographer who also trained as a fine artist. They had met at the 1904 St. Louis World's Fair and become lovers.[26] In New York they lived together at 55 Irving Place, just down the street from their early client, *The House in Good Taste* author and decorator Elsie de Wolfe (1865–1950) sharing a house with theatrical agent Elisabeth Marbury (1856–1953).[27] In 1911 Johnston and Hewitt opened a studio at 628 Fifth Avenue, a prestigious address for artists and galleries. Five years later they moved to 536. From this year they no longer lived together.[28]

FBJ and Hewitt began circa 1909 photographing gardens while on architecture assignments.[29] Johnston, the experienced professional, had the contacts needed to succeed in the world of property owners who could afford garden photography. By 1912 she decided to "specialize" and to pursue the "great work yet to be done in photographing beautiful homes"[30] She had already photographed the Princeton garden of banking heir Moses Taylor Pyne and the James Lawrence Breese house in Southampton. In 1913 she was established as a leader in house and garden photography when *The House Beautiful* published as its April and June covers her hand-colored photographs of an unidentified sunroom and a colored image of the Breese garden. Though FBJ had been working with Hewitt for four years, the magazine credited only Johnston.

The year of her garden covers, Frances Benjamin Johnston formed a business partnership with Mattie Edwards Hewitt. That same year, wealthy women members of 12 local garden clubs met in Philadelphia and founded The Garden Club of America. The association of women with gardens, the craft of gardening and flora culture extends back millennia. By 1900, as Thaïsa Way writes, women believed that the home garden had always been "a woman's domain."[31] Gardening was associated, by both men and women, with motherhood, good health, and, for wealthy women, good taste, the ability to recognize and cultivate beauty. When the City Beautiful movement gave voice to the 19th-century ideal articulated by Andrew Jackson Downing (1815–52), Catharine Esther Beecher (1805–78), and Frederick Law Olmsted (1822–1903) that a designed and tended American landscape reflected a civilized society's moral and mental health, the nation's gardeners, guardians of home and community, participated through associations and societies.

The mission of The Garden Club of America was "to stimulate the knowledge and love of gardening among amateurs, to share the advantages of association through conference and correspondence in this country and abroad; to aid in the protection of native plants and birds; and to encourage civic planting."[32] By 1930 it had become, in its own words, "the Mother of

[Fig. 9] Près Choisis, Albert Herter House, East Hampton, New York, Color in The New Country Life, *May 1917. Photographers, Frances Benjamin Johnston and Mattie Edwards Hewitt, 1913. The magazine presented the partners' autochromes of a garden and house interior. FBJ worked in the early color process before converting to hand-colored slides.*

Garden Clubs," with 88 local clubs whose 6,275 members, all women except a small minority of men, paid dues to support the national office in New York.[33] With the rise of the professionally designed landscape, the club extended its objectives. Board member and gardener Helen Stafford Thorne (1866–1952) explained in 1931 that members should raise "the standard of the fine art of gardening among the amateurs of America." By participating in events and tours sponsored by the national club, the regional gardener moved beyond "the highly *localized* garden club … to enter a wider sphere" of influence.[34]

Conferencing and corresponding comprised a wide range of activities. Beginning in 1913, the national club published a quarterly bulletin with articles on gardening by members and leading voices of the garden renaissance. Botanist Charles Sprague Sargent (1841–1927), English Arts and Crafts gardener Gertrude Jekyll (1843–1942), and publisher John Horace McFarland (1859–1948) contributed essays on the Arnold Arboretum, color in the garden, and cultivating roses. Members organized annual trips to visit American and international gardens, donated money to the Ambler and Lowthorpe programs, and sponsored lectures by amateur and professional gardeners. Through photographs and lantern slides they collected of member gardens, The Garden Club of America brought gardening to the progressive efforts of the City Beautiful movement.

Long Island South Shore residents founded the Garden Club of Southampton in February 1912 and the club was admitted to The Garden Club
of America the following year.[35] Georgina Bonner Boardman (1855–1916),
daughter of *Harper's Weekly* editor John Bonner and wife of a New York
lawyer, was its first president. The national club initiated in 1914 the collecting of photographs of member gardens. Living on her Southampton
estate with a garden designed by Marian Cruger Coffin (1876–1957),
Boardman led a local initiative to hire Johnston and Hewitt. From 1914
through the fall of 1916, the partners photographed East Hampton and
Southampton gardens, working in black and white and autochrome. FBJ
had been using the early color process since meeting its inventor Claude-
Antoine Lumière (1840–1911) at the Saint Louis World's Fair. On trips
to France in 1905 and the following year, she advanced her technique by
visiting the inventor at home.[36] Sculptor Thomas Shields Clarke (1860–
1920), a garden club member and amateur photographer, recommended
the process for photographing gardens. The "autochrome glass plates give
us the real charm of the garden, its feat of color. Those made in Paris by
the Lumière Company seem to be the best. Snapshots cannot be made on
these plates."[37]

Johnston wrote that the "beautiful collection" she made of Hampton
gardens was prepared "to stimulate local interest in gardening and civic
improvement."[38] She extended this effort by producing her first illustrated
lecture, "Our American Gardens." Initially she presented autochromes
but converted to hand-painted plates that were simpler to project.[39] The
more than 100 slides and related print photographs she assembled vaulted

Johnston to prominence.[40] Her first documented lecture was in September 1915 at the Southampton house of garden club member Cora Dillon
Wyckoff (1852–1925). The same year, writer Louise Kirtland Shelton
(1867–1934) published her best seller *Beautiful Gardens in America*, with
two autochromes and 15 black-and-white photographs by "Miss Johnston–Mrs. Hewitt," of Long Island, New Jersey, and Rhode Island gardens.
In May 1917, Doubleday, Page & Company launched a redesigned *Country Life* with "features being more especially valuable *because they are in
color.*"[41] A two-page spread presented four autochromes of the Albert and
Adele Herter East Hampton house and garden by the "Johnston-Hewitt
Studio." Ten pages later, as part of the same article on country house

decorating, were two autochromes of an unidentified sunroom by "Mattie E. Hewitt," her first solo credit in the magazine.[42] Today, the *Country Life* photographs and the two pale plates in Shelton's book are the only identified autochromes by the photographers.[43]

Two months before the color-illustrated issue of *The New Country Life* landed on newsstands with differing credits for the autochrome plates, Frances Benjamin Johnston and Mattie Edwards Hewitt ended their four-year partnership. When a reporter asked in late 1912 the role of Hewitt in their business, Johnston answered dismissively, "She develops and enlarges the pictures."[44] This may have been the case in their first years together, but by 1917 Hewitt was an accomplished residential photographer who continued to photograph houses and gardens for 25 years. A comparison of FBJ's disparate images of the Phoebe A. Hearst garden with her composed Long Island photographs from 1915 makes clear that Johnston advanced with her younger colleague.

FBJ resumed her independent practice as owner of the lantern slides and prints produced during the Johnston–Hewitt years.[45] For the next decade she lived in New York and earned a living as a garden photographer, author, and lecturer.[46] She traveled by train and car with camera cases, a book box, slides, a typewriter, and a suitcase.[47] She worked in black and white and abandoned the autochrome that was difficult to project and print.[48] Before the mid-1920s, when competition for exclusives pushed magazines to commission photographs and offer first-refusal agreements, Johnston photographed on speculation. Commissions came from wealthy women who were members of local garden clubs and the national Garden Club of America. By its very nature, writes historian Vera Norwood, the garden photograph was for and about affluent women, a "public display of American imperialism" and "a portrait of 'womanhood' associated with plant cultivation and gardening."[49] As a woman and professional photographer, Johnston considered herself particularly suited to garden work. Photography, Johnston told a reporter, was feminine because of a woman's "greater delicacy of touch and fineness of perception."[50] FBJ remained a single woman pursuing a career as a professional observer, a hired hand, never elected a member of The Garden Club of America.

Limited to houses she could visit and in response to editorial interest, Johnston assembled portfolios representing the eclectic English, French, Italian, and Japanese Revivals in American gardens. Because the club women who bought Johnston's photographs, attended her lectures, and purchased magazines focused on the design and care of flower gardens, FBJ photographed herbaceous borders, rose arbors, and parterres. She included walls, gates, fountains, pools, and houses to show the relationship of architecture to the landscaped garden.

Johnston sustained her long career by accommodating cultural change. As publishers responded to the evolving American home, FBJ adapted her practice. She began photographing East Coast gardens in 1910 and continued in California in 1917. As urban renewal gained momentum in the 1920s, she joined the city garden movement. Encouraged by editors turning to the Colonial Revival and historic preservation, she moved back to Washington, D.C., before the Depression to photograph in southern states. Related to the four collections from these periods that formed her "Our American Gardens," "Gardens of the West," "Gardens for City and Suburb," and "Gardens of the South" lectures were FBJ's 1925 photographs of European gardens influencing American design. By assembling these defined collections that were representative, not encyclopedic, FBJ circumscribed travel, reduced production expense, learned regional conditions, and developed professional contacts. Collections led to articles in magazines and exhibitions in galleries.[51]

By 1923 clubs and magazine editors considered Johnston a leading photographer. She had photographed gardens on both coasts, published widely in magazines of class, and exhibited her prints of East and West Coast gardens at New York's Touchstone Gallery. That year, Leonard Barron, editor of *The Garden Magazine,* approached FBJ for an interview. She responded directly: "Whatever you publish … I am anxious to have from [you] an understanding and sympathetic angle, brief if you like but discriminating which will relieve me of the banal curse of being just a photographer."[52]

This pointed request spoke to the challenges Johnston faced as a magazine photographer. Editors considered illustrators "artists," portrait photographers "professionals," and landscape and building photographers "commercial."[53] Garden photography, wrote sociologist Catherine Filene (1896–1994) in 1920, was an "Arts and Crafts" profession, not a fine art.[54] Consequently, the house and garden photographer struggled for recognition in reviews of exhibitions and for credit in magazines and books. Edith Wharton's *Italian Villas and Their Gardens* (1904) was "Illustrated with Pictures by Maxfield Parrish and by Photographs." *American Landscape Architecture* (1924), edited by Philip Homer Elwood Jr. (1884–1960), cited architects of featured work, but no photographers. Elwood considered photography a documentary tool for landscape architects to "preserve impressions of their work as it grows towards the realization of the picture held in the mind of the artist."[55] In his terms, the professional photographer was a technician who preserved in film the pictures that designers conceived in gardens.

Though they consistently collected and exhibited photographs to inform growing memberships, garden clubs contributed to the photographer's fundamental anonymity. When the *Bulletin of The Garden Club of America* listed the winners of its 1922 photography show in Detroit, it reported that Helen S. Thorne had won the prize for best photograph "of a vista or view from a garden." The *Bulletin* did not credit FBJ, the actual photographer of the winning image, a perspective of Thorne's California garden[56]

[Figs. 11a, 11b] *Frances Benjamin Johnston Wearing Her Palme Académique Ribbon, circa 1923, and Smoking a Cigarette,* The Garden Magazine, *December 1923. Photographer, Anthony Bacon and unknown photographer. The two FBJs: the lady lecturer, purveyor of beauty and class, in a publicity photograph she mailed to garden clubs and journalists; and Johnston the activist-artist New Woman, wearing what she called "barbaric" jewelry.*

Author Louise Shelton altered the status quo. In 1924, Scribner's published a second edition of *Beautiful Gardens in America*, with photographs selected by writer Mrs. Francis "Louisa" King (1863–1948), peony expert Alice Howard Harding (1872–1938), garden fine art painter Helen Shelton Clarkson (1857–1937), and landscape architect Edith Ripley Kennaday (1873–1926). Commenting on this committee, *Landscape Architecture* magazine wrote critically that captions credited the photographers, not the landscape or house architects.[57] The reviewer did not note that Shelton had chosen a painter, not a photographer, to represent the artist's voice on the selection committee. In a period when both photography and landscape architecture were new professions struggling for recognition as arts, the shaky status of each impeded the progress of both.

Commercial photographers of gardens overcame the critical and financial limitations of their profession variously. Ella M. Boult and Antoinette R. Perrett wrote and illustrated articles; Mary H. Northend authored books on the Colonial Revival, illustrated with photographs by her and photographers she employed;[58] John Wallace Gillies taught photography and wrote manuals;[59] Arthur Grenville Eldredge (1880–1972), through his association with Wilhelm Miller, taught photography and contributed to the

FRANCES BENJAMIN JOHNSTON
Interpreter of gardens East and West

She promoted photography as art and women as photographers through articles, interviews, and exhibitions. She continued this dual role of practitioner and activist as a garden photographer who endorsed the Garden Beautiful with illustrated lectures.

Lantern-slide presentations originated in the 17th century with glass plates painted in watercolor or oil. The first photographic slides were produced from 1849 as popular entertainment, 10 years after the invention of photography. Production for teaching art history and design gained momentum when the Metropolitan Museum of Art in New York initiated its slide collection after opening in 1870. In 1874 Harvard professor Charles Eliot Norton (1827–1908) introduced lantern slides to his influential course in the "History of fine arts and their relation to literature." From the 1880s, institutions and community organizations formed extensive lantern collections presented with increasingly sophisticated projectors until 35mm slides began to replace glass plates in the 1950s.[63]

The illustrated lecture was ideal for Johnston seeking to be a garden authority. It was visual, informative, and associated with education. After breaking with Hewitt, FBJ exhibited her colored slides at garden club meetings and shared programs with scientists, landscape architects, and gardeners hired to speak at horticultural societies, museums, and private houses in Cincinnati and Akron, Ohio; Rockford, Illinois; and Flushing, New York. Between 1915 and 1923, FBJ delivered more than 100 lectures in 11 states, charging $75 ($816 in 2011) per show in 1920 and, by 1928, $100 ($1,270) for a lecture and $10 ($127) for one print and a slide of local

landscape architecture program at the University of Illinois at Urbana;[60] Gabriel Moulin and his sons established a firm photographing houses, gardens, family events, and new city buildings;[61] and Samuel H. Gottscho wrote books on architecture and American wildflowers.[62] Writing and teaching, prestigious endeavors in a society that valued the literary over the photographic, brought status to the American garden photographer.

Advocating American Beauty

Like her colleagues, Frances Benjamin Johnston pursued varied professional work to augment her income and enhance her professional standing. Coming of age at the turn of the century, when social change permeated American life, she combined progressive advocacy and career.

member garden, the top of the garden club scale. Word of mouth, self-published brochures, and reviews in local papers made FBJ a celebrity on the garden talk circuit. By 1930, with her reputation established, FBJ was asking $150 ($1,960) a lecture, travel included.[64]

Journalists wrote enthusiastically about Johnston's colored images of East Coast estates, enumerating by house and location the gardens she showed. The *Post-Star* in Glen Falls, New York, reported that home owners "actuated by a desire to aid the nation-wide movement for better gardens and more beautiful cities … [had] graciously consented to have them photographed."[65] With rare exceptions, first- and second-generation rich Americans, with banking, railroad and industrial fortunes, owned the gardens pictured in FBJ's lantern slides. Unlike old New York, Philadelphia, and Boston society, they welcomed publicity and assumed leadership, living lavishly to secure their status while progressively supporting top-down civic improvement.[66] They took their lead from professors at universities they endowed and journal editors who concurred with Harvard president Charles William Eliot (1834–1926) that wealth had increased faster than public taste. To correct this imbalance and beautify America, standards were needed. The wealthy, avatars of success in a capitalist democracy, were the logical leaders.[67] They had the money to build houses that could be models of domestic design for all classes.

In this social Darwinian world that assumed money knows best, the professionally landscaped garden owned by a Morgan banker or New York Central Railroad heir offered the greatest influence. "It is more than personal belonging. It is a national asset increasing the value and interest of the whole community," wrote the editors of Arts and Crafts magazine *The*

Touchstone in an article illustrated with FBJ photographs. "Such beautiful gardens are great object lessons. Without them, small gardenmakers would perhaps have little incentive to work." The "sense of beauty" in the estate garden was "a constructive, uplifting force for refinement and sense of loveliness."[68]

The beauty of the wealthy person's garden was the moralizing beauty associated in the 19th century with the English critic and cultural philosopher John Ruskin (1819–1900). His thinking influenced the work of landscape gardener Andrew Jackson Downing (1815–52), Downing's follower Frederick Law Olmsted, and educator Charles Eliot Norton (1827–1908).[69] Beauty was an object's outward appearance that provided pleasure on contemplation.[70] It was recognized and created by the morally and spiritually elevated artist. However, the "sensibility to the beautiful," wrote Downing, could be "cultivated and ripened into good taste by the study and comparison of beautiful productions in nature and art."[71] When nature's beauty was discernible in painting, sculpture, and architecture, it brought

[Fig. 13] Beacon Hill, Arthur Curtiss James House, Newport, Rhode Island, Gardener Posed Mowing in the Blue Garden, July 1917. FBJ photographed the estate's gardeners performing tasks to illustrate Rudyard Kipling's poem, "The Glory of the Garden." Associating photography with poetry gave literary patina to the commercial photograph and the photographer.

meaning and social improvement to everyday living. The potential for beauty to transform life informed the Arts and Crafts and City Beautiful movements and drove the funding of schools in building and landscape architecture. Beauty would "hardly grow of itself," wrote Charles W. Eliot's son, landscape architect Charles Eliot (1859–97), in 1891. "If we want it, we shall have to work for it through that arduous process which is called design."[72]

An Arts and Crafts enthusiast, Frances Benjamin Johnston subscribed to Ruskinian beauty. She befriended and photographed Elbert Hubbard (1856–1915) and visited his upstate New York Roycroft community. She decorated her woodsy Washington studio with Mission furniture, collected Japanese prints and art pottery, and published her photographs in *The Craftsman* and *The Touchstone* magazines. When she herself became an advocate for social improvement through design in nature, FBJ made beauty central to her crusading lectures. Every house owner, she wrote, had a "responsibility … to beautify their yard, no matter how small…. As

Ruskin once said, 'Sir the exterior of your house *is not* private property!'"[73] Gardens of "splendid establishments, which cost fortunes to develop," designed by landscape architects and garden authorities trained in beauty, were fine examples, but "the real charm and atmosphere of a community is determined by the beauty, fitness and all-around attractiveness of its small homes and little gardens."[74] Progress in cities and towns depended on the local gardener to learn through lecture slides and illustrated books how to bring taste and refinement to American neighborhoods.

FBJ's beauty-in-every-backyard message was consistent with her stance as a cultivated popularizer of garden club orthodoxy. She collected and studied the era's books and magazines to inform her lectures and garden selections. "Famous American Gardens," "Intimate Gardens," "Planning and Planting the Garden," "The Small Garden," and "The Rose in American Gardens" were among her more than a dozen presentations, arranged, she wrote, "to appeal not only to garden clubs, but also to organizations featuring civic improvement, art and literary study."[75] Her topics were consistent with lectures by competing landscape architects, amateur gardeners, and photographers, who included J. Horace McFarland and Mary H. Northend.[76]

Wearing the purple ribbon of the Palme Académique, awarded by France for her work at the Louisiana Purchase Exposition, Johnston spoke extemporaneously and from notes.[77] She projected 100 to 175 slides, weaving a familiar tale of garden design from Babylon and Rome to the Renaissance hillside villa; from the French parterre to the English

[Figs. 15a, 15b top] *Williams Bridge and Gun Hill Road, Bronx, New York, Before and After Restoration, circa 1907–20. Photographs from Bronx River Parkway Commission. Manufactured products brought new convenience to the American home, but advertising spoiled roadside views. FBJ promoted billboard regulation, showing slides of sites before and after beautification.*

[Figs. 16a, 16b bottom] *Worker Houses and Gardens, National Cash Register Company, Dayton, Ohio, John Charles Olmsted, Landscape Architect, from 1895, Before and After Landscaping, circa 1895 and 1900. Photographer, National Cash Register Company. Company founder John Henry Patterson transformed an urban ghetto into a company town where children learned to garden. FBJ showed NCR slides to demonstrate how greening backyards could transform all American lives.*

park. She promoted the adaptation of the formal, natural, and Colonial Revival "grandmother" garden to new American houses designed in related styles. Three things to bear in mind, she advised women in South Bend, Indiana: "plant in masses, leave open spaces and avoid straight lines. Americans are beginning to realize that terraces and gardens should bear distinct relation to the architecture of the house; the old Colonial home should have an appropriate setting of old-fashioned flowers and the bungalow a more simple arrangement as there is architecture in the plans of gardens as well as of houses."[78] This eclectic mélange of accepted themes, animated by colorful slides of pergolas and grass paths, brought FBJ national success.

Garden club audiences received Johnston as a design professional and connoisseur of literature and poetry. Some slide lecturers approached the garden as "a chemical laboratory," others as "seed catalogue, mostly in Latin," wrote a reporter in Massachusetts. In favorable contrast, Frances Benjamin Johnston was "an interpreter of garden beauty and the meaning

of gardens."[79] Quoting poets and famous authors was a sign of culture in turn-of-the-century America, and Johnston waxed poetic for her upper-class garden audience. She spoke and wrote lyrically about flowers, window boxes, and mountain views. In Santa Barbara she discovered that "Fountains float cups of fragrance and deep crimson on their clear hearts."[80] To the New York City gardener renovating tenement yards, she quoted Frances Bacon's *Of Gardens; An Essay* (1625): "A garden is the purest of human pleasures; it is the greatest refreshment to the spirits of man, without which buildings and palaces are but gross handy works."[81]

On occasion, poetry alone sufficed to describe a garden. At the Rhode Island house of mining heir Arthur Curtiss James, FBJ performed in "Gardening with the Poets," a Red Cross fund-raiser. She projected her garden slides as poet Gertrude Moore Richards (1859–1927) read verse.[82] While in Newport, she photographed gardeners performing tasks in the James Blue Garden. She intended the posed series to illustrate "The Glory of the Garden" (1911) by the British poet and novelist Rudyard Kipling (1865–1936), whom she met while traveling in England in 1906.[83] This association of photography with poetry by FBJ and magazine editors was a late manifestation of *Ut pictura poesis* ("As is painting, so is poetry"). Poetry, the highest literary form, had elevated the status of painting. Now it was lifting garden photography and landscape architecture to the status of literature and fine art.

[Fig. 17] *The City Gardens Club of New York City Exhibit, 8th Annual International Flower Show, Grand Central Palace, New York, New York, Rosalie Warner Jones, Landscape Gardener, Row House Before and After Renovation, March 1921. Launched in 1913, the same year as The Garden Club of America, the International demonstrated horticultural progress by suppliers, clubs and estate owners. A critic wrote in 1921 that among miniature gardens exhibiting Gertrude Payne Whitney's primroses and executive William Robertson Coe's camellias was this "forceful object lesson … which makes words quite unnecessary." FBJ, the first photographer to exhibit at the annual show, recounted to audiences that a set painter created the controversial backdrop to encourage renovation.*

Johnston added "saving what we have for the next generation" to her poetic advocacy of beauty.[84] To inform her talks on native plants, she researched wildflowers at the U.S. Department of Agriculture and attended lectures and exhibitions by horticulturists Albert Cameron Burrage (1859–1931) and Edgar Theodore Wherry (1885–1982).[85] With slides from New York's Museum of Natural History and the Bronx River Parkway Commission, she lectured on birds and their habitats wrecked by urban development, nature education in public schools, and billboard regulation.[86] In the 1920s she joined the urban backyard movement, promoting worker gardens at the National Cash Register Company in Dayton, Ohio, and The City Gardens Club of New York City renovating row-house yards and apartment courts.[87]

FBJ's role as a prophet of civic beauty made her more than "just a photographer." In December 1923, Leonard Barron at the *The Garden Magazine* published "Garden Photography as a Fine Art: How Frances Benjamin Johnston Turned from the Brush to the Camera as a Means to Artistic Expression." The following year the magazine featured "The Art in Garden Photography … How Photography Captured the Imagination of Mattie Edwards Hewitt in Her Student Days."[88] As biographies of garden photographers, these profiles were unique in *The Garden Magazine* and publications that presented Johnston's work.

Johnston's professional story was distinct. Hewitt made her living only as photographer, but FBJ, in contrast, was a garden celebrity. The article, as Johnston had requested, was sympathetic, describing her Washington connections, the fame of her family garden, her association with women, her book collecting, her lectures, and the "uncanny truthfulness" of her color

[Figs. 18a, 18b] Arkady, Frances Benjamin Johnston House, New Orleans, Louisiana, Frances Benjamin Johnston, Landscape Gardener, Patio Court, Before and After Renovation, August 1945, Spring 1946. Following years promoting reform through beautification, FBJ in retirement brought urban renewal to her first and only garden.

slides.[89] A photo portrait illustrated Barron's deferential essay. Johnston, in a spare interior, hair groomed and wearing an exotic necklace, glanced out at the reader while smoking a cigarette, a signifier of independence.[90] This was FBJ, a New Woman, a friend of presidents and plutocrats, a bohemian, a social reformer, and Arts and Crafts devotee. She was literate, an artist, not a technician, an aesthete who in black-and-white photography captured the color and spirit of a garden. Through words and photography, Barron had successfully profiled the image Johnston crafted in her first decade of garden photography.

Conclusion

At the close of the 19th century, there had been both hope and dissent. The genteel tradition of American arts and letters, embraced by Charles Eliot Norton, *The Century Magazine* editor Richard Watson Gilder (1844–1909), and Chicago exposition architect Charles Follen McKim (1847–1909), held that literature, fine art, classical music, and architecture could change through beauty a world barbarized by industrialism and unfettered wealth.[91] In opposition to their high-culture mantra that informed the City Beautiful, artists and writers called for a new realism to reveal the era's social inequities ignored by American litterateurs who defiled thought with what Mark Twain (1835–1910) mocked as "meretricious artificialities and affectations."[92] Writers Jacob August Riis (1849–1914), Ida Minerva Tarbell (1857–1944), and Twain himself, all photographed by FBJ, exemplified a modern critical commitment.[93]

Frances Benjamin Johnston was of both the old and new worlds of American thought and engagement. As the dedicated D.A.R. member, rallying garden club women with verse and beautiful pictures, she exemplified the genteel artist–stateswoman, a master of diverse interests, a model of the civilized American.[94] As the smoking, ambitious professional photographer, she made her art a force for social change by bringing Old World art conventions to New World photographs promoting American backyard beauty.

FBJ's blend of advocacy and poetic musings earned her a decade of garden work in the prosperous 1920s. When the Depression shattered this interlude between two world wars, Johnston turned to photographing the Old South. The 1930s was a period of introspection when the documentation and study of the past became a national interest. Johnston reflected the new ethos by photographing southern buildings and donating photographs to the Library of Congress. In 1926 FBJ wrote that without a backyard of her own, she had "every garden I have ever seen in vivid, colorful, fragrant impressions, none the less actual and real because they flower only in fancy."[95] Today, her virtual garden, preserved by the Library, is a public document contributing to the history of the American house and garden beautiful.

In 1945 FBJ retired to a house she purchased in New Orleans' Vieux Carré. There, for the first time, she made a garden of her own. She cleared rubble from an interior court and built a lily pool to bring interior rooms into harmony with the out-of-doors. "Hobbies in general are the only effective insurance against boredom," wrote Johnston. "The garden hobby is a freemasonry of which the necessary high sign is merely a kindling glean of the eye over a garden hedge."[96]

Living in her private urban renewal with cats Herman and Vermin, tending goldfish while sipping afternoon bourbon, FBJ became, in her words, an "octo-geranium."[97] On March 16, 1952, she died at 88.

The Garden Photograph

There is more to photography than just taking pictures! —1922

In 1894 Harper Brothers in New York published a slim volume, *Italian Gardens,* written and illustrated by Bostonian Charles Adams Platt (1861–1933). He had trained as a fine artist at the Académie Julian, entering in 1884 as FBJ began her final year at the school.[1] Charles Percier and Pierre Fontaine's 1809 treatise on the villas of Rome, illustrated with engravings, inspired his book, but since the time of the French publication, wrote Platt, "the art of photography had been perfected."[2] He considered himself a landscape painter yet illustrated his treatise not only with etchings and drawings, but with finely detailed photographs to "illustrate as far as possible the more important gardens in Italy."[3]

From photography's rise in the 1840s, gardens and houses had been photographic subjects in Europe and America. Beginning in the 1880s, Underwood & Underwood, Wurtz Brothers, the Detroit Photographic Company, and the Keystone View Company introduced to American parlors the period's new urbanized world. Vistas from buildings and rooftops showed new streets and shady park squares. Johnston's photographs from the 1890s of the Chicago exposition, a Washington convent garden, and The White House are in this late 19th-century documentary tradition.[4]

The photographs by Platt were different. Influenced by commercial and naturalistic photography, he composed pictures with fine-art conventions to convey what architects were beginning to study—how to integrate house and garden through design. His point of view was not of the distanced documentarian, but of the artist experiencing nature in a designed world of stone terraces, balustrade walls, and fountain terraces.[5] The year Platt published his book, FBJ, another fine artist turned photographer, composed one of her first photographs of a designed landscape as experienced by a garden visitor. It was an on-the-ground view of Mount Vernon's vegetable garden. Three years later she similarly photographed the south lawn fountain of The White House.[6] The era of the modern landscape photograph was dawning, and FBJ, attuned to opportunity, recognized the potential for the garden image to be artistic and for the garden photographer to be an artist participating in the house and garden movement.

Garden photography advanced with new camera technology, the maturing of professional landscape design, and the publication of photo-illustrated magazines showing what a commercial garden photograph needed to be. When *Country Life in America* launched in 1901, its editors sponsored a contest for the best four photographs of American nature and rural life. This appeal reached out to the expanding world of amateur and professional photographers that might depict gardens and houses in ways that sold magazines and promoted advertised products. As *Town & Country* editor Henry James Whigham (1869–1954) noted, "one could not be done without the other."[7] The winner of the competition was Henry Troth

(circa 1860–1945), a nature photographer who had been a juror with FBJ in 1899 at the second annual Philadelphia Photographic Society exhibition. As judges, both earned the disdain of Alfred Stieglitz, who rejected photographers with practices combining art and commercial photography.[8] A Stieglitz acolyte, Joseph Turner Keiley (1869–1914), observed that Johnston was a "refined and ambitious worker" but her artistic progress was "retarded by the continual requirements of an onerous professional life."[9]

J. Horace McFarland, the polymath founder of the American Rose Society, printer of *Country Life in America* and *The Garden Magazine*, photographer and leader of the national park movement, announced the prize as consulting editor. He explained that Troth's photographs of men harvesting hay followed "the simplest rules of composition." Technical proficiency was never enough to make a photograph "'artistic.' The camera, the lens, the plates and the chemicals—they are but tools. As with any form of art, it is the conception of the thing to picture that is primarily important. In these days of facility with things cameristic, millions may photograph, and only scores make pictures." Troth won for creating images that were romantic in the tradition of mid-19th-century landscape painting yet retained the details that readers expected from a magazine describing nature and rural life.[10]

Making a photograph that was both expressive and illustrative was the challenge for the contemporary magazine photographer wanting to be an artist, not a technician. Since the 1880s, Pictorialists had explored techniques to shift the photograph away from scientific verisimilitude towards artistic impression by disrupting the recessional perspective, surface detail, and clarity of the photographic image. In contrast, the commercial magazine photographer had to preserve form without losing the abstract values associated with art.[11] Representational photography, wrote naturalistic photographer Peter Henry Emerson (1856–1936), had to be poetic, achieving naturalism, not realism. Through framing and selective focus, the "realist shows, or attempts to, things as they are, not as they look."[12] The landscape and garden photograph had unique potential for beauty and expression because of nature's inherent spiritualism, associated in American thought with Emerson's cousin Ralph Waldo Emerson (1803–82) and the Transcendentalists.[13]

Two decades after Johnston took her first garden photographs, Jessie Tarbox Beals wrote in 1920 that there were no schools teaching the art of garden photography. The profession was suitable for women, "natural makers and lovers of gardens," but the aspiring garden photographer needed to abstract rules for an artistic photograph from manuals on landscape and flower photography already associated with painting genres. She recommended *The Photo-Miniature* series and J. Horace McFarland's *Photographing Flowers and Trees and the Use of Natural Forms in Decorative Photography* (1911). Beals noted that the photo portrait also offered outdoor experience. Clarence Hudson White (1870–91), a founder of the Photo-Secessionist movement and an eponymous photography school, trained students in portraiture by having them design and plant a garden where they posed models for portraits.[14]

Picturing the Garden

FBJ learned to work out-of-doors as a photojournalist and aspiring artist photographer in the 1890s. She photographed Niagara Falls, a coal miner's house and vegetable garden, and Washington mansions. On weekends she composed low-horizon scenes of Maryland waterways indebted to Barbizon

landscape painting, which was then influencing Pictorialist photography.[15] The landscaped garden as subject emerged as Johnston moved from portraiture to architectural photography. In 1912 Mrs. Frank "Narcissa" Vanderlip (1879–1966) and her children posed on the terrace at their Hudson River estate landscaped by William Welles Bosworth (1868–1966). FBJ's print and autochrome of the Vanderlip family were portraits of motherhood consciously alluding to paintings by Mary Stevenson Cassatt (1844–1926) and photo portraits by Johnston's friend Gertrude Käsebier (1852–1934).[16]

In the second half of the 19th century, scholars advancing art and art history codified pictorial aesthetics. Rutgers University historian John Charles Van Dyke (1856–1932), author of *How to Judge of a Picture ...* (1899), wrote that the skilled artist must harmonize the relation of "proportion, color, light" and unite "all the parts into a perfect whole."[17] When the conception of photography as more than a mechanical art emerged at the turn of the century, critics and photographers called for harmonious unity in

[Fig. 21] Cow Grazing Along Waterway Below Alexandria, Virginia, circa 1895. FBJ experienced photographing out-of-doors on weekends in the country, creating pastoral landscapes inspired by French Barbizon painting.

OUT-DOOR PORTRAIT GROUP—MRS. FRANK VANDERLIP AND HER CHILDREN
1 A KODAK FITTED WITH ZEISS PROTAR LENS STOPPED TO F 32   BY FRANCES B. JOHNSTON—MATTIE E. HEWITT
SLOW SHUTTER

[Fig. 22] Narcissa Cox Vanderlip and Her Children at Beechwood, Scarborough, New York, 1912. Influenced by French and American Impressionists, FBJ and her colleagues learned garden photography while making portraits of garden owners.

the new artistic photograph. Carl Sadakichi Hartmann published *Landscape and Figure* (1912), a manual on photographing outdoor scenes, and garden photographer John Wallace Gillies wrote "The Significance of Design in Picture Making" for *The Photo-Miniature* (1919).[18] Both presented how-to illustrations for composing landscape photographs. A comparison of their illustrations with FBJ's garden photographs reveals how closely FBJ conformed to conventions, making her direct photography acceptably artistic, not only in art circles, but in the world of commercial publishing pursued by Gillies and Johnston's contemporaries. Despite the rise of modernist photography in the 1920s, FBJ never deviated from academic composition. "I will do anything to get a picture," she noted in 1947. "But I leave the trick angles to Margaret Bourke-White and Salvador Dali."[19]

Johnston's adherence to traditional form brought her early recognition in the emerging field of garden photography. In 1917 the Touchstone Gallery mounted "Gardens East and West and Other Studies: An Exhibition of Pictorial Photographs by Frances Benjamin Johnston." The show was both the gallery's and FBJ's first garden photography exhibit. The exhibition title made clear that the images of California and Long Island gardens were artistic pictures, not illustrations. To coincide with the opening in December, the editors of the gallery's eponymous magazine published their manifesto, "Garden Photography as a Fine Art: Illustrated by Rare Photographs of Beautiful Gardens." The new field of landscape design, they wrote, had made gardening a fine art, and new gardens had "helped turn photographers into artists, [had] lifted the mechanical science to the plane of the arts." Limited to black and white, the "object of garden photographers should be to attain the feeling and to convey the sense of color and not clearly delineate every leaf and petal." Johnston's garden photograph was "a portrait, not a mechanical exposure." She studied and understood the character of every garden, and her modulation of black and white tone conveyed a "true feeling of color." Her image of the Robert C. Hill East Hampton blue, gray, and pink garden entrance, though in shades of black and white, functioned as a "rarely beautiful color picture," a photograph as artistic as a painting, as composed and harmonious as the garden itself.[20]

The interrelation of picture and garden making was long established by the time garden design and garden photography emerged in the 20th century.[21] Painting traditions had been fundamental to England's Picturesque movement and, in turn, to American landscape design through Andrew Jackson Downing and Frederick Law Olmsted. Charles A. Platt, whose plans and photographs inspired Johnston's garden images and lectures, followed this pictorial tradition.[22] For *Country Life* editor Liberty H. Bailey, landscape gardening was "to make a picture. All grading, seeding, shaping planting are incidental.... The green sward is the canvas, the house or some other prominent point the central figure, the planting completes the compositions and adds color."[23] When the photograph emerged as a new

[Figs. 23a, 23b, left] Diagram for a Tree-Lined Road¸ Carl Sadakichi Hartmann, Illustration, 1912; El Fureidis, James Waldron Gillespie House, Montecito, California, Bertram Grosvenor Goodhue, Landscape Architect, 1902–06, Entrance Drive, Spring 1917. [Fig. 23c center and right] Diagram for Drawing and Photographing the Williamsburg Bridge, New York, New York, John Wallace Gillies, Illustrator and Photographer, 1912; [Fig. 23d, far right] Anne Tracy Morgan House, 3 Sutton Place, New York, New York, Mott Brooshouft Schmidt, Architect, Nellie Beatrice Osborn Allen, Landscape Architect, View from Garden to Queensboro Bridge, Spring 1926. FBJ used picturesque conventions shared by fine artists and photographers to make artistic garden photographs.

pictorial, fine art, the link of photography to landscape design was a logical next chapter in the landscape-as-picture history.

Frances Benjamin Johnston read and collected historic and contemporary books guiding American landscape design. She owned essential volumes including *Art-Out-of-Doors: Hints on Good Taste in Gardening,* by garden critic Mariana Griswold Van Rensselaer (1851–1934), published the year of the Chicago World's Fair, and *An Introduction to the Study of Landscape Architecture,* by Harvard professor Henry Vincent Hubbard (1875–1947) and his wife, Theodora Kimball (1887–1935). These texts and others defined American landscape design and its relation to art for FBJ and her generation of garden photographers and architects.

Landscape designer and educator Frank Albert Waugh (1869–1943) founded in 1903 the landscape gardening program at the Massachusetts Agricultural College, today the University of Massachusetts, Amherst. He was an early promoter of photographs for teaching landscape design and admired FBJ's garden images.[24] He wrote *Book of Landscape Gardening,* published in 1899 and revised in two editions. Following the lead of Van Rensselaer, Waugh distinguished landscape gardening as a fine art that "attempts to create organized beauty—to unite several dissimilar parts in one harmonious whole."[25] The landscape architect achieved this unity by building "the largest number of possible pictures, supposing them all to be consistent with the main theme, upon every piece of land placed in his hands."[26] For the architect designing pictures, the camera was utilitarian. The measure of his or her achievement in "landscape-composition," wrote Waugh, was a landscape's "photographability." The photograph was "an absolutely reliable report of light and shade … [it] shows textures and gives a very good approximation of color-values."[27]

Hubbard and Kimball shared Waugh's regard for landscape architecture as art. In their 1917 *Introduction,* they applied to garden design Beaux-Arts principles that FBJ had learned in Paris and that guided American landscape programs. The authors illustrated their text outlining the components of unified design—progression, sequence, balance, symmetry, monotony,

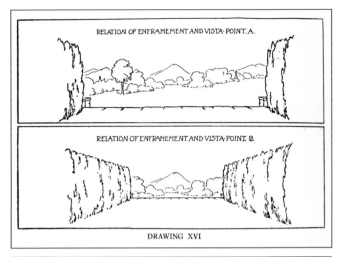

RELATION OF ENFRAMEMENT AND VISTA-POINT. A.

RELATION OF ENFRAMEMENT AND VISTA-POINT. B.

DRAWING XVI

[Figs. 24a, 24b] Top: Landscape "Enframement" Diagram for Designing a Garden with a Mountain View, Illustration, Henry Vincent Hubbard and Theodora Kimball, 1917; Bottom: Arcady, George Owen Knapp House, Montecito, California, Francis Townsend Underhill, Architect and Landscape Architect, 1914, Lower Garden, View to Santa Ynez Mountains, Spring 1917. In new design programs, landscape architects learned to compose garden pictures that FBJ interpreted in garden photographs. She trained through practice and study.

reflect what a landscape architect and garden owner could, in reality, see. In analyzing the "enframement" of a view by hedges, they wrote that "a very distant mountain of marked form but not notable size may serve in a landscape view as a perfectly satisfactory climax, but in no ordinary photograph of that view will it appear other than insignificant."[29] Using pictorial conventions familiar to the viewer from fine art and commercial illustration, the professional photographer assured that beauty made by the landscape architect on the land was seen in the photographic print.

Having studied painting and drawing, read contemporary landscape writings and learned through portraiture in the 1890s to construct photographic realties, FBJ succeeded as a professional photographer selling garden photographs to publishers and women's clubs. Landscape designers and editors, trusting her perceptual experience, left Johnston to compose photographs of the pictures they conceived for clients and readers learning to garden through magazines and books. Washington, D.C., landscape architect John Henry Small III (1889–1965) wrote to Johnston that "no one … seems to understand the photographing of gardens so well as you do; in fact, I think most landscape men should admit that nine times out of ten your photographs are very flattering to their work, due entirely to your selection of the proper view point and composition."[30] Using new lenses that produced undistorted, wide-field images, FBJ photographed popular garden elements—flower parterres, ornamental pools aligned with terraces, pavilions, and herbaceous borders along pergola walks.[31] Modulating tone in prints and slides, Johnston further enhanced both natural and

variety, color, and atmosphere—with engravings and photographs that were "in themselves good examples of composition in various modes."[28] Hubbard, Mary H. Northend, and others were the artists of these images. They, like Johnston, used picturesque devices: natural and man-made elements framing main subjects, balance of foreground and middle with lights and darks, and diagonals leading to distant scenes. While Waugh idealized the photograph as scientific and depicting an unmediated reality, Hubbard and Kimball understood that the camera image had to be composed to man-made features, making them, at a minimum, as significant in photographs as they were in life.

House owners and designers who commissioned photographs thought that Johnston brought more to garden photography than fine composition. Landscape architect Beatrix J. Farrand encouraged FBJ to photograph her gardens, writing that she had "personally not been satisfied with [pictures] which a local photographer took, as they don't seem to me to have got quite the character that I hoped it might be possible to bring out."[32] Through differential focus, light, and tone, Johnston evoked the "poetry and mystery" Sadakichi Hartmann found lacking in her 1900 art photograph, "Cigarette," of a woman wearing a kimono. In Johnston's prints and slides, viewers discovered what Hildegarde Hawthorne described as the "spirit that broods over Eastern as well as Western Gardens," the Emersonian transcendence that garden club members were seeking in magazines and lectures.[33] "To be worthy of the name, a garden, like a person, must have three sides: physical, intellectual and spiritual," wrote landscape architect and Johnston friend Rose Ishbel Greely (1887–1969). "The charm of the walled garden, of the half-open gate, of the screening rose arbor, and of the curving path, lies in what they only half reveal" of the "mystery" in the garden.[34] FBJ made these details consistent features of her photographs, combining poetic and informative detail to make photographs salable to house owners and magazine editors.

In the Picturesque tradition, FBJ's generation of landscape architects, writers, and editors conceived and perceived the designed landscape as interdependent scenes related, as Kimball instructed, through progression and sequence. Artist and garden editor for *The Craftsman* Eloise Jenkins Roorbach (1886–1961) discovered that dealer George Turner Marsh (1857–1932) had composed his 1906 Japanese garden at the Hotel del Coronado in San Diego "for vistas and pictures."[35] Johnston herself experienced the Italian villa garden as "a series of pictures painted with growing things carefully related and set in their proper frame."[36] To reflect photographically the American landscaped garden, FBJ made 15 to 50 exposures,

from different angles and distances, to create a composite, albeit fractured, overview of a garden's design. On her trip to Southern California in 1917, Johnston's process evolved. Landscape architects there had addressed the challenges of landscaping hillside lots by adapting Italian traditions. FBJ reflected their designs by sequencing photographs as garden walks up and down terraced steps.

FBJ's efforts to convey the three-dimensionality of the landscaped garden were largely futile in the day-to-day world of photo publication. Writers, landscape architects, and publishers, despite their concurrence that gardens were interrelated compositions, selected single photographs that served professional needs, editorial agendas, and budgets. At exhibition and in slide presentations, however, Johnston controlled what was seen, preserving a photographic order corresponding to her experience of gardens. This control allowed the viewer, as a relative discovered at FBJ's 1917 Touchstone exhibition, to "follow the progress of garden making from the beginning."[37]

The inherent narrative arc of the lantern-slide presentation, with a beginning and an end, deepened the virtual garden experience. Johnston used the medium's dynamic potential to tell stories and teach design principles.[38] She compared gardens didactically, arranged California slides as a travelogue, and sequenced slides to walk viewers along flower borders. Beauty had to be experienced, not just observed, and the more a lantern-slide presentation reenacted the direct experience of a garden, the deeper the understanding of its design and spirit.[39]

Sequential presentation of prints and the projection of lantern slides were steps in the cultural evolution from books to movies, from understanding the world through reading to experiencing it through seeing.[40] Already in 1915, Louise Shelton sensed the new visual literacy, explaining in *Beautiful Gardens in America* that borders and fountains in photo vignettes "spoke so eloquently for themselves that there seems but little need of detailed verbal description."[41] *The Garden Magazine* took a further step, introducing in 1918 its "Garden Movies" column, illustrated with staged, sequential photographs of gardeners performing tasks graphically framed as film strips. By the 1920s, when the middle and upper middle classes were accepting film as authentic culture, not just low-art immigrant entertainment, garden clubs began to feature movies on national parks and wildflowers. Frances Benjamin Johnston, alert to this cultural shift, pursued movie production.[42] "The Garden Isle, Long Island"; "Gardens of a Little Paradise, Italy"; "Gardens of the Kings of France and Their Nobles"; and "Gardens of Holy Places, Palestine" were among the productions FBJ envisioned but never realized before she began documenting buildings in the South.[43]

Writers and lecturers from the turn of the century debated color appropriate for the American flower garden. Influenced by Arts and Crafts design and English Romantic and French Impressionist painting, designers rejected the brilliant contrasts of 19th-century flower bedding. Gertrude Jekyll and William Robinson (1838–1935), influential in England and America, advocated for graduated shades and color themes to avoid what New York gardener Helen S. Thorne discovered at a local flower show, a "hopeless clash of color and type" versus "a harmonious and lovely glowing border."[44] They and their followers wrote books and

articles to define the new palettes. With the autochrome difficult to produce and print, authors commissioned paintings and hand-tinted photographs to illustrate their garden essays. Gertrude Jekyll collaborated with watercolorist George Samuel Elgood (1851–1943), whose paintings Johnston included in her slide collection.[45] America's Louise Beebe Wilder (1878–1938) illustrated her 1918 best seller *Colour in My Garden* with paintings by her neighbor Anna Lillian Winegar (1870–c. 1941), a student of American Impressionist painter Frank Edwin Scott (1863–1929). Its title-page quotation, "Colour is the most sacred Element of all things," was from John Ruskin's *The Stones of Venice* (vol. 2, 1852).[46] His conception of spiritual redemption through beauty continued to inspire American garden design.

Johnston endeared herself to clubs by promoting her sense for color, akin to the musician's "true pitch," she told *The Garden Magazine* in 1924.[47] Like American artists, she had developed this sensibility while studying in France at the time of the Impressionists.[48] What FBJ saw and understood in modern art is not known, but she kept a list of works by Cézanne, Matisse, and Picasso published in Alfred Stieglitz's *Camera Work*.[49] She participated in Washington's art community at the turn of the century and later photographed the gardens of post-Impressionist painter Gari Melchers (1860–1932) and of Annie May Hegeman (1859–1948), an artist in the Southampton, New York, circle of William Merritt Chase (1849–1916).

[Figs. 25a, 25b] Biltmore, George Washington Vanderbilt House, Asheville, North Carolina, Richard Morris Hunt, Architect, Frederick Law Olmsted, Landscape Architect, 1888–95, FBJ with Camera and Photographing the Garden, circa 1938. Photographer unknown. In the Depression, Johnston and her driver Huntley Ruff, seen here in a cap, traveled through the South photographing houses and gardens. They stopped at this Vanderbilt estate landscaped by Olmsted as FBJ was launching her career. Just under half a century later, the famous photographer added the Gilded Age château to her survey of southern buildings. She recalled that, "when I went trudging about carrying a big 11-by-14 camera, they used to tell me that I looked like an ant with a huge last year's grasshopper."

[Figs. 26a, 26b] Top: Villa Farnese, Caprarola, Italy, Giacomo Barozzi da Vignola, House and Landscape Architect, from 16th Century, View to Casino, Summer 1925; Bottom: Las Tejas, Oakleigh Thorne House, Montecito, California, Francis William Wilson, Architect, Helen Stafford Thorne, Landscape Gardener, from 1918. View from Swimming Pool Pavilion to House, Spring 1923. FBJ photographed thematically for instructive comparisons. With these two slides, garden club members learned that Wilson remodeled an adobe to be a Californian Villa Farnese. The garden, combining Western drought-resistant shrubs and flowers cultivated in the East, was a synthesis of America and Europe. Las Tejas, wrote Johnston, "breathed Italy," and so did this award-winning photograph composed as a Renaissance panel with color "notes of rose & orange in the shrubbery."

Her association of color with music reflected 19th-century thought that interwove music and painting as allied arts in the formulation *Ut pictura musica* ("As is painting, so is music").[50] In the 20th century Henri Matisse (1869–1954), whose paintings Johnston admired at the Corcoran Gallery of Art in 1910, wrote that "colors have a beauty of their own which must be preserved, as one strives to preserve tonal quality in music."[51]

To convey to garden club audiences the correct colors for the American flower border, Johnston tinted her garden photographs. As was customary, she commissioned production specialists for this work. From the 1910s until the mid-1920s, her lead colorist was Grace Adele Smith Anderson (b. 1873), who began her career in Dayton, Ohio, at the National Cash Register Company. Its founder, John Henry Patterson, was a media enthusiast who set up studios in New York and Dayton to produce slides and movies.[52] Grace Smith moved to New York by 1906 and worked freelance, painting slides for the Museum of Natural History. Curator of ornithology Frank Chapman (1864–1945) considered her the most proficient of the museum's artists at the exacting skill of coloring birds. In 1908 she married sales manager Frank Carson Anderson and moved to Philadelphia, where she worked from her house for Columbia University and Amherst College.[53] Smith painted for both FBJ and Mattie Edwards Hewitt, who did not lecture but, like Johnston, sold slides to garden clubs and landscape architects.

In late 1925 or early 1926, Johnston turned to Edward van Altena to produce her European garden slides. By 1928 Grace Smith, for unknown reasons, was no longer working for FBJ.

Using transparent glazes, Smith tinted black-and-white photo positives transferred to 3¼- by 4–inch glass plates.[54] Like drawing in fine art painting, the lightly developed images guided tone and form. Before beginning,

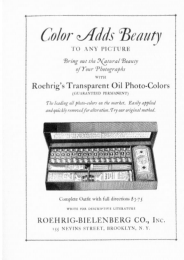

[Figs. 27a, 27b] *Top: Unidentified Artist Painting Lantern Slides, Slide Room, National Cash Register Company, Dayton, Ohio, Photographer unknown, January 25, 1903; Bottom: Advertisement for Roehrig-Bollenberg Lantern-Slide Paints, 1922. Grace Smith Anderson, who tinted FBJ's slides, began her career at the Ohio factory studio. Artists painted with both oils and watercolor to bring beauty to luminous slide paintings.*

Smith, in consultation with FBJ, applied a pre-cut mat or black tape to frame an image. At first, the artist referred to Johnston and Hewitt autochromes for color guidance. After FBJ abandoned the French process circa 1917, Smith studied notes Johnston transcribed to photograph prints.[55] Smith protected each finished painting with a clear glass plate, forming a two-layer packet. This consistent production by Smith and photo houses conventionalized the lantern slide, making it a medium in itself.[56]

No less than her print photographs, FBJ's slides were works of imagination and art, not science and nature, competing aesthetically with watercolors by Mary Helen Carlisle (1869–1925) and Ella du Cane (1870–1940). Just as Johnston moved plants, stopped traffic, photographed at full bloom, and processed negatives to achieve balanced composition and tone, so did Grace Smith Anderson and Edward van Altena perfect coloring to make a slide artistic.[57] Colorists painted brown window mullions green, smoothed patchy turf into carpets, and made water turquoise blue.[58] To tint flower borders, they used graduated palettes paralleling color manuals published for the new flower garden. Architect Leicester Bodine Holland's 1915 *The Garden Blue Book* was an early example of a how-to-color-a-garden manual, with plant charts printed in color to show the "arrangement of flower harmonies and flower sequences" to make a "garden picture."[59]

In contrast to the soft grayness of the black-and-white print and the atmospheric but opaque world of the autochrome, Johnston's lantern slides were translucent, light-filled miniatures.[60] Her California field of purple lupine and yellow poppies, her daffodil ravine at Lob's Wood outside Cincinnati, and her perennial borders at the Kies garden in Scarborough, New York, are color symphonies with spots of bright hues rivaling paintings by John Singer Sargent, Charles Courtney Curran (1861–1942), and Childe Hassam (1859–1935), all artists who, like FBJ, attended the Académie Julian.[61] Her 1915 images of the Stephen Swete Cummins water garden were Monet harmonies in blue, violet, yellow, and green.

Johnston's transference of painterly color to the lantern slide was a critical turn. Nineteenth-century Impressionism, in part, was a response

[Figs. 28a, 28b, 28c, top row] left to right: Casa de Mariposa, Walter Franklin Cobb House, Montecito, California, Cary Fish Cobb, Landscape Gardener, circa 1916. Rock Garden Photograph, Verso and Recto, with FBJ's Notes for Coloring; Rock Garden Slide, Spring 1917. A lantern slide was a collaboration between FBJ, who took notes in the field, and the slide colorist who interpreted them in paint.

[Figs. 29a, 29b, 29c, bottom row] left to right: Près Choisis, Albert Herter House, East Hampton, New York, Grosvenor Atterbury, Architect, 1898–99, Albert and Adele McGinnis Herter, Landscape Gardeners, from 1898. Blue-and-White Garden Terrace: Black-and-White Photograph, Autochrome, and Lantern Slide, Fall 1913. FBJ used these three formats for garden photography. An unidentified autochrome guided the tinting of the slide, a perfected view.

to photography's challenge to realist painting. Representation became the domain of the mechanical image and impression the objective of fine-art photography. As discussed, the commercial photographer wanting to be an artist had to retain form and be expressive. Johnston achieved this balance by modulating values in black and white and composing slides with palettes that harmonized blues and greens highlighted with what she called "notes" of bright colors. This painterly approach conformed to landscape design practices. In a 1922 article illustrated with gardens by Marian C. Coffin, Beatrix J. Farrand, and Ellen Biddle Shipman (1869–1950), *The Architectural Record* wrote that the contemporary designer was "keeping pace in garden planting with the impressionists, the luminarists, and leaders in the most modern schools of landscape painting."[62] FBJ, the modern

[Figs. 30a, 30b, top row] Claude Monet, Le Bassin Aux Nymphéas, Harmonie Verte *("The Lily Pond, Green Harmony"), 1899; Grey-Croft, Stephen Swete Cummins House, East Hampton, New York, Emma Woodhouse Cummins, Landscape Gardener, Circa 1903, Lily Pool, July, 1913. [Figs. 30c, 30d, bottom row] Lilla Cabot Perry,* Stream Beneath Poplars, *Circa 1890–1900; Michael Cochrane Armour House, Pasadena, California, Robert Gordon Fraser and/or Thomas Chisholm, Landscape Gardeners, from 1910, Native Plant Garden Pathway, Spring 1917. Monet and the Impressionists influenced American painters and landscape architects coloring the new American garden. FBJ reflected this influence in slide paintings that conveyed her impressions of a garden.*

photographer, did the same in lantern slides with colors conveying the impression of the new American garden. She pitched her slides as being in "natural colors," but in their perfected reality, they were artistically naturalistic.[63]

Unlike Impressionist artists, who pictured children and parents out-of-doors, FBJ rarely included garden owners in prints and slides. Men and women, wrote *Country Life* contributor Arthur G. Eldredge, "added a touch of sentiment" to the garden image, but the photographer needed to "subordinate" either person or garden when determining a photographic subject.[64] Whenever a human figure looks at a camera, wrote J. Horace McFarland, "the whole thing becomes a portrait, with landscape accessories … not an outdoor picture." The farmers in Henry Troth's 1901 award-winning photographs enriched his harvest story because they were posed at work. In an outdoor composition, children, "in their grace and freedom from conventional pose," were the exception.[65]

For magazine editors and authors, the garden, as FBJ explained, "reflected the personality of the gardener as much as the interior reflected the personality of the housewife."[66] Consequently, the owner's presence in a photograph was redundant, disrupting readers' experience of a garden as potentially their own.

Already an experienced portraitist when she became a professional garden photographer, Johnston understood the perceptional effects of people in photograph images. By 1917, when magazines were regularly purchasing her garden images, she rarely photographed owners and did not exhibit the portraits she made. Her lantern slides, with the exception of Rear Admiral Aaron and Elizabeth Cairns Ward at Willowmere, included only children and adults engaged in garden activities. For slides of Hickory

Hill in Virginia, Johnston included owners to establish the garden's scale, a convention used by period engravers and recommended by Frank A. Waugh for slides educating landscape architects.[67]

Weedless, ever-blooming, flawless, and without people, the photographed garden was timeless and authoritative, ideal for persuasive lectures and magazines delineating American design. Editors universalized the garden photograph by presenting it as art, not contemporary illustration or document. They did not date published images and often did not identify location.[68] In the 1920s *House & Garden* ran its "Garden in Good Taste" feature with toned and framed photographs, and *Country Life* regularly published garden photographs as art pictures.[69] Editors poetically titled Johnston's spring bulbs at the estate of Fitz Eugene Dixon, the locale not identified in print, "Spring Is Just Around the Corner." One-line captions were verse quotations from Proverbs (13:26): "Scattered Gold," "Ways of Pleasantness," and "Ways of Peace."[70] FBJ, the photographer–artist, received credit under the title. When gardener Elinore Harde launched in 1917 her

GARDEN SENTINELS

Our Garden Journal   Photographed by Frances B. Johnston   September 1917

[Fig. 31] "Garden Sentinels," Our Garden Journal, September 1917, Photo-Reproduction of Hand-Tinted Black-and-White Photograph. A print of Johnston's 1917 soft-focus image of the Mrs. Dudley Peter Allen stairway in Pasadena, California, illustrated the poetry of a hillside garden.

[Fig. 32a, 32b] Villa Bel Riposo, George Gregory Smith House, San Domenico, Italy, Cedars of Lebanon, Summer 1925, Exhibition Print, Ferargil Gallery, New York, New York, 1926; Philipland, Philip Laird House, New Castle, Delaware, Robert Buist, Landscape Gardener, 1847, Grape Arbor, Spring 1928. FBJ exhibited and sold her garden photographs as art, producing Pictorialist silver gelatin prints and mounting images on hand-blocked paper.

short-lived journal for wealthy "amateur flower gardeners," she reproduced Johnston's print of the garden stairs at Mrs. Dudley "Elisabeth" Allen's Pasadena house. Hand-colored and tipped-in, the artistically blurred photograph, "Garden Sentinels," was the frontispiece to the first issue. Harde credited FBJ but not the owner, location, or landscape designer. Unrelated to the articles that followed, the photograph was a work of art conjuring up the elusive beauty experienced in a designed American garden.[71]

The publication and exhibition of Johnston's photographs as art reflected FBJ's conception of herself and her work. Her early V-Street atelier had been "more like a painter's workshop than a photographer's room," and her garden series were "collections."[72] She printed, matted, and presented photographs in ways considered artistic by art-photography circles, offering

rice paper and embossed mounts. Through the 1920s she continued to develop prints using a soft-focus, Pictorialist style. These embellishments added status and presence to Johnston's garden images, but finally for FBJ, a straight photographer, traditional composition and tone were the qualities that made a photograph artistic.[73]

Conclusion

The Architectural League of New York held annual exhibitions of members' work illustrated by photographs of building and landscape architecture. The 1927 exhibit at New York's Arden Gallery, which sold garden accessories, was the first devoted solely to landscape design. In a review for The Garden

Club of America, designer Ruth Bramley Dean (1889–1932) wrote that "the most significant thing about these exhibits" was "their bringing together of the various artists and artisans who may co-operate to produce the perfect garden." Dean included "the photographs of executed work, carefully framed and hung" as contributing to the exhibition's success.[74]

FBJ advanced in this new professional world, when the fates of the garden photographer and landscape architect were intertwined as American house building and gardening evolved. To participate in the era's high-art culture, both needed acceptance as fine artists. One designed gardens, and the other interpreted them in picturesque ways that assured their mutual success. "My slides are as beautiful as is possible to produce short of the Autochrome plate," wrote Johnston, "but what I consider much more important, they have invariably been taken for a definite purpose and *mean* something."[75] Through composition and color conforming to design ideals guiding fine art and garden design, she produced views of the American garden embodying the beauty that architects and garden owners sought to elevate American taste through "beautiful productions in nature and in art."

By the late 1920s, Johnston and her colleagues were influencing garden design as The Garden Club of America had anticipated. FBJ client Anna Gilman Hill (1872–1955) personally planned her gardens in East Hampton and Englewood, New Jersey, in the 1910s. When she moved to her family house above the Hudson River in the late 1920s, she "studied photographs of other old places which had been remodeled and discovered [the] work of Miss Marian Coffin." On the basis of these photographs, Hill selected

[Fig. 33] Auld Lang Syne, James Herndon Lightfoot House, Takoma Park, Maryland, Virginia Dorsey Lightfoot, Landscape Gardener, 1935. Frances Benjamin Johnston Under an Arbor, 1938. Photographer unknown. Garden photographs educated the new American gardener. After attending a slide lecture by FBJ, Virginia D. Lightfoot planted her backyard and dedicated this shady corner to the photographer. A hand-carved plaque thanked Johnston for making a "dream come true."

the landscape architect to redesign her rocky site.[76] A Connecticut resident, expanding his garden, purchased from Johnston a print of a garden gate he was having "his gardener reproduce … beside an old apple orchard."[77] And gardener Virginia Dorsey Lightfoot, after attending FBJ's "Old World Garden" lecture in the late 1930s, transformed her one acre in Takoma Park, Maryland, into an ornamental flower garden based on FBJ slides. Under an arbor planted with varieties of wisteria and roses that Johnston remembered from her family garden, Lightfoot placed a plaque inscribed: "To Frances Benjamin Johnston whose lore and art of Old World gardens have made a dream come true. VDL"[78] At 76, FBJ visited the suburban garden. In the shade of the bower, the photographer experienced in living color the meaning her photographs had to an American backyard gardener.

[Figs. 34a, 34b, 34c top row]: Beacon Hill, Arthur Curtiss James House, Newport, Rhode Island, Olmsted Brothers, Landscape Architects, 1908–13, 1915–16, Blue Garden, Gate, July 1917; Enniscorthy, Albert Henry Morrill House, Green Mountain, Virginia, Birdbath, 1932; Claverack, Colonel Thomas Henry Barber House, Southampton, New York, Frederick Law Olmsted, Landscape Architect, 1893–94, Rustic Gate, circa 1915.

[Figs. 34d, 34e, 34f, bottom row]: Vivian Spencer Town House, New York, New York, Marian Cruger Coffin, Landscape Architect, circa 1921, Garden in Two Seasons, Exhibition Display at The City Gardens Club of New York City, December 1922; Daniel Elezer Pomeroy House, Englewood, New Jersey, Ruth Bramley Dean, Landscape Architect, circa 1915, Iris Pathway, Spring 1918; Villa Lante, Bagnaia, Italy, Giacomo Barozzi da Vignola and Carlo Maderno, Landscape Architects, 1568–1600, Water Chain, Summer 1925.

Though slides consistently measured 3 ¼ by 4 inches, FBJ framed images variously to enhance subject focus.

Plates

The garden photographs that follow are a selection from the more than 1,100 Frances Benjamin Johnston lantern slides at the Library of Congress. The five chapters represent the five collections Johnston formed from her travels, beginning with American estate gardens in the 1910s and concluding with southern gardens in the 1930s. For clarity, slide images are presented geographically by garden location. FBJ, in fact, rearranged slides within and between collections for different lectures. Unless otherwise noted, images dated 1895–1909 and 1917–35 are by Frances Benjamin Johnston; those dated 1910–16 are by the Johnston-Hewitt partnership.

[*Frontispiece*] THE APPLETREES, HENRY EUGENE COE HOUSE, SOUTHAMPTON, NEW YORK

View from Porch, 1914

Gardens of the East

The exterior of your home and its surroundings are not private property. Your neighbors and every person
who sees your home are impressed by its charm or its unattractiveness. —1924

The flight of the rich to greener pastures outside cities at the turn of the century led to country house building. For the three decades before the Depression, the wealthy hired architects educated in professional programs to design estates as small as 10 acres and as large as 1,000. These designers, both men and women, turned to American antebellum and European precedents to distill a new aesthetic after the prior generation's eclecticism. By 1913 Boston architect Ralph Adams Cram (1863–1942) was able to write that America was finally lifting itself up from the "hopeless vulgarity and ignorance and tawdriness that followed after the last flicker of native taste" in the 1850s.[1] Enclaves with revivalist houses had emerged along the East Coast with flower parterres and pergola walks that Frances Benjamin Johnston photographed at the beginning of her garden photography career.

After moving to New York from Washington, D.C., in 1909, FBJ, with her partner Mattie Edwards Hewitt, photographed, in both black and white and autochrome, gardens in Rhode Island, Massachusetts, and Connecticut, as well as in New York, where she focused on Long Island's South Shore. Mrs. Charles Frederick "Zelia" Hoffman Jr. (1867–1929), wife of a New York real estate heir, was an early ally. She arranged the photography of Newport gardens in summer 1914 and was the first to publish photographs by Johnston–Hewitt in a garden club journal, the

1915 *Annuaire of the Garden Club of Newport.*[2] In fall of that year, the partners photographed the Bronx, New York, garden of the International Garden Club, founded in summer 1914 by Hoffman and English garden designer Alice Vaughan-Williams Martineau (1865–1956). The club's members were wealthy gardeners who became Johnston clients.[3] In August 1917, the organization published its first *Journal of the International Garden Club,* illustrated with East Coast gardens photographed by Johnston and Hewitt before they ended their partnership that year.

Johnston lived in New York, the center of magazine publishing and commercial photography. For garden assignments, she relied on business contacts and landscape architects including Bryant Fleming (1877–1946), Clarence Fowler (1870–1935), and Fletcher Steele (1885–1971). Designers worked directly with FBJ, recommending recently completed projects, or through magazine editors who purchased photo prints directly from the photographer. She advertised in the *Bulletin of The Garden Club of America* and mailed promotional brochures to local affiliates, offering discounts to members who wanted their gardens photographed while she was in town to lecture.[4]

From March through October, FBJ visited gardens in the East, Northeast, and Midwest. Staying with house owners or friends for a day or two, Johnston, sometimes with an assistant, worked from early morning through afternoon, looking for the light that "gives roundness."[5] She stood on a ladder and leaned out windows, choosing points of view she thought conveyed in print a garden's design and character.

Before motoring to New England in summer 1920, just months after The Garden Club of America held their annual meeting north of Boston, FBJ wrote Beatrix Jones Farrand (1872–1959), seeking gardens to photograph. The landscape architect, niece of Edith Wharton and early Garden Club of America advisor, replied from her cottage in Maine. She sent a list of gardens of possible interest and explained, "While I do not of course dare to say that all the owners would consent indiscriminately to the publication of their garden photographs, I can say that I have not yet been refused where I asked for permission."[6] With this contact, FBJ photographed in August Farrand's garden, the architect's Italian terrace for John Stewart Kennedy, and Massachusetts North Shore gardens belonging to brothers Charles William and Frederick Strong Moseley. In the coming decade, FBJ followed established protocol, explaining to an inquiring editor, "I never use any material for publication that is not properly authorized."[7]

House owners, participating in the competitive worlds of magazine profiles and garden clubs, coordinated photo shoots to capture peak bloom before seasonal rains and summer heat. In April 1921 The Garden Club of America board member Mrs. Robert "Virginia" Low Bacon requested that FBJ photograph as soon as possible the dogwoods in her Old Westbury garden designed by Martha Brookes Brown Hutcheson (1871–1959). Four days later, FBJ arrived by train in time for the garden's flowering trees and shrubs.[8] Similarly, she returned to estates over several years to update private and institutional photo collections with images of recent plantings and improvements.

A property that Johnston visited at least twice was Dosoris, the Long Island North Shore family compound assembled by Charles Pratt, an oil refiner whose Brooklyn business became part of the Standard Oil Company. From the end of the 19th century through the 1930s, his children built and then rebuilt houses on the 1,100-acre property overlooking Long Island Sound. The two Pratt gardens represented in the Johnston slide collection are Killenworth and Welwyn, owned by brothers George Dupont Pratt, manager of the family's holdings, and Harold Irving Pratt, trustee of the Pratt Institute and husband of Garden Club of America leader and Johnston supporter Harriet Barnes Pratt. Frederick Law Olmsted Jr. oversaw the planning of shared drives and garden projects at Dosoris. Martha B. Hutcheson in 1911 and 1913 designed flower gardens at Welwyn, with James Leal Greenleaf contributing, and circa 1913 Greenleaf, influenced by Hutcheson, designed the roads and overall plan for Killenworth.

What it is notable about these two gardens is the similarity of their sunken terraces, both to each other and to gardens along the Eastern Seaboard.[9] The sharing of picturesque aesthetics and good taste by landscape designers and garden photographers contributed to what John Dixon Hunt calls "the pervasive bland uniformity of design," when "keeping up with the Joneses meant having our garden look like the Joneses'."[10] Johnston and her colleagues helped bring beautiful gardens to America in the country house era, but with individual expression confined by creative conformity.

From Johnston–Hewitt photographs of the Pratt, Hoffman, and other eastern estates, FBJ produced her talk "Our American Gardens" and its variants, adding and deleting slides as her work progressed over 20 years. Her collection, eventually comprising over 300 slides, was not encyclopedic, but representative of contemporary garden design. Color palettes and planning a garden in relation to the house were among the subjects she presented.

FBJ opened her "Our American Gardens" presentation with a slide of Mount Vernon's vegetable garden. Saved by women before the Civil War, the Virginia plantation was a shrine to national taste and design. Critics Harry William Desmond (1863–1916) and Herbert David Croly (1869–1930) similarly introduced their 1903 summa *Stately Homes in America from Colonial Times to the Present Day* with George and Martha

Washington's Potomac River house. It confirmed that America had a tradition of estate building, albeit more restrained than the one developing at the turn of the century. From this historic garden, Johnston progressed to present-day exemplars: J. Pierpont Morgan's Hudson River spring bulb garden, a naturalized planting in the spirit of William Robinson (1838–1935); Isabel and Larz Anderson's formal Italian Garden in Brookline, Massachusetts; and the Olmsted Brothers' Blue Garden at Beacon Hill in Newport, a color-themed flower garden. With each slide, FBJ identified the garden's owner, enhancing his or her reputation as a cultural leader and her own as a society photographer.

In 1917 and in 1923 Johnston traveled in California from March through May. The early spring of West Coast gardens extended her annual June-through-October photography calendar by two months. After these western trips, FBJ created new lectures, "Gardens of the East" and "Gardens of the West." This vision of two Americas reflected not only a geographical and horticultural divide, but a cultural bias that defined western gardens through contrast with establishment eastern gardens, standard-bearers of national design.

Johnston's mastering of the garden photograph as both art and document brought her new stature a decade after she entered the field of professional house and garden photography. In May 1919, at the annual meeting of the Women's National Farm and Garden Association held at the Pennsylvania School of Horticulture for Women at Ambler, Johnston was among the speakers, who included Charles Lathrop Pack (1858–1937), millionaire president of the War Garden Commission, and Elizabeth Price Martin (1865–1932), president of The Garden Club of America. Minutes of the meeting reported that "Miss Johnston urged owners of small gardens to make more use of cameras to show results obtained." In the movement to beautify America through education and example, both professional and amateur photographers were needed to document gardens. For direct experience of progress in the new field of landscape design in harmony with architecture, conference attendees visited over two days

the houses of Mrs. Joseph Coleman Bright, Mrs. William Warner Harper, Mrs. Charles William Henry, Mrs. Horatio Gates Lloyd, and Mrs. Frederick Winslow Taylor, all photographed by Johnston while on this trip.[11]

In 1922 and 1923 FBJ returned to Pennsylvania to photograph her final Pennsylvania estate, Whitemarsh Hall. Horace Trumbauer (1868–1938), the architect of The Elms in Newport, an early Johnston assignment, designed the 1920 house for Philadelphia financier Edward Townsend Stotesbury. Balustrade terraces and lawn parterres by French landscape architect Jacques-Auguste-Henri Gréber (1882–1962) overlooked the Whitemarsh Valley in Wyndmoor.[12] Johnston took more than 225 photographs of interiors and exteriors, making this her most extensive garden and house commission. Lucretia Cromwell Stotesbury paid for the photographs and kept the rights to reproduction.[13]

Johnston made no slides of this lavish Georgian Revival house. Federal income taxation from 1913, immigration reform in 1917 and 1924, and the Depression ended the American estate era. By the early 1920s, Johnston's clients and their heirs were subdividing land for development. Magazines began to publish Spanish Revival villas and colonial manors on three-acre lots appealing to new affluent middle- and upper-middle-class readers, now members of Garden Club of America affiliates. In 1926 Johnston submitted to Mary Fanton Roberts (1880–1956), editor of *Arts & Decoration*, photographs of an unidentified estate, possibly Whitemarsh Hall. Roberts rejected the images, explaining that the house "seems so formal and so very expensive in every way that I fear it holds very little in it for the readers who are interested in building up gardens."[14] Responding to this changing world, Johnston turned to city and suburban backyards for new work.

[1]   THE ELMS, EDWARD JULIUS BERWIND HOUSE, NEWPORT, RHODE ISLAND

Boxwood Parterre, Summer 1914

[2] THE ELMS, EDWARD JULIUS BERWIND HOUSE, NEWPORT, RHODE ISLAND

Fountain Alley, Summer 1914

[3]   THE BREAKERS, CORNELIUS VANDERBILT II HOUSE, NEWPORT, RHODE ISLAND

Loggia Parterre, Summer 1914

[4] HAMMERSMITH FARM, HUGH DUDLEY AUCHINCLOSS HOUSE, NEWPORT, RHODE ISLAND

Rock Garden, July 1917

{ 5 } HAMMERSMITH FARM, HUGH DUDLEY AUCHINCLOSS HOUSE, NEWPORT, RHODE ISLAND

Lily Pool in Sunken Garden, July 1917

[6] HAMMERSMITH FARM, HUGH DUDLEY AUCHINCLOSS HOUSE, NEWPORT, RHODE ISLAND

Pergola Overlooking the Sunken Garden, July 1917

[7]   BEACON HILL, ARTHUR CURTISS JAMES HOUSE, NEWPORT, RHODE ISLAND

Blue Garden, View to Pergola, Summer 1914

[8] BEACON HILL, ARTHUR CURTISS JAMES HOUSE, NEWPORT, RHODE ISLAND

Blue Garden, Pergola, Summer 1914

[9] BEACON HILL, ARTHUR CURTISS JAMES HOUSE, NEWPORT, RHODE ISLAND

Blue Garden, View to Pergola, July 1917

[10] BEACON HILL, ARTHUR CURTISS JAMES HOUSE, NEWPORT, RHODE ISLAND

Blue Garden, Flower Border, Summer July 1917

[11] BEACON HILL, ARTHUR CURTISS JAMES HOUSE, NEWPORT, RHODE ISLAND

Vegetable Garden, July 1917

[12]   SURPRISE VALLEY FARM, ARTHUR CURTISS JAMES ESTATE, NEWPORT, RHODE ISLAND

Farmer Cottages, July 1917

[13] ARMSEA HALL, CHARLES FREDERICK HOFFMAN JR. HOUSE, NEWPORT, RHODE ISLAND

Flower Garden Gate, Summer 1914

[14]   ARMSEA HALL, CHARLES FREDERICK HOFFMAN JR. HOUSE, NEWPORT, RHODE ISLAND

Flower Garden, Summer 1914

[15] MARIEMONT, THOMAS JOSEPHUS EMERY HOUSE, MIDDLETOWN, RHODE ISLAND

Rockery, Summer 1914

[16] MARIEMONT, THOMAS JOSEPHUS EMERY HOUSE, MIDDLETOWN, RHODE ISLAND

Flower Garden, Summer 1914

[17–18]   KENARDEN LODGE, JOHN STEWART KENNEDY HOUSE, BAR HARBOR, MAINE

Italian Garden. Above: View from Pergola; Opposite: View to Pergola and Champlain Mountain; Summer 1920

[19–20] REEF POINT, BEATRIX JONES FARRAND HOUSE, BAR HARBOR, MAINE

Pathway to House and Stone Pathway, Summer 1920

[21] ROOKWOOD, EVELYN RUSSELL STURGIS HOUSE, MANCHESTER, MASSACHUSETTS

View to Atlantic Ocean, Summer 1924

[22]   CHAILEY, CHARLES WILLIAM MOSLEY HOUSE, NEWBURYPORT, MASSACHUSETTS

Flower Garden, Summer 1920

[23] DR. CHARLES WILLIAM RICHARDSON HOUSE, DUXBURY, MASSACHUSETTS

Native Plant Garden, August 1927

[24] DUDLEY LEAVITT PICKMAN JR. HOUSE, BEVERLY, MASSACHUSETTS

Fountain Basin, 1926

[25] DUDLEY LEAVITT PICKMAN JR. HOUSE, BEVERLY, MASSACHUSETTS

View from House, 1926

[26] HOLM LEA, CHARLES SPRAGUE SARGENT HOUSE, BROOKLINE, MASSACHUSETTS

Crab Apple (Malus), *circa 1914*

[27]   WELD, LARZ ANDERSON HOUSE, BROOKLINE, MASSACHUSETTS

Herms at Pathway from House Lawn, the Bowling Green, to Italian Garden, circa 1914

[28–29] WELD, LARZ ANDERSON HOUSE, BROOKLINE, MASSACHUSETTS

Italian Garden, Stairway and Terrace, circa 1914

[30–31] WELD, LARZ ANDERSON HOUSE, BROOKLINE, MASSACHUSETTS

Italian Garden, View from Terrace to Cupid Fountain and View from Cupid Fountain to Terrace, circa 1914

[32–33] WELD, LARZ ANDERSON HOUSE, BROOKLINE, MASSACHUSETTS

Above: Willow Alley from the Rond Point to Temple, circa 1914; Opposite: Temple in Water Garden, circa 1914

[34] BROOKSIDE, WILLIAM HALL WALKER HOUSE, GREAT BARRINGTON, MASSACHUSETTS

Boat Landing, circa 1916

[35]   BROOKSIDE, WILLIAM HALL WALKER HOUSE, GREAT BARRINGTON, MASSACHUSETTS

Perennial Garden Fountain, circa 1916

[36] WAVENY, LEWIS HENRY LAPHAM HOUSE, NEW CANAAN, CONNECTICUT

View From House Terrace, circa 1915

[37] WAVENY, LEWIS HENRY LAPHAM HOUSE, NEW CANAAN, CONNECTICUT

Fountain, circa 1915

[38] ARNOLD SCHLAET HOUSE, SAUGATUCK, CONNECTICUT

View from House to Sunken Garden, circa 1915

[39] ARNOLD SCHLAET HOUSE, SAUGATUCK, CONNECTICUT

View from Pergola, circa 1915

[40] CHELMSFORD, ELON HUNTINGTON HOOKER HOUSE, GREENWICH, CONNECTICUT

Brook Garden, circa 1914

[41] CHELMSFORD, ELON HUNTINGTON HOOKER HOUSE, GREENWICH, CONNECTICUT

Vegetable Garden, circa 1914

[42]   THE PAVILION, STEPHEN HYATT PELHAM PELL HOUSE, FORT TICONDEROGA, NEW YORK

Pathway to Teahouse in Walled Garden, August 1927

[43] THE PAVILION, STEPHEN HYATT PELHAM PELL HOUSE, FORT TICONDEROGA, NEW YORK

Pathway in Walled Garden, August 1927

[44] THORNEDALE, OAKLEIGH THORNE HOUSE, MILLBROOK, NEW YORK

Lawn Terrace and Pond, 1919

[45]   THORNEDALE, OAKLEIGH THORNE HOUSE, MILLBROOK, NEW YORK

Pond at House Entrance, 1919

[46] THORNEDALE, OAKLEIGH THORNE HOUSE, MILLBROOK, NEW YORK

Sugar Maple Hedge Along Alley to Rose Garden, 1919

[47] THORNEDALE, OAKLEIGH THORNE HOUSE, MILLBROOK, NEW YORK

Canal, 1919

It is not what you crowd into an allotted space that makes

it beautiful but what you judiciously leave out.   —1923

[49] BARTOW MANSION, INTERNATIONAL GARDEN CLUB HEADQUARTERS, PELHAM BAY, NEW YORK

Terrace Fountain, Fall 1915

[50] SAMUEL KNOPF HOUSE, LAWRENCE, NEW YORK

Flower Garden, circa 1913

[51] WILLOWMERE, REAR ADMIRAL AARON WARD HOUSE, ROSLYN HARBOR, NEW YORK

Rear Admiral Aaron and Elizabeth Cairns Ward, circa 1914

[52] WILLOWMERE, REAR ADMIRAL AARON WARD HOUSE, ROSLYN HARBOR, NEW YORK

Rose Garden, circa 1914

[53] CLARABEN COURT, BENJAMIN STERN HOUSE, ROSLYN HARBOR, NEW YORK

Terracing to Harbor, circa 1914

[54] FANNY A. MULFORD HOUSE, HEMPSTEAD, NEW YORK

Arbor Seat, circa 1916

[55] MARSHFIELD, GEORGE WOODWARD WICKERSHAM HOUSE, CEDARHURST, NEW YORK

Pond Before Landscaping, 1914

[56] MARSHFIELD, GEORGE WOODWARD WICKERSHAM HOUSE, CEDARHURST, NEW YORK

View from House to Japanese Garden, circa 1915

[57] BARBERRYS, NELSON DOUBLEDAY HOUSE, MILL NECK, NEW YORK

Garden Gate, 1921

[58] OLD ACRES, ROBERT LOW BACON HOUSE, OLD WESTBURY, NEW YORK

Steps from Rose Garden to Wild Flower Sanctuary, April 1921

[59] WELWYN, HAROLD IRVING PRATT HOUSE, GLEN COVE, NEW YORK

Sundial, "The Fruit Bearer," by Edward Francis McCartan, circa 1918

[60] WELWYN, HAROLD IRVING PRATT HOUSE, GLEN COVE, NEW YORK

View from Living Room to Sunken Garden, 1915

[61] KILLENWORTH, GEORGE DUPONT PRATT HOUSE, GLEN COVE, NEW YORK

View to Tea House from Swimming Pool, circa 1915

[62]   KILLENWORTH, GEORGE DUPONT PRATT HOUSE, GLEN COVE, NEW YORK

View from Terrace to Swimming Pool, circa 1918

[63]   BURRWOOD, WALTER JENNINGS HOUSE, COLD SPRING HARBOR, NEW YORK

View from Drive to Sunken Garden, 1916

[64] BURRWOOD, WALTER JENNINGS HOUSE, COLD SPRING HARBOR, NEW YORK

Sunken Garden, Fountain, 1916

[65–66] BURRWOOD, WALTER JENNINGS HOUSE, COLD SPRING HARBOR, NEW YORK

Sunken Garden. Opposite: Evergreens; Above: Pathway; 1916

[67] PLANTING FIELDS, WILLIAM ROBERTSON COE HOUSE, OYSTER BAY, NEW YORK

View to Blue Pool Garden and Tea House, Spring 1926

[68]   LAURELTON HALL, LOUIS TIFFANY FOUNDATION, COLD SPRING HARBOR, NEW YORK

Octagonal Garden, circa 1918

[69] CLAVERACK, COLONEL THOMAS HENRY BARBER HOUSE, SOUTHAMPTON, NEW YORK

View to House from Garden, circa 1915

[70] MILLEFIORI, ALBERT BARNES BOARDMAN HOUSE, SOUTHAMPTON, NEW YORK

Garden Gate, Summer 1914

[71]   WOOLDON MANOR, DR. PETER BROWN WYCKOFF HOUSE, SOUTHAMPTON, NEW YORK

View from East Terrace, 1914

[72]   WOOLDON MANOR, DR. PETER BROWN WYCKOFF HOUSE, SOUTHAMPTON, NEW YORK

View to East Terrace, 1914

[73] THE STEPPINGSTONES, ANNIE MAY HEGEMAN HOUSE, SOUTHAMPTON, NEW YORK

Sunken Garden, circa 1915

[74]   BLACK POINT, COLONEL HENRY HUTTLESTON ROGERS JR. HOUSE, SOUTHAMPTON, NEW YORK

Children's Garden, circa 1916

[75] GARDENSIDE, FREDERICK AUGUSTUS SNOW HOUSE, SOUTHAMPTON, NEW YORK

View North to Flower Garden, circa 1914

[76-79] THE ORCHARD, JAMES LAWRENCE BREESE HOUSE, SOUTHAMPTON, NEW YORK

Above: Entrance Drive, 1912; Gatefold, Left to Right: Pergola Garden Pathway, Herms Along Pathway, Fountain, 1912

[80] PRÈS CHOISIS, ALBERT HERTER HOUSE, EAST HAMPTON, NEW YORK

View to House from Orange-and-Yellow Garden, Fall 1913

[81] BALLYSHEAR, CHARLES BLAIR MACDONALD HOUSE, SOUTHAMPTON, NEW YORK

Flower Garden, circa 1915

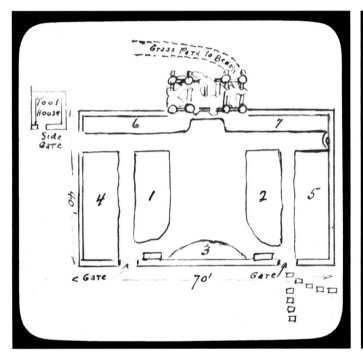 

[82–83] GRAY GARDENS, ROBERT CARMER HILL HOUSE, EAST HAMPTON, NEW YORK

Left: Plan; Right: View from House; 1914

[84]   GRAY GARDENS, ROBERT CARMER HILL HOUSE, EAST HAMPTON, NEW YORK

View West to Pergola, 1914

[85] GREY-CROFT, STEPHEN SWETE CUMMINS HOUSE, EAST HAMPTON, NEW YORK

Rustic Bridge in Japanese Iris Garden, July 1913

[86]   GEORGE FISHER BAKER HOUSE, TUXEDO PARK, NEW YORK

Rockery Pool, circa 1913

[87] GEORGE FISHER BAKER HOUSE, TUXEDO PARK, NEW YORK

Bridge, circa 1913

[88] GEORGE FISHER BAKER HOUSE, TUXEDO PARK, NEW YORK

Rhododendron, circa 1913

[89] DRUMTHWACKET, MOSES TAYLOR PYNE HOUSE, PRINCETON, NEW JERSEY

House Overlooking the Italian Garden, 1911

[90] DRUMTHWACKET, MOSES TAYLOR PYNE HOUSE, PRINCETON, NEW JERSEY

Italian Garden Stairway, 1911

[91] ANDORRA, WILLIAM WARNER HARPER HOUSE, WYNDMOOR, PENNSYLVANIA

Garden Bench, Spring 1919

[92] ANDORRA, WILLIAM WARNER HARPER HOUSE, WYNDMOOR, PENNSYLVANIA

Fountain, Spring 1919

[93] ALLGATES, HORATIO GATES LLOYD HOUSE, HAVERFORD, PENNSYLVANIA

View to House. Spring 1919

[94] ALLGATES, HORATIO GATES LLOYD HOUSE, HAVERFORD, PENNSYLVANIA

View from House, Spring 1919

[95] BOXLEY, FREDERICK WINSLOW TAYLOR HOUSE, CHESTNUT HILL, PENNSYLVANIA

Boxwood Path, Spring 1919

[96] THE CAUSEWAY, JAMES PARMELEE HOUSE, WASHINGTON, D.C.

Walkway, 1919

[97] LOB'S WOOD, CARL H. KRIPPENDORF HOUSE, PERINTOWN, OHIO

Woodland Daffodils, circa 1920

[98] LAKE TERRACE, JOHN STOUGHTON NEWBERRY JR. HOUSE, GROSSE POINTE FARMS, MICHIGAN

Pergola Garden, Summer 1917

[*Frontispiece*] SANTA BARBARA MISSION, SANTA BARBARA, CALIFORNIA

Friar in the Garden Court, Spring 1917

Gardens of the West

No matter how well one knows California, or how often one has made the long journey overland from the East, arriving in that golden, flower-decked Southland in late March or early April, affords one a new thrill every time. —1923

Historian William Deverell writes that California, spared the bloodshed of Antietam and Gettysburg, held out the promise of redemption after the Civil War, with railroads promoting the state as a refuge for rest and health.[1] Travel advertisements pictured what Frederick Law Olmsted Jr. called "Sunny Land," a paradise of snow-capped mountains and orange groves far from industrial pollution and the war-torn South.

To this Golden State of promise Frances Benjamin Johnston headed by train on April 4, 1917, days after she broke with photographer Mattie Edwards Hewitt and two days before President T. Woodrow Wilson declared war on Germany. She was 52 years old, alone, and embarking on a career as an independent garden photographer. Underrepresented in eastern magazines, California estates offered the enterprising Johnston places of renewal for her and her garden portfolio.

FBJ traveled from New York through Chicago, where she visited, on the recommendation of author Louise Shelton, Mrs. Walter S. "Katherine" Brewster (1879–1947), Lake Forest estate owner and editor of The Garden Club of America *Bulletin*.[2] "She promised," Johnston noted in her diary, "to be of great assistance." From the Windy City FBJ went to Albuquerque, New Mexico, "very picturesque with Indians in bright colors," and then to Arizona, where on Easter Sunday, April 8, she stood on the rim of the Grand Canyon, "the Throne of God." For her, the view

was "more than words can paint." The following week she arrived in Los Angeles.[3]

California had matured since FBJ's visit in 1903, when she photographed the estate of Phoebe A. Hearst. In the south, streetcars connected Pasadena and outlying towns to downtown Los Angeles. In the north, the rich lived in Classical Revival houses they built south of San Francisco after the 1906 earthquake. Santa Barbara, between the two cities, was a vacation retreat for wealthy easterners who chose California over Florida.

Johnston went west with the introduction of a New York client, architect Bertram Grosvenor Goodhue, prominent in California for his Hispanic style buildings at the San Diego 1915 Panama-California Exposition.[4] She photographed Goodhue's villa for New York financier Herbert Coppell, his neo-Persian estate for New York real estate heir James Waldron Gillespie, and the modest Pasadena backyard of that estate's supervising architect, Myron Hunt (1868–1952). By the time FBJ arrived in 1917, the wood bungalow in a garden was synonymous with California. Brothers Charles Sumner Greene (1868–1957) and Henry Mather Greene (1870–1954) were its leading architects. While in Los Angeles she photographed their David Berry Gamble garden and the hillside terrace at the Cordelia Culbertson house, recently purchased by Ohio Standard Oil heiress Elisabeth Severance Allen.

Johnston took west her "Our American Gardens" lecture, presenting slides at the Neighborhood Club in Pasadena and at the San Francisco store of garden book publisher Paul Elder & Company. Charles Templeton Crocker, a railroad heir and lantern-slide amateur whose Hillsborough estate she photographed, sponsored a private viewing.[5] FBJ was 3,000 miles from home but still traveling in elite circles to secure exclusive photography assignments.

At the end of May, Johnston returned to the East, stopping in Detroit along the way. In December she mounted her first exhibition of garden photographs at the New York town-house gallery of *The Touchstone*.[6] In the following years, the magazine continuously published FBJ's California images. The editors thought they were fine art, and contributor Hildegarde Hawthorne (1871–1952) wrote what FBJ considered the "most perfect tribute I have ever received as appreciation of the feeling I try to put into my photographs of gardens."[7] In black and white, Hawthorne wrote, FBJ had captured the "gradations of light and shade … the radiance and the glow, the hot sunlight, the veils of green" in California gardens. Considering that "no picture painted by man can give such color," this was a significant achievement for an artist working in a mechanical medium.[8]

Johnston created her slide presentation "California Gardens" with images from her 1917 tour. For lectures on eastern gardens, FBJ ordered and reordered unnumbered slides to illustrate garden themes. In contrast to this interchangeability, FBJ sequenced her California slides to reflect her trip by car and train, from Los Angeles, where she arrived in April, up to Santa Barbara, and finally north to San Francisco in May. Since the last quarter of the 19th century, hotels, railroads, and tour companies had promoted this south-to-north trip, and its counterpart, north to south, as the route through America's Eden. Wherever the visitor to California looked, wrote Aaron Augustus Sargent (1827–87), a native of Newburyport, Massachusetts, "he finds the bounties of nature prodigally displayed, as if this far West bordering the Sea had been chosen out as the favored of Providence."[9] By sequencing her slides, FBJ made her lecture an illustrated pilgrimage through what she called the "fabled land."[10] "California Gardens," through association, became "Gardens of Paradise."

FBJ returned to California in late March 1923. As in the East, suburban development was taking hold. Wealthy Angelenos were moving to hillside lots and into neighborhoods Johnston had photographed in 1917. Professionally landscaped houses provided FBJ work opportunities. She photographed gardens designed by Paul George Thiene (1880–1971) for clients of architects Reginald Davis Johnson (1882–1952) and Gordon Bernie Kaufmann (1888–1949), including the Pasadena houses of Wellington Stanley Morse and John Long Severance, the brother of Elisabeth S. Allen. Landscape architect Charles Gibbs Adams (1884–1953) commissioned photographs of his recently completed work for Arthur G. Reynolds and William Meade Orr.

With movies the new American culture and Los Angeles the center of studio production, the enterprising Johnston tried unsuccessfully to organize a business photographing soundstage sets, working with Douglas Fairbanks and Mary Pickford.[11] Myron Hunt recommended a distributor who thought FBJ's photographs were not only "charming from an artistic point of view," but had "the elusive quality of an etching, something not usually found in a photograph."[12] Her foray into Hollywood was unsuccessful, but through art dealer Joseph Duveen (1869–1939) FBJ met Henry Edwards Huntington.[13] She photographed his San Marino gardens and his library designed by Myron Hunt. An art and antiquarian book collector, the millionaire was an heir of railroad pioneer Collis Potter Huntington, an early patron of the Hampton Normal and Agricultural Institute and Johnston's portrait subject, Booker T. Washington (1856–1915). This connection may have secured the bibliophile's purchase of FBJ's photo-portraits from the turn of the century, a fortuitous sale that financed Johnston's tour of European villas and châteaux in 1925[14]

Myron Hunt introduced Johnston to the local design community, organizing an exhibition of her garden photographs at the Architectural Club of Los Angeles. There she presented "Our American Gardens" to an audience of landscape and architecture professionals that included Frederick Law Olmsted Jr. The designer, Johnston recalled, considered her slides "the finest existing on the subject of American gardens."[15]

When she finished lecturing and photographing in Los Angeles and Santa Barbara, FBJ traveled north to Portland, Oregon. She photographed the Thomas and Peter Kerr gardens before moving on to the Tacoma, Washington garden designed by Olmsted Brothers for banker Chester Thorne. Over the border in British Columbia was Benvenuto, the estate of Portland cement producer, Robert Pim Butchart. There "the chatelaine's cordial invitation to tea somehow miraculously extended itself into a three day's visit."[16] FBJ photographed the Butcharts' rose garden and rockery pools in an abandoned quarry before returning to New York.

Johnston was in the forefront of eastern photographers in Californian gardens. West Coast publications *Architectural Digest* (founded 1920) and *California Southland* (founded 1918) hired local photographers Albert Herbert Hiller (1877–1944) and Gabriel Moulin, and architects who were also photographers, William Mycajah Clarke (1872–1953) and George Delos Haight (1885–1965). Eastern magazines acquired prints from Johnston and Jessie Tarbox Beals, who was in Southern California from 1928 to 1929.[17] Johnston's California portfolio achieved a rare prominence in Louise Shelton's revised 1924 *Beautiful Gardens in America.* Twenty-two of the book's 31 photographs of California gardens were by FBJ. In contrast, California writer Winifred Starr Dobyns (1886–1963) included only five FBJ photographs in her 1931 *California Gardens.*[18]

West Coast gardens received mixed reviews from horticulturists and landscape designers. Frank A. Waugh thought Southern Californians had produced fine lawns and successfully substituted evergreen *Escallonia,*

Abelia, Osmanthus, and *Pittosporum* for East Coast deciduous *Spiraea, Caprifolium,* and *Forsythia.*[19] Arnold Arboretum associate director Ernest Henry Wilson (1876–1930), however, found that house owners in "the most favored as a garden region" had selected predictable varieties when there was potential for experimentation.[20] For the usually dour Mrs. Francis King, California gardens were all about color. "Not climate first, not fruits or flowers, forest or valley, seas or mountains—but color, color ineffable, color like a miracle."[21] English landscape gardener Alice Martineau, in contrast, thought Californians had used their palette "in too indiscriminate a way."[22]

FBJ distilled these views to appeal to national audiences paying to hear her presentations "California Gardens" and "Gardens of the West." She had discovered in Southern California horticultural variety, with eastern favorites heliotrope and fuchsia planted with "exotics usually restricted to hot-house culture." The amateur gardener in San Diego appeared to "scorn the subtleties of color harmonies and contrasts," ignoring "the important factors of continuous bloom, or of carefully considered design in their garden plans."[23] In showing Massachusetts, New York, and Connecticut gardens to gardening West Coasters, FBJ intended not to "reform, but to offer new standards" by comparing Los Angeles and San Francisco efforts to established achievements in the East.[24]

Late in the 1940s when FBJ had retired to New Orleans, a friend recalled that the photographer, for all her success in the West, found California and its sunshine "reprehensible." But the state before the Depression had made for her, as it had for prospectors, land developers, and hoteliers since the Civil War, very good business.[25]

[99] JOHN HENRY FISHER ADOBE, REDLANDS, CALIFORNIA

Water Garden, Spring 1917

[100] JOHN HENRY FISHER ADOBE, REDLANDS, CALIFORNIA

Trophy Room, Spring 1917

[101] KIMBERLY CREST, JOHN ALFRED KIMBERLY HOUSE, REDLANDS, CALIFORNIA

Italian Garden, Spring 1917

[102] MYRON HUNT HOUSE, PASADENA, CALIFORNIA

View to House, Spring 1917

[103–104] MRS. ELDRIDGE MERICK FOWLER HOUSE, PASADENA, CALIFORNIA

Terrace Wall and Terrace Wall Steps, Spring 1917

[105–106] MRS. ELDRIDGE MERICK FOWLER HOUSE, PASADENA, CALIFORNIA

Wall Fountain and Fountain in Flower Garden, Spring 1917

[107–108] MRS. FRANCIS LEMOINE LORING HOUSE, PASADENA, CALIFORNIA

View to Staircase Landing, Spring 1917; Staircase Landing, Spring 1917

[109] MRS. FRANCIS LEMOINE LORING HOUSE, PASADENA, CALIFORNIA

Staircase from Landing, Replanted, Spring 1917

[110] MRS. FRANCIS LEMOINE LORING HOUSE, PASADENA, CALIFORNIA

Flower Garden, Spring 1917

[111] MRS. FRANCIS LEMOINE LORING HOUSE, PASADENA, CALIFORNIA

Bougainvillea Pergola, from Flower Garden to House, Spring 1917

[112] MI SUEÑO, HERBERT COPPELL HOUSE, PASADENA, CALIFORNIA

Pergola, from House to Flower Garden, Spring 1917

[113] MI SUEÑO, HERBERT COPPELL HOUSE, PASADENA, CALIFORNIA

Water Rill, Spring 1917

[114] IL PARADISO, MRS. DUDLEY PETER ALLEN HOUSE, PASADENA, CALIFORNIA

Loggia, Spring 1917

[115–116] IL PARADISO, MRS. DUDLEY PETER ALLEN HOUSE, PASADENA, CALIFORNIA

Ornamental Pool and Lower Garden Stairs, Spring 1917

[117]   DAVID BERRY GAMBLE HOUSE, PASADENA, CALIFORNIA

Water Terrace, Spring 1917

[118] MICHAEL COCHRANE ARMOUR HOUSE, PASADENA, CALIFORNIA

Lily Pool, Spring 1917

[119] JOHN CONSTANTINE HILLMAN HOUSE, PASADENA, CALIFORNIA

Pergola Porch, Spring 1917

[120]   WELLINGTON STANLEY MORSE HOUSE, PASADENA, CALIFORNIA

Terrace Gate, Spring 1923

[121] GLENN-ORR, WILLIAM MEADE ORR HOUSE, ALHAMBRA, CALIFORNIA

The Secret Garden, Spring 1923

[122] WILLIAM ALEXANDER SPINKS JR. RANCH, DUARTE, CALIFORNIA

Fish Pond, Spring 1917

[123] HENRY EDWARDS HUNTINGTON HOUSE, SAN MARINO, CALIFORNIA

Drum Bridge in the Japanese Garden, Spring 1923

[124] CASA DE MARIPOSA, WALTER FRANKLIN COBB HOUSE, MONTECITO, CALIFORNIA

Garden Gate, Spring 1917

[125–126]   INELLAN, WALTER DOUGLAS HOUSE, MONTECITO, CALIFORNIA

Above: Garden Facade, Spring 1917; Opposite: Pergola at the Pacific Ocean, Spring 1917

[127] GLENDESSARY, ROBERT CAMERON ROGERS HOUSE, SANTA BARBARA, CALIFORNIA

Shaded Terrace, Spring 1917

Many of these great estates may be regarded as among the finest examples of landscape or formal gardening in California, and as such lend a rare distinction to Santa Barbara.... The real character of any town or city, however, does not depend upon such splendid establishments.... On the contrary, the real charm and atmosphere of a community is determined by the beauty, fitness, and all-round attractiveness of its small homes and little gardens which line the more unpretentious thoroughfares. —1923

[128-130, *gatefold*] GLENDESSARY, ROBERT CAMERON ROGERS HOUSE, SANTA BARBARA, CALIFORNIA

Left to Right: Walk from Terrace to Fountain, Along the Fountain Walk, Fountain, Spring 1917

[131-133] SOLANA, FREDERICK FORREST PEABODY HOUSE, MONTECITO, CALIFORNIA

Above, left to right: Entrance Drive, View to Interior Court, Interior Court, Spring 1917

[134] SOLANA, FREDERICK FORREST PEABODY HOUSE, MONTECITO, CALIFORNIA

Terrace, Spring 1917

[135–136] EL FUREIDIS, JAMES WALDRON GILLESPIE HOUSE, MONTECITO, CALIFORNIA

Above: Interior Court, Spring 1917; Opposite: Banksia Roses (Rosa banksiae) Along Terrace, Spring 1917

[137–140] EL FUREIDIS, JAMES WALDRON GILLESPIE HOUSE, MONTECITO, CALIFORNIA

Opposite: View from Casino to House, Spring 1917; Above, left to right: View from House to Casino, Water Terrace on Stairs to Casino, Stairs at Water Terrace, Spring 1917

[141–143, *following pages*] PIRANHURST, HENRY ERNEST BOTHIN HOUSE, MONTECITO, CALIFORNIA

Left to right: View to Outdoor Theater Boxes, Wings, and Stage, Spring 1917

[144–146] ARCADY, GEORGE OWEN KNAPP HOUSE, MONTECITO, CALIFORNIA

Above: Lower Garden, Pool House and View to Swimming Pool; Opposite: Lower Garden, View to Santa Ynez Mountains; Spring 1917

[147–148]   ARCADY, GEORGE OWEN KNAPP HOUSE, MONTECITO, CALIFORNIA

Above: Lower Garden, Marble Seat at Terminus, Spring 1917; Opposite: Yellow Garden in Upper Garden, Spring 1917

[149] VILLA ROSE, JOSEPH DONOHOE GRANT HOUSE, HILLSBOROUGH, CALIFORNIA

Garden Gate, Spring 1917

[150] VILLA ROSE, JOSEPH DONOHOE GRANT HOUSE, HILLSBOROUGH, CALIFORNIA

View from House Library to Swimming Pool, Spring 1917

NEW PLACE, WILLIAM HENRY CROCKER HOUSE, HILLSBOROUGH, CALIFORNIA

Exedra, Spring 1917

[152] NEW PLACE, WILLIAM HENRY CROCKER HOUSE, HILLSBOROUGH, CALIFORNIA

Reflecting Pool, Spring 1917

[153] UPLANDS, CHARLES TEMPLETON CROCKER HOUSE, HILLSBOROUGH, CALIFORNIA

View to Porte Cochere Terrace, Spring 1917

[154] UPLANDS, CHARLES TEMPLETON CROCKER HOUSE, HILLSBOROUGH, CALIFORNIA

View to Porte Cochere Terrace with Herbaceous Border, Spring 1917

[155] NEWMAR, SENATOR GEORGE ALMER NEWHALL HOUSE, HILLSBOROUGH, CALIFORNIA

Rose Garden, Spring 1917

[156] NEWMAR, SENATOR GEORGE ALMER NEWHALL HOUSE, HILLSBOROUGH, CALIFORNIA

House Terrace, Spring 1917

[157–158] JAMES KENNEDY MOFFITT HOUSE, PIEDMONT, CALIFORNIA

View from House to Water Terrace and Steps from Water Terrace, Spring 1917

[159] THORNEWOOD, CHESTER THORNE HOUSE, LAKEWOOD, WASHINGTON

View to House from Flower Garden, Spring 1923

[*Frontispiece*] DEMONSTRATION GARDEN, BRYANT PARK, NEW YORK, NEW YORK

Visitors Studying Gardening Notices, August 1918

Gardens for City and Suburb

*What must be the sensations of the visiting Martian, when after thrilling to the matchless beauty of the
New York skyline from the harbor, and the soaring Gothic perfection of the Woolworth Tower, the squalor
and sordidness of many of our city districts stand revealed to his shocked and startled gaze?   —1922*

New York was "cursed with its universal chocolate-covered coating of the most hideous stone ever quarried, this cramped horizontal gridiron of a town without towers, porticoes, fountains or perspectives, hide bound in its deadly uniformity of mean ugliness."[1] This is how upper-class Edith Wharton famously remembered her childhood city after the Civil War. For journalist Jacob A. Riis, the author of *How the Other Half Lives* (1890), New York was a dark world of immigrants living in cellars and feeding hogs in houses built in old gardens where "the stolid Dutch burgher grew his tulips or early cabbages."[2] The brown and squalor of these two New Yorks existed variously in urban centers across America, motivating officials to remake cities into metropolises worthy of a rich nation. Based in New York from 1909 until 1927, FBJ experienced firsthand the outcome of Gotham's City Beautiful achievements.

From 1900, row-house renovation brought lightness and convenience to middle- and upper-class New Yorkers. Backyards relegated to ash heaps and dumps improved when planting for food in World War I became a civic duty shared by men, women, and children. In 1918 the National War Garden Commission, headed by lumberman Charles L. Pack, with members Charles W. Eliot and plantsman Luther Burbank (1849–1926), organized a demonstration garden in Bryant Park, named for editor, poet, and early park advocate William Cullen Bryant (1794–1878).[3] This was

the first New York garden photographed by Frances Benjamin Johnston. Conforming to photo conventions of the time, FBJ included men and children reading displays to convey that the garden was for learning, not recreation.

After the war, ornamental planting of city streets and backyards took hold. Women, now America's "municipal housekeepers," formed clubs to bring gardening to urban centers just as The Garden Club of America had done in the suburbs.[4] These organizations realized Johnston's call to improve "the shabby, neglected appearance of the surroundings of our cities and towns" and presented opportunities for garden photography.[5] With commissions from club members, Johnston photographed city houses owned by the era's professionals. They included attorney Charles Clinton Marshall, who challenged Governor Alfred Emanuel Smith's run for president as a Catholic, and Dr. Henry Alexander Murray Jr., an experimental psychologist trained in analytic theories.

Across America, Johnston promoted her membership in the first city garden club, The Society of Little Gardens, founded in Philadelphia in 1915. Long gone was the hometown of Mary Cadwalader Jones (1850–1935), mother of Beatrix J. Farrand. In the 1850s, "halberd-headed railings guarded sunny squares where fat squirrels hoped in greedy peace," she wrote in her memoir *Lantern Slides*.[6] In the 20th-century city, society member Bertha A. Clark (b. 1860) found dead trees and backyards with "board fences painted a depressing drab." Concrete pavement stopped "the growth of promiscuous blades of grass."[7] The Society of Little Gardens, like its more than 100 affiliated clubs, promoted "the love of growing plants and making gardens within small city limits."[8]

In 1918 activist Frances Peters (1862–1924) founded an affiliate, The City Gardens Club of New York City, to transform apartment courts, hospital yards, and church cloisters. She and her board, which included Charles L. Pack, organized exhibitions at flower shows, contests to plant window boxes, and annual presentations at New York's Museum of Natural History, where president Henry Fairfield Osborn (1857–1935) supported nature education.[9] By 1924 the club had 900 members.

FBJ was an early member of Peters' organization. In 1921 she became its Chairman of Pictorial Records, responsible for collecting photographs of member gardens and civic projects. Once again, Johnston was at the beginning of a garden club's archival efforts, but now in a leadership role. An experienced curator from her work at the 1900 Paris Exposition, FBJ organized a contest for the best backyard, roof, window box, and park. From the end of 1921, she reached out to private owners, gardeners, and professional photographers. In the advocacy voice she perfected to promote garden beauty, FBJ wrote to *Gardeners' Chronicle* readers: "The object of the club is to turn unsightly backyards into gardens, to beautify all waste places, to plant trees near important buildings and on long treeless streets, to encourage window-box planting, and to be observant of the workings of the park department, in order that we may make city life richer by fostering the love of beauty … we feel that it is very necessary to have photographs for successful developments, so that people can clearly see the possibilities of their own backyards, and receive inspiration."[10]

In December 1922, The City Gardens Club opened a two-week exhibition of garden photographs by FBJ and others at the New York Camera Club in cooperation with the Clarence H. White School of Photography. Judges included landscape architect Martha B. Hutcheson, *House &*

Garden editor and garden book author Richardson Little Wright (1887–1961), and Clarence White, a strident critic of amateur and commercial photography. The selection of winning gardens was a model of reform-era democracy. It included the town-house gardens of landscape architect Ruth B. Dean and New York Central Railroad president Charles Hoadly Ingalls, the community gardens of the Jackson Heights apartment development, and the basement planting by an unnamed janitor at East 30th Street.[11] Johnston explained to friends and to the public that she had launched the exhibition "under many unforeseen difficulties," which likely included the uneven quality of the amateur and professional images exhibited at a club dedicated to art photography. But the exhibition succeeded at "showing almost every type of horticulture the city affords," wrote Johnston, furthering the cause to bring "the inner spiritual meaning of the garden to city life."[12]

Johnston added images of Turtle Bay Gardens and Jones Woods to her collection of City Gardens Club photos. These row-house renovations were around garden courts designed with the fountains and perspectives Edith Wharton expected in a civilized New York. At Sutton Place along the East River, FBJ photographed in 1926 the town houses of the development's independent women residents: Mrs. William Kissam "Anne" Vanderbilt (1862–1952); Anne Tracy Morgan (1873–1952), the daughter of J. Pierpont Morgan; and Elisabeth Marbury, living with Elsie de Wolfe.[13] Their communal garden designed by Nellie Beatrice Osborn Allen (1869–1961) was "a simple English plan … there are tall trees already there and there will be green turf and a terrace with a balustrade, from which one may look down to the river, far enough below to keep its smoke at a pleasant distance." De Wolfe's society friends, wrote *Vogue* magazine, were escaping the "noise and congestion of the city center … to be free, also, from something of the burden of great establishments."[14] Just as they were building smaller houses in the country, the wealthy were leaving Fifth Avenue mansions that had been photographed by Johnston when she first arrived in New York.

FBJ produced slides of the Camera Club exhibition winners and of gardens just miles from city centers for her lecture "Gardens for City and Suburb." These town lots and three- to four-acre gardens, more modest than the miniature park at Sutton Place, introduced to audiences in Akron, South Bend, Kansas City, and Baltimore lessons for designing and planting beautiful yards. With The Garden Club of America growing to over 6,000 members by 1930, Johnston's audience now included gardening home owners living in new developments, for whom FBJ's 1914–15 Long Island and Newport estates were magazine fantasies of a fading past.

For her city garden presentations, FBJ used a before-and-after format to dramatize a garden's from-death to-life transformation. Photographs of backyards before renovation were in black and white. The same spaces with gardens followed in blooming color. She illustrated the social benefits of urban improvement with slides supplied by the National Cash Register Company in Dayton, Ohio, where Johnston's colorist Grace S. Anderson began her career working for the company's founder, John H. Patterson. In return, Johnston spoke from 1917 through the 1930s to factory employees about flower gardens, staying with Patterson's sister, Mrs. Joseph "Julia" Halsey Crane.[15]

Johnston promoted the progressive cause of teaching city kids to understand the natural world. With "horror in her voice," she recounted to audiences the tale of schoolchildren who "in one day in the wood brought back 450 of the plants called Jack-in-the-Pulpit, killing the plant that they might satisfy a passing desire for flowers."[16] Johnston included children in her city garden images to show the benefits of outdoor life and projected slides of New York's School Nature League. Hunter College botany teacher Alice Rich Northrop (1864–1922) organized the public school alliance in 1917 to promote plant and animal study. The private and public gardens in FBJ's city slides were for pleasure *and* for educating a new generation growing up in an industrialized world.

In January 1925, FBJ ended her association with The City Gardens Club of New York City when she headed to Europe. Her town-house photography in New York prepared her for commissions in the late 1920s when she photographed gardens in Washington, D.C., and Richmond, Virginia, cities then undergoing their own garden renewals.

[160] THE TOUCHSTONE GARDEN, NEW YORK, NEW YORK

Sculpture Exhibition, Summer 1918

[161] TURTLE BAY GARDENS, NEW YORK, NEW YORK

View East to Common Garden, Fall 1920

[162] TURTLE BAY GARDENS, NEW YORK, NEW YORK

Charlotte Hunnewell Sorchan House Garden, Fall 1920

[163] TURTLE BAY GARDENS, NEW YORK, NEW YORK

Charlotte Hunnewell Sorchan House, Loggia, Fall 1920

[164–165] JONES WOOD, NEW YORK, NEW YORK

Opposite: North Terrace Fountain, 1921; Above: View to North Terrace, 1921;

The most ardent and enthusiastic horticulturist I ever met was an eastside janitor who gave the best of the sunlight that filtered into his gloomy basement to his window boxes filled with 'Old Man' and stunted geraniums and who rescued the faded Easter plants thrown out on the ash-heap to nurse them back to semblance of green in his little sky-high roof garden.   —1926

Stairwell Garden, circa 1922

[167–168] GEORGE HOADLY INGALLS HOUSE, NEW YORK, NEW YORK

Above left and center: View from Garden to Terrace, View from Terrace to Garden, 1921

[169–170] DR. ALEXANDER MURRAY JR. HOUSE, NEW YORK, NEW YORK

Above right: View to Terrace from Garden; Opposite: View from Terrace to Sandbox, 1922

[171–173] FLAGSTONES, CHARLES CLINTON MARSHALL HOUSE, NEW YORK, NEW YORK

Above: Porch and Laundry, 1922; Opposite: Tea House/Sleeping Porch, 1922

[174] QUIET CORNER, JOHN WESLEY BAXTER HOUSE, GREENWICH, CONNECTICUT

View from Terrace, Winter 1920

[175] QUIET CORNER, JOHN WESLEY BAXTER HOUSE, GREENWICH, CONNECTICUT

Macaws on Terrace, Summer 1920

[176] AXARIAN PLEASURE GARDEN, SAINT PETERSBURG, RUSSIA

View to Trellis, Engraving, 1780

[177] LATHROP COLGATE HOUSE, BEDFORD VILLAGE, NEW YORK

View to Garden Trellis, 1921

[178–179] FENIMORE, JAMES STETSON METCALFE HOUSE, BEDFORD HILLS, NEW YORK

Above: Portrait of Gardener, 1922; Opposite: View to Lake Marie from Terraced Garden, 1922

[180–182] WILLIAM SAMUEL KIES HOUSE, SCARBOROUGH, NEW YORK

Walking sequence, left to right: Pergola, Walkway to Vegetable Garden, Further Along Walkway, 1922

[183] BEECHGATE, ROBERT CARMER HILL HOUSE, ENGLEWOOD, NEW JERSEY

View from Flower Garden to House, 1918

[184]　BEECHGATE, ROBERT CARMER HILL HOUSE, ENGLEWOOD, NEW JERSEY

Flower Garden Gate, 1918

[185] WILLOWBANK, JOSEPH COLEMAN BRIGHT HOUSE, BRYN MAWR, PENNSYLVANIA

Pathway to House, Spring 1919

[186] WILLOWBANK, JOSEPH COLEMAN BRIGHT HOUSE, BRYN MAWR, PENNSYLVANIA

Pathway to Fountain, Spring 1919

[187] THE WHITE HOUSE, WASHINGTON, D.C.

Southeast Garden, Spring 1921

[188] WEST POTOMAC PARK, WASHINGTON, D.C.

Irises Along the Embankment, 1921

[189] EDGAR THEODORE WHERRY HOUSE, CHEVY CHASE, MARYLAND

Bull Frog in the Native Plant Garden, July 1921

[190] EDGAR THEODORE WHERRY HOUSE, CHEVY CHASE, MARYLAND

The Wherrys in Their Native Plant Garden, July 1921

[191] WILLIAM CORCORAN EUSTIS HOUSE, WASHINGTON, D.C.

Courtyard Gate, circa 1895–1900

[192] SAMUEL HILLS TAFT HOUSE, CLIFTON, OHIO

Walkway to Lily Pool from Drive, April 1922

[*Frontispiece*] PAVILLON COLOMBE, EDITH JONES WHARTON HOUSE, ST. BRICE-SOUS-FORÊT, FRANCE

Terrace, Summer 1925

Gardens of the Old World

We have, to be sure, garden spots. Richly, rapidly do they develop throughout our wide handsome land, but
these playhouses of Europe … these gardens of the old world hold much for which we long. —1927

From the 1880s, a question for newly rich Americans was, how should an elite competing for world authority live? Steamship travel and tours of European palaces known through illustrated magazines and books introduced industrialists and their architects to Old World culture. With these experiences, a New World cosmopolitanism entered life coast to coast. To be upper class in Greenwich or Cleveland was to live American, with efficiency and convenience, but to feel European in Tudor Revival manors and French pavilions overlooking wooded lanes and flower parterres. This synthesis had reassuring precedents for the new house builder. George Washington and his generation had landscaped Virginia plantations, influenced by the "'gardens of intelligence,' planned in France and England by Lenôtre and his followers," wrote illustrator and critic Ernest Clifford Peixotto (1869–1940) in 1923.[1]

Students preparing to be landscape architects and club members planting beautiful backyards studied Old World gardens. "A child does not progress the more by refusing to accept the knowledge of his parents," wrote landscape architect George Elberton Burnap (1885–1938). Careful study of palaces and villas revealed the "universal laws of composition." When owners and architects applied these classical standards to new house plans, their Connecticut and Delaware gardens acquired

"meaning through association with what has gone before as much as by adaptation to an immediate end."[2] For the garden photographer, the same enduring conventions guided photo prints and lantern slides, making them works of art.

Educated in Europe and defined by Old World culture, FBJ and her generation of artists and writers continued to advocate Renaissance traditions, a generation after Charles A. Platt's *Italian Gardens* (1894) and *English Pleasure Gardens* (1902) by landscape architect Rose Standish Nichols (1872–1960), volumes illustrated with author photographs. Editors at Doubleday, Page & Company and Condé Nast annually issued books and magazines picturing Florentine palazzos and cottages in Kent. Recognizing this continuing and profitable interest, FBJ sailed from New York in January 1925 to take photographs for her own guide to continental gardens.[3] After stops in Spain, North Africa, Turkey, Palestine, and Egypt, she headed north to Italy, France, and England. With limited time and three countries to cover, FBJ intended, as she wrote a colleague, to "make pictures of certain types, which [might] be regarded as representative of the best."[5]

FBJ arrived in Europe well prepared, having traveled abroad since the 1890s. She knew the French countryside from her student days and in

1907 had photographed the English cottage of *The Secret Garden* author Frances E. H. Burnett.[6] To plan garden visits, she contacted government officials, including the former French ambassador to the United States, Jean Adrien Antoine Jules Jusserand, and the cultural exchanges Bienvenue Française and the English Speaking Union.[7] A "compact tripod camera tucked away in an unobtrusive, black bag" made photography possible in discreet, civilized Europe, where disciplined children still played in parks "minus ear-splitting screams" while their parents quietly read the daily paper "without leaving behind them a disgusting litter of eggshells."[8]

Beginning in June, Johnston traveled along the French Riviera to reach Tuscany and Rome. In July she headed north to Paris and the Isle de France. Aristocrats and wealthy expatriates welcomed her, "for beauty is a glorious host to those who court her quality," FBJ recounted on return to America.[9] Cosmopolitan Americans living in Europe, including Matilda Travers and Walter Gay, Adele McGinnis and Albert Herter, Mary Smith and Bernard Berenson, and Consuelo Vanderbilt Balsan, offered recommendations and entrée to private estates. To her collection of famous Italian villas accessible by advance *permesso,* Johnston added George Wurts's Villa Sciarra in Rome, Arthur Acton's Florentine Villa La Pietra, Edith Wharton's Pavillon Colombe, Elsie de Wolfe's Villa Trianon, and Côte d'Azur Mediterranean Revival gardens recently completed by Raffaele Mainella (1856–1941) and Ferdinand Bac (1859–1952). In England she enthusiastically met and photographed Alice Martineau at her Oxfordshire cottage. She stayed overnight at Cliveden for the gardens of Waldorf Astor and his wife Nancy Langhorne Astor, whose Virginia family manor, Mirador, FBJ photographed four years later.[10] Her composed photographs of these private gardens and water terraces offered glimpses into lives revered by America's gardening rich and magazines of class.

After nine months abroad, Johnston sailed from Liverpool to New York, in September 1925. On return she did not find a publisher for her garden guide but sold illustrated articles to *Town & Country* and *Arts &*

Decoration, edited by early supporter Mary Fanton Roberts. FBJ based her profiles of villas and châteaux on research in the English edition of *Country Life* magazine, and in books: Luigi Dami's, *Il Giardino Italiano* (1924), John Chiene Shepherd and Geoffrey Alan Jellicoe's, *Italian Gardens of the Renaissance* (1925), and Henry Avray Tipping's *English Gardens* (1925).[11] Blending fact with reminiscence, Johnston enhanced her image as an educated observer of continental culture and mores.

Johnston's photographs of European gardens brought her new visibility. In 1926 she opened "In Old World Gardens" at New York's Ferargil Gallery, which represented established post-Impressionist and New Realist painters including Arthur Bowen Davies (1862–1928) and Ernest Lawson (1873–1939). This was the gallery's second garden photography show. In 1924, at the second annual exhibition of garden paintings and sculpture sponsored by The Garden Club of America, Ferargil displayed 110 photographs of garden sculpture by club members. Gallery judges Charles A. Platt, art critic and beauty advocate Royal Cortissoz (1869–1948), and editor and photographer James Beebee Carrington (b. 1860) awarded Mrs. Harold I. "Harriet" Pratt a prize for best photograph, a close-up view of a sundial by Edward Francis McCartan (1879–1947) at Welwyn, her Glen Cove estate.[12] Though self-serving for a dealer in sculpture collected by club members, the exhibition reflected the new status of the garden photograph as gallery-worthy.

At Ferargil in February and March, FBJ exhibited 148 silver-toned prints mounted on black board, with simple titles naming garden locations.[13] The response to her soft, tonal vistas, some inspired by illustrations in Edith Wharton's and Charles A. Platt's books on Italian villas, was enthusiastic. Cortissoz thought the gardens of Italy, France, and England had been "reproduced with feeling and taste, and we are glad to say, with no forcing of the note to get 'composition.'"[14] Success followed, with an exhibition in March at the International Flower Show, the first for a photographer, and shows at the New York Botanical Garden in May 1926, at Boston's Horticultural Hall in December 1927, and at George

Washington University and the United States National Museum in January 1929.[15] These latter two were professionally efficacious, returning FBJ to the capital-city limelight while she was photographing Virginia gardens and buildings. A *Washington Post* reviewer, however, was less impressed by FBJ's Europe than New Yorkers had been. She thought the photographs "sincere, straightforward … realistic yet so lovely are the gardens that they stimulate the imagination in spite of the scientific manner of presentation."[16]

From her 1925 photographs, Johnston created her lecture "Gardens of the Old World." Edward Cornelius van Altena (1873–1968) in New York prepared and painted more than 75 colored lantern slides of water chains, parterre arabesques, and shaded allées that brought a vivid dimension to gardens many Americans knew only in black and white. [17] FBJ's choice of exclusively French, Italian, and English gardens reflected the Anglo-Italian bias of American establishment garden club taste.

In an unpublished essay on European gardens submitted to the *Saturday Evening Post*, FBJ asked rhetorically why middle-class Americans, "industriously cultivating the flower borders and pruning the young shrubbery of their small suburban plots," should emulate the gardens of "monumental villas of the golden age of the Italian Renaissance." One might as well, she wrote, "question Chaucer and Shakespeare as the fountainheads of English Literature, Bach's supremacy in music, or the undying flame of Michelangelo's creative genius." As landscape architects had written since the turn of the century, the Italian garden "embodied the basic principles of design which apply to any garden, whether acres or square feet," that bring the house and garden into a "harmonious relation."[18]

For Johnston and club members, classical art, music, and literature were important not only for aesthetic pleasure, but for their power to transform public taste. They believed that high art transcended class, elevating the lives of all house owners and gardeners. FBJ's slides of painter Jean-Antoine Watteau's 1721 *A Garden Party* and of the Villa d'Este, photographed in 1925, resonated with the harmonies of Jean-Phillipe Rameau and the ancient falls at Tivoli, enriching Johnston's message of beauty in the New World through association with the Old.

[193] VILLA D'ESTE, TIVOLI, ITALY

View to Sabine Mountains from Villa, Summer 1925

[194] VILLA D'ESTE, TIVOLI, ITALY

View to Villa, Summer 1925

[195] VILLA BORGHESE, ROME, ITALY

Piazza di Siena, Summer 1925

[196] VILLA TORLONIA, FRASCATI, ITALY

Water Theater, Summer 1925

[197]   VILLA GAMBERAIA, BARONESS CLEMENS AUGUST FREIHERR VON KETTELER HOUSE, SETTIGNANO, ITALY

Grotto, Summer 1925

[198] VILLA GAMBERAIA, BARONESS CLEMENS AUGUST FREIHERR VON KETTELER HOUSE, SETTIGNANO, ITALY

Water Terrace, Summer 1925

[199] VILLA I TATTI, BERNARD BERENSON HOUSE, SETTIGNANO, ITALY

View to Villa, Summer 1925

[200]   VILLA I TATTI, BERNARD BERENSON HOUSE, SETTIGNANO, ITALY

View from Villa, Summer 1925

[201–202] VILLA LA PIETRA, ARTHUR ACTON HOUSE, FLORENCE, ITALY

Above: Entrance Drive, Summer 1925; Opposite: Stairway to Lower Terrace, Summer 1925

[203–204] VILLA ALDOBRANDINI, FRASCATI, ITALY

Above: Water Theater; Opposite: Steps to Water Theater; Summer 1925

It is really difficult to forgive the misguided genius who has here labored industriously to crush one's most treasured ideal [of the Hanging Gardens of Babylon] under tons of Rococo embellishment, which in any contest would capture the final award of bad taste. Where time and nature have been allowed to cover up its crudities, there are parts of this famous garden which still retain a certain romantic charm. —1926

[205] VILLA BORROMEO, ISOLA BELLA, LAKE MAGGIORE, ITALY

Terrace Garden, Summer 1925

[206–207] VILLA TORRE CLEMENTINA, LOUIS ANTOINE STERN HOUSE, ROQUEBRUN-CAP-MARTIN, FRANCE

Left: View to Ruins; Right: Pansy Ribbon, Summer 1925

[208] CHÂTEAU D'USSÉ, COMTE LOUIS DE BLACAS CASTLE, RIGNY-USSÉ, FRANCE

Parterre, Summer 1925

[209] CHÂTEAU DE COURANCES, MARQUIS JEAN DE GANAY CASTLE, COURANCES, FRANCE

View to Castle from Canal, July 1925

[210] CHÂTEAU DE COURANCES, MARQUIS JEAN DE GANAY CASTLE, COURANCES, FRANCE

Plane Trees Along Canal, July 1925

[211] CHÂTEAU DE BRÉAU, WALTER GAY CASTLE, DAMMARIE-LÈS-LYS, FRANCE

Alley, July 1925

[212] CHÂTEAU DE VAUX-LE-VICOMTE, EDME SOMMIER CASTLE, MAINCY, FRANCE

View from Château, July 1925

[213] WELLSBRIDGE COTTAGE, PHILIP HERBERT MARTINEAU HOUSE, WELLSBRIDGE, ENGLAND

Entrance Walk, August 1925

[214] WELLSBRIDGE COTTAGE, PHILIP HERBERT MARTINEAU HOUSE, WELLSBRIDGE, ENGLAND

Garden Doorway, August 1925

[215] CLIVEDEN, VISCOUNT WALDORF ASTOR HOUSE, TAPLOW, ENGLAND

Water Garden, August 1925

[216]   CLIVEDEN, VISCOUNT WALDORF ASTOR HOUSE, TAPLOW, ENGLAND

Long Garden, August 1925

[*Frontispiece*] TUCKAHOE, NEHEMIAH ADDISON BAKER HOUSE, RICHMOND, VIRGINIA

View from Thomas Jefferson's Schoolhouse to Boxwood Maze, April 1936

Gardens of the South

*It was during my travels after gardens that I noticed the fine old houses which figured so importantly in
colonial history and which are falling to wrack and ruin unhonored and unsung.*   —1935

The Renaissance spectacle of the 1893 World's Fair in Chicago, photographed by FBJ, was only one vision for America evolving from an agrarian past into an urban present. Another was the Colonial Revival, energized by the Centennial International Exhibition, organized in Philadelphia in 1876 to celebrate the republic a decade after the Civil War.[1] As immigration, industrialization, and international political engagement changed the contours of daily life, knowing how Washington, Jefferson, and Adams had lived was reassuring to some Americans. To honor and study a fading past, they founded associations and preservation societies. From 1928, John Davidson Rockefeller funded the restoration of Williamsburg, and in 1930 and 1934 The Garden Club of America published *Gardens of Colony and State,* a two-volume history of American gardening before 1840 by club member Alice Gardner Burnell Lockwood (1874–1954).[2] Illustrated with engravings and amateur and professional photographs of eastern and southern gardens, the books reflected the continuing interest of members in the boxwood "Grandmother Garden."

For FBJ, the colonial past was throughout her life a source of identity. She joined the Society of the Daughters of the American Revolution (D.A.R.) in 1892, and researched her family's Kentucky Baptist heritage.[3] When she briefly owned a house in Alexandria, Virginia, in the 1930s,

Johnston ordered sycamore saplings from Mount Vernon for "sentimental reasons."[4]

In the late 1920s a new generation of garden photographers received commissions to photograph suburban gardens in New York, Connecticut, and Long Island. FBJ, responding to this competition, reconnected with her southern heritage. From August through October 1926, the 62-year-old photographer scouted for gardens in Maryland, Delaware, Washington, D.C., Virginia, and Tennessee. She stopped in Baltimore and Wilmington, green with the estates of E. I. du Pont de Nemours & Company heirs, including Longwood, where she photographed the new Water Garden designed by Pierre Samuel du Pont.[5] Near the end of the three-month trip, FBJ sent an update on her progress to Augusta Owen Patterson (1873–1964), her editor at *Town & Country* magazine that was financing the photographer's tour in exchange for first refusal rights.[6] Johnston had encountered "unbelievably bad weather" but had photographed "historic old box gardens in Virginia" and secured for publication "important and exclusive features."[7] Always alert to cultural change, FBJ foresaw in the historic garden revival underway in southern states the potential for new photography commissions.[8] In February 1927 she gave up her New York apartment and returned to America's capital, leasing a studio at the Washington Arts Club.[9]

From 1927 until the mid-1930s, Johnston worked for revival architects Waddy Butler Wood (1869–1944) and William Lawrence Bottomley (1883–1951). Commissions to photograph new Washington gardens came from landscape architects Rose I. Greely and Nellie B. Allen. Through professional organizations, real estate brokers, and garden club members, Johnston extended her reach into Virginia, assembling slides colored by Edward van Altena for her talks "Gardens of the South," "Old Gardens and Old Houses along Colonial By-Paths," and "A Ramble in Old Gardens," which she delivered to her chapter of the D.A.R. in 1929.[10] FBJ became an honorary member of the Georgetown Garden Club and contributed to the James River Garden Club's 1935 guide to historic gardens.[11] The club was documenting the region's gardening past and exhibited Johnston photographs through the 1930s. Members added images to the club's photography collection, purchasing slides produced by FBJ and colored by artist William Oscar Hazard (1862–1943).[12]

Editors enthusiastically received FBJ's southern photographs, but increased publication of the region's houses and gardens also brought criticism. Taylor Scott Hardon (1904–76), editor at the short-lived *Home & Field* magazine, found FBJ's Middleton plantation "incomplete," her Magnolia Plantation "hackneyed," and her David C. Sands house in Benton, South Carolina, lacking "instruction or fascination."[13] *The House Beautiful* was more positive, turning to FBJ to enhance a profile on Brandon at the James River. The assignment introduced Johnston to Edith Tunis Sale (1877–1932), whose 1924 *Historic Gardens of Virginia*, with accounts and photographs by members of the James River Garden Club, was a landmark in the southern Colonial Revival.[14]

Robert Williams Daniel, banker and distant relative of its 18th-century builder, acquired Brandon in 1927. He and his wife, automobile heiress Marjorie Campbell Daniel, restored the house and expanded its gardens. At first Mrs. Daniel consented to an article by Edith Sale if *The House Beautiful* would publish the author's amateur photographs. "I cannot believe she would not much prefer the photographs that you have

taken," wrote editor Ethel Brown Power (1881–1969) to FBJ.[15] Johnston met with Sale and together they produced for the magazine a 1928 feature on Brandon, with photographs by FBJ and text by the author.[16] For Johnston and her colleagues, the garden photograph was always a negotiated portrait of ownership informed by demands from proprietors, editors, and landscape architects.

During her 1926 trip, FBJ met Mrs. Daniel Bradford "Helen" Devore (1875–1960). An heir to a Wisconsin lumber fortune, she was restoring the 18th-century Chatham house, which overlooked the Rappahannock River and colonial Fredericksburg. Johnston photographed the manor's garden for Helen Devore the following spring and produced slides for its landscape architect, Ellen B. Shipman.[17] With Devore's patronage, Johnston between 1927 and 1929 photographed domestic and public buildings in and around the preserved 18th-century town. In May 1929 she presented at its town hall her exhibition "Pictorial Survey, Old Fredericksburg, Virginia, Old Falmouth and Other Nearby Places." The exhibit's notice explained that FBJ had assembled the 267 pictures for Mrs. Devore as an "historical record."[18] In 1930 the Library of Congress displayed selected photographs from the Fredericksburg survey, opening the final chapter of Johnston's life as a professional photographer.

FBJ's pragmatic response to cultural change in an era of transitions—from farm to city, from making to consuming, from revivalism to modernism in design—sustained her long career. She never regained the prominence in house magazines she had in the 1920s, but her move south and subsequent Fredericksburg commission landed her front and center in the American preservation movement.

"Our architectural heritage of buildings from the last four centuries diminishes daily at an alarming rate," wrote Charles Emil Peterson (1906–2004), the founder of the Historic American Buildings Survey (HABS) in 1933. "The ravages of fire and the natural elements together with the demolition and alterations caused by real estate 'improvements' form an inexorable tide of destruction…. It is the responsibility of the American people that if the great number of our antique buildings must disappear through economic causes, they should not pass into unrecorded oblivion."[19]

Peterson's clarion call echoed the sentiments of local historical museums and of individuals as the Depression brought cultural introspection. They hired photographers to document present-day conditions, to illustrate books and magazines, and to produce lantern-slide lectures educating Americans about their colonial past. FBJ was well suited to this blend of photography and advocacy. She had photographed and promoted gardens to make America beautiful and to save "what we have for the next generation" through wildflower preservation and urban renewal. Now she would photograph and lecture on historic houses to secure an informed American future.

Johnston entered the preservation world working on speculation and commission. From photographs of Virginia made at the turn of the century and in the late 1920s, combined with images from the Fredericksburg–Falmouth commission, FBJ produced her lantern-slide lecture "The Tales Old Houses Tell" and its variants, "Old Gardens and Old Houses along Colonial By-Paths" and "Old Virginia Rediscovered."[20] After the Library of Congress received a grant in 1930 from the Carnegie Corporation to create the Pictorial Archives of Early American Architecture, she sold the library 156 negatives of Virginia buildings. Through this acquisition, and through gifts and purchases from other participating photographers, the Library assembled 10,000 photographs.

FBJ's sense of opportunity was unfailing. In the collecting of photographs by the Library of Congress she recognized the potential for paying work. She petitioned the Carnegie Corporation to support her photography of historic buildings, both interiors and exteriors. In 1933 it initiated funding of a photo survey of southern architecture to be produced by Johnston in coordination with the Library of Congress. Monies lasted until 1939, with FBJ taking over 7,000 photographs of buildings and coauthoring books.[21] This project, as well as additional financing from the library to catalog her photograph collections, and an inheritance from Cornelia J. Hagan, supported FBJ through the Depression until her retirement in 1945.

Johnston adapted her picturesque style for the Carnegie Survey of the Architecture of the South, assuming a documentary approach that was, by standards of the time, pictorial and romantic. She took photographs of houses and commercial buildings with a direct foreground and middle perspective. As she had in garden photography, Johnston constructed her seemingly straight views. She photographed antebellum churches and stores by standing on railcars, cajoling officials to cut down trees, and posing children and adults.[22] People added scale to her photographs of crumbling buildings and country lanes, but they did more. In tattered clothes and bare feet, these southerners, like their buildings, signified the failure of the City Beautiful to reach all Americans 70 years after the close of the Civil War.

Leicester Bodine Holland (1882–1952) oversaw Johnston's Carnegie survey. He was chief of the Fine Arts Division at the Library of Congress and chairman of the American Institute of Architects' Committee on the Preservation of Historic Buildings, which assisted Charles E. Peterson in the creation of HABS. Holland trained as an architect in the office of Wilson Eyre (1858–1944) and was a garden enthusiast. "I don't know whether you realize how particular an interest your gift has for me," he wrote FBJ in 1929. "In the days when I practiced architecture it had been my fortune to lay out gardens ... one of the most fascinating phases of architecture. I was even lead by my enthusiasm to compile a book!"[23] He was the author of *The Gardening Blue Book: A Manual of the Perennial Garden*. It was an early color guide, published in 1915, the year Frances Benjamin Johnston first showed her lantern slides promoting the American Garden Beautiful.

[217]   HAMPTON, JOHN RIDGLEY HOUSE, TOWSON, MARYLAND

House Facing South to Hillside Parterre Garden, circa 1915

[218] HAMPTON, JOHN RIDGLEY HOUSE, TOWSON, MARYLAND

First Parterre, circa 1915

[219–221] CHATHAM, COLONEL DANIEL BRADFORD DEVORE HOUSE, FREDERICKSBURG, VIRGINIA

Opposite: West Garden; Above: Porch and Service Court, 1927

[222–223]   CHATHAM, COLONEL DANIEL BRADFORD DEVORE HOUSE, FREDERICKSBURG, VIRGINIA

East Garden Gate and East Flower Garden, 1927

[224–225]   CHATHAM, COLONEL DANIEL BRADFORD DEVORE HOUSE, FREDERICKSBURG, VIRGINIA

View to Kitchen from East Flower Garden and East Flower Garden Pergola, 1927

[226]   THOMAS R. BOGGS HOUSE, FREDERICKSBURG, VIRGINIA

Terrace at The Quarters, 1927

[227] BELMONT, GARI MELCHERS HOUSE, FREDERICKSBURG, VIRGINIA

Arbor at the Long Walk, 1927

[228]   REVEILLE, ELMER MULFORD CRUTCHFIELD HOUSE, RICHMOND, VIRGINIA

Servant's Cottage, 1929

[229] MARY BALL WASHINGTON HOUSE, FREDERICKSBURG, VIRGINIA

View to Flower Garden, 1927

[230] YORK HOUSE, CAPTAIN GEORGE PRESTON BLOW HOUSE, YORKTOWN, VIRGINIA

Guest House in Memory Garden, 1929

[231]   YORK HOUSE, CAPTAIN GEORGE PRESTON BLOW HOUSE, YORKTOWN, VIRGINIA

Gardener's Cottage in Memory Garden, 1929

[232] WILLIAM ALBERT SMOOT JR. HOUSE, RICHMOND, VIRGINIA

Rose Garden, 1920

[233–234] HICKORY HILL, HENRY TAYLOR WICKHAM HOUSE, ASHLAND, VIRGINIA

Elise W. B. Wickham at End of Boxwood Walk and with Henry T. Wickham at the Entrance Gate to Boxwood Walk, 1927

[235]   PINE BARRENS NEAR WILMINGTON, NORTH CAROLINA

American Pitcher Plant (Sarracenia flava)*, April 1929*

Bowling along, I saw what appeared to be the most gorgeous clear yellow iris I ever saw in my life, which on investigation proved to be a large pitcher plant in full flower. My [standby] reference book, Lyons' "Plant Names and Synonyms" … gives the botanical name as Sarracenia flava *(Linnaeus), perennial marsh or bog herbs native to southeast U.S. … Very near to the groups of* S. flava, *I found whole colonies of the weird little Venus flytrap,* Dionaea, *also of the* Sarraceniaceae, *one species only in all of the world of plants, and that peculiar to your Carolinas. Then I had the Great Idea burst upon me. Why not start "MICHAUX'S GARDEN" on some favorable tract at Middleton Place and make it the botanical shrine of the native flora of the region which all the world would journey to see and study? So with some lovely wild cranberry vine, I dug up a lot of plants carefully with a shoe-horn loaned by James, wrapped them in damp moss and shipped them from New Bern, as the living memorial to Michaux. I think you could really do something quite wonderful with this idea, as you could start in a very small way and develop it as time and material offer.*

—Frances Benjamin Johnston to Heningham Ellett Smith, Owner of Middleton Place, April 30, 1929

I have never seen anyone have so many great ideas! It is good of you to be so interested … I put the plants you sent down by the edge of the lake, so shall leave them there. I love them.

—Heningham Ellett Smith to Frances Benjamin Johnston, May 13, 1929

[236-237, *gatefold*]   MIDDLETON PLACE, JOHN JULIUS PRINGLE SMITH HOUSE, CHARLESTON, SOUTH CAROLINA

Left: The Middleton Oak, March 1928; Right: Butterfly Lake, March 1928

[238] MAGNOLIA PLANTATION, CHARLESTON, SOUTH CAROLINA

Azalea Reflections in Cypress Swamp, March 1928

[239] MAGNOLIA PLANTATION, CHARLESTON, SOUTH CAROLINA

Azaleas Along Pathway, March 1928

[240] SMALLWOOD-WARD HOUSE, NEW BERN, NORTH CAROLINA

Entrance, circa 1930

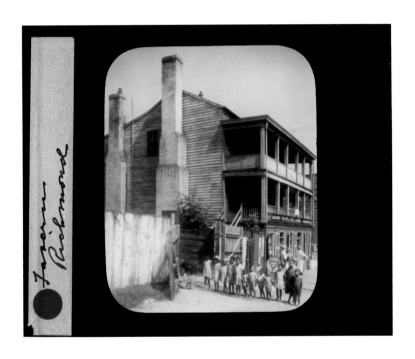

[241] TAVERN, RICHMOND, VIRGINIA

Children Pose for the Photographer, circa 1933 to 1935 (Lantern slide reproduced to scale, 3 ¼ by 4 inches)

Notes to Figures and Plates

Unless noted, the photographs published here and dated from 1895–1909 and from 1917–36 are by Frances Benjamin Johnston. Photographs from 1910–16 are by the Johnston-Hewitt partnership known as "Miss Johnston–Mrs. Hewitt," "Frances Benjamin Johnston, Mattie Edwards Hewitt, 628 Fifth Avenue, New York" and "The Johnston Hewitt Studio, 536 Fifth Avenue, New York." Magazines and books also credited "Miss Johnston and Mrs. Hewitt" and "Johnston & Hewitt." Photographs by Frances Benjamin Johnston were credited: "Johnston," "Miss Johnston," "Frances B. Johnston," and "Frances Benjamin Johnston."

All images, unless specified otherwise, are from glass lantern slides measuring 3¼ by 4 inches. Print photograph and document dimensions are to the closest ¼ inch. All colored slides are hand-tinted.

FBJ did not date any slides. In the 1940s she and an assistant cataloged some print photographs and negatives that correspond to the lantern slides. The dates associated with this cataloging are unreliable. Only when letters, invoices, or publications confirmed a year or year and month were specific dates assigned to slides. Otherwise dates are approximate. Slides with seasons correspond to months: Winter (December, January, and February); Spring (March, April, and May); Summer (June, July, August, and September); Fall (October and November).

In lectures Johnston identified Grace Adele Smith Anderson as her colorist from circa 1914 until circa 1928. It is not possible to determine which slides Anderson painted since she did not sign or label her work. Edward van Altena, 71–79 West Fourth Street, New York, New York, labeled his workshop's production. He produced Johnston's European garden slides and some of her images of southern gardens. From time to time T. H. McAllister-Keller Co., at 176 Fulton Street, New York, New York, worked for FBJ. The names of slide producers, when known, are found in the Library of Congress Prints & Photographs Online Catalog (www.loc.gov/pictures).

Identification of garden location, owners, landscape and house architects was achieved through research of archival photographs, landscape plans, descriptions in periodicals, newspapers, and historic collections. Johnston summarily noted owner names and location, sometimes inaccurately, on some slide labels of East Coast and California gardens. More than 600 of the 1,134 slides have no identifying marks.

In notes to individual plates and in the online catalog, only landscape architects and gardeners known to have contributed to garden features in the photographs are listed. For present day clarity, the term *landscape architect* distinguishes designers with professional training from landscape gardeners, though this distinction did not always apply in the period when Johnston worked.

All photographs and illustrations are in the Library of Congress Catalog Prints & Photographs Division, unless otherwise noted. Reproduction numbers for use with the Prints & Photographs Online Catalog are (LC-DIG-ppmsca—*XXXXX*). Call numbers for research of original photographs at the Library of Congress are (Lot *XXXX-X*).

LOC: Library of Congress, Washington, D.C.

LOCFBJ: Frances Benjamin Johnston papers, Manuscript Division, Library of Congress, Washington, D.C. (MSS27995)

LOCFBJphot: Frances Benjamin Johnston photographs, Prints & Photographs Division, Library of Congress, Washington, D.C.

LOCOA: Olmsted Associates Records, Manuscript Division, Library of Congress, Washington, D.C. (MSS52571)

Figures

[Fig. 1] *Gertrude Käsebier and Frances Benjamin Johnston Dining, Venice, Italy, August, 1905*. Photographer unknown. 6½- by 10½-inch gelatin silver print. Letter from FBJ to Frances A. B. Johnston, Hotel de Milan-Bristol, Venice, August 24, 1905, LOCFBJ reel 1. (LC-DIG-ppmsca-31670)

[Fig. 2a] *Students at the Académie Julian, Paris, France, circa 1885*. Photographer unknown. 6½- by 9-inch albumen print. (LC-DIG-ppmsca-04833)

[Fig. 2b] *Students at the Art Students League, Washington, D.C., circa 1889*. Scan from 8- by 10-inch dry plate glass negative. (LC-DIG-ppmsca-31735)

[Fig. 3] *Anderson Doniphan Johnston House, Washington, D.C., Studio Interior, circa 1898*. 8- by 10-inch modern black-and-white print. FBJ, "The Old World Gardens" press release n.d. [1925 or 1926]: 2. (LC-DIG-ppmsca-04835)

[Fig. 4] *Anderson Doniphan Johnston House, Washington, D.C., Studio Garden, 1898*. 16- by 20-inch gelatin silver print. For this photograph FBJ was a winner in the contest "Inside of Gardens" initiated in *The Ladies' Home Journal* 15, no. 6 (May 1898): 36. Announced in "For Pictures of Pretty Gardens" 16, no. 1 (December 1898): 37, and published by Eben E. Rexford, "Inside of a Score of Gardens," in 16, no. 3 (February 1899): 18. A close-up of the garden and house appeared in 16, no. 5 (April 1899): 25. FBJ won $10.00. (LC-DIG-ppmsca-31736)

[Fig. 5] *North View over South Canal, World's Columbian Exposition, Chicago, 1893*. 10- by 13½-inch platinum print. (LC-DIG-ppmsca-31678)

[Fig. 6] *Pennsylvania School of Horticulture for Women, Ambler, Pennsylvania, Demonstration Kitchen and Flower Garden, May 1919*. (LC-DIG-ppmsca-16732)

[Fig. 7] *Hacienda del Pozo de Verona, Phoebe Apperson Hearst Ranch, Pleasanton, California,* Country Life in America, *June, 1904*. Photographs by Frances Benjamin Johnston, October, 1903. Charles F. Lummis, "The Greatest California Patio House," *Country Life in America* 6, no. 6 (June 1904): 533–40. LOC General Collections (LC-DIG-ppmsca-31748).

[Fig. 8] *The Orchard, James Lawrence Breese House, Southampton, New York, McKim, Mead & White, Architects and Landscape Architects, 1898–1907, Conservatory Entrance with Hydrangeas,* Ageratum, *and White Clematis.* The House Beautiful, *34, no. 1 (June 1913),* Cover. Acanthus Press Collection, New York, New York. The image was a tinted, black-and-white photograph credited by the magazine to Frances Benjamin Johnston only. (Corresponding slide LC-DIG-ppmsca-16896)

[Fig. 9] *Près Choisis, Albert Herter House, East Hampton, New York, Color in* The New Country Life, *May 1917*. Photo mechanical reproduction of autochromes by Frances Benjamin Johnston and Mattie Edwards Hewitt, 1913. Agnes Rowe Fairman, "Furnishing and Decorating the Summer House," *The New Country Life* 32, no. 1 (May 1917): 36–37. (LC-DIG-ppmsca-31746)

[Fig. 10] *Frances Benjamin Johnston, "Vaux-le-Vicomte, near Melun,"* Town & Country, *1927.* Town & Country *82, no. 3974 (December 15, 1927): 54.* (LOCFBJ Box 46)

[Fig. 11a] *Frances Benjamin Johnston Wearing Her Palme Académique Ribbon, circa 1923*. Photographer, Anthony Bacon. 10- by 8-inch gelatin silver print. (LC-DIG-ppmsca-31674)

[Fig. 11b] *Frances Benjamin Johnston Smoking a Cigarette,* The Garden Magazine, *December, 1923*. Photographer unknown. [Leonard Barron], "Garden Photography as a Fine Art," *The Garden Magazine* 38, no. 4 (December 1923): 205; "Barbaric Jewelry." LOCFBJ reel 32. (LC-DIG-ppmsca-31772)

[Fig. 12] The Art of Gardens *brochure, circa 1923, reproduced to scale, 2¾ by 4 inches, paper*. Measuringworth.com for conversion from $75.00. For fees, see here "A Garden Photographer" p. 24 and p. 341, note 64. (LOCFBJ Box 45, folder 3)

[Fig. 13] *Beacon Hill, Arthur Curtiss James House, Newport, Rhode Island, Gardener Posed Mowing in the Blue Garden, July 1917*. 8- by 10-inch gelatin silver print. (LC-DIG-ppmsca-31668)

[Fig. 14] *Horticultural Hall, Massachusetts Horticultural Society, Boston, Albert Cameron Burrage, Landscape Gardener, Wild Flower Exhibition Garden, May 1921.* Albert Emerson Benson, *History of the Massachusetts Horticultural Society* (Boston: Massachusetts Horticultural Society, 1929), 488. Magazines and exhibition organizers urged visitors to take notes at horticultural exhibits, which they shared later at garden club meetings. FBJ made a plant list in consultation with Douglas Eccleston, Albert C. Burrage's assistant. "List of Wild Flowers…." LOCFBJ reel 9. (LC-DIG-ppmsca-16566)

[Fig. 15a] *Williams Bridge and Gun Hill Road, Bronx, New York, Before Restoration, circa 1907–15.* Photograph from Bronx River Parkway Commission. (LC-DIG-ppmsca-16126)

[Fig. 15b] *Williams Bridge and Gun Hill Road, Bronx, New York, After Restoration, circa 1920.* Photograph from Bronx River Parkway Commission. (LC-DIG-ppmsca-16127)

[Fig. 16a] *Worker Houses and Gardens, National Cash Register Company, Dayton, Ohio, John Charles Olmsted, Landscape Architect, from 1895, Before Landscaping, circa 1895.* Photographer, National Cash Register Company. (LC-DIG-ppmsca-16131)

[Fig. 16b] *Worker Houses and Gardens, National Cash Register Company, Dayton, Ohio, John Charles Olmsted, Landscape Architect, After Landscaping, 1900.* Photographer, National Cash Register Company. (LC-DIG-ppmsca-16124)

[Fig. 17] *The City Gardens Club of New York City Exhibit, 8th Annual International Flower Show, Grand Central Palace, New York, New York, Rosalie Warner Jones, Landscape Gardener, Row House Before and After Renovation, March 1921.* 8- by 10-inch gelatin silver print. "City Gardens Club at the International Show," *New York Sun*, March 15, 1921; "New York's Spring Feast of Flowers," *The Garden Magazine* 33, no. 3 (May 1921): 186 and 33, no. 8 (August 1921): 386. (LC-DIG-ppmsca-31671)

[Fig. 18a] *Arkady, Frances Benjamin Johnston House, New Orleans, Louisiana, Frances Benjamin Johnston, Landscape Gardener, Patio Court, Before Renovation, August 1945.* 8- by 5.7-inch gelatin silver print. The house was at 1132 Bourbon Street. (LC-DIG-ppmsca-31676)

[Fig. 18b] *Arkady, Frances Benjamin Johnston House, New Orleans, Frances Benjamin Johnston, Landscape Gardener, Patio Court, After Renovation, Spring 1946.* 8- by 10-inch gelatin silver print. (LC-DIG-ppmsca-31677)

[Fig. 19] *Georgetown Convent and Academy of the Visitation, View to Garden, Washington, D.C., 1892.* 7½- by 9½-inch cyanotype. Johnston used the blue process for test prints. (LC-DIG-ppmsca-31919)

[Fig. 20] *The White House, Washington, D.C., James Hoban and others, Architects, from 1792, Henry Pfister, Landscape Gardener, View North to House, 1897.* Administrations determined what the public saw. Theodore Roosevelt's secretary George Bruce Cortelyou authorized FBJ to photograph the north grounds "with the distinct understanding that no photographs are to be taken upon the front portico…."

Letter from Cortelyou to FBJ, March 2, 1901, LOCFBJ reel 6. William A. Bushong, "Frances Benjamin Johnston's White House," *The White House, Actors and Observers*, edited by William Seale (Boston: Northwestern University Press, 2002), 97–102. The first credited FBJ photograph in *Country Life in America* was a version of this view, circa mid-1890s, illustrating a Faxon's Favorite Flower Seeds advertisement, 2, no. 1 (May 1902): xi. The other advertisement identified to date with an FBJ photograph, not credited, is for Farr's Gold Metal Irises, *The Garden Magazine* 17, no. 7 (July 1917): final page, featuring a hand-colored image of the Rear Admiral Aaron Ward house iris border. A version of this tinted photograph is the 7¼- by 9½-inch hand-colored gelatin silver print, LOCFBJphot LOT 12637-3; and lantern slide LC-DIG-ppmsca-16823. Photographs for advertising were not significant to FBJ's career. (LC-DIG-ppmsca-21855)

[Fig. 21] *Cow Grazing Along Waterway Below Alexandria, Virginia, circa 1895.* 5¾- by 8-inch platinum print. (LC-DIG-ppmsca-31669)

[Fig. 22] *Narcissa Cox Vanderlip and Her Children at Beechwood, Scarborough, New York, 1912.* Photomechanical print of black-and-white photograph, taken with "A Kodak fitted with Zeiss Protar lens stopped to f. 32 slow shutter." Eva Vom Baur, "Frances Benjamin Johnston, Mattie Edwards Hewitt," *Wilson's Photographic Magazine* 50, no. 6 (June 1913): 251. See black–and–white reproduction of autochrome version in "Newest Portraits Are Color-Photo Transparencies," *The Evening Sun*, October 28, 1912, LOCFBJ reel 34. (LC-DIG-ppmsca-31754)

[Fig. 23a] *Diagram for a Tree-Lined Road, Carl Sadakichi Hartmann, Illustration, 1912.* Carl Sadakichi Hartmann, *Landscape and Figure Composition* (New York: The Baker Taylor Co., 1912), 29. (LC-DIG-ppmsca-31750)

[Fig. 23b] *El Fureidis, James Waldron Gillespie House, Montecito, California, Bertram Grosvenor Goodhue, Landscape Architect, 1902–06, Entrance Drive, Spring 1917.* (LC-DIG-ppmsca-16100)

[Fig. 23c] *Diagram for Drawing and Photographing the Williamsburg Bridge, New York, New York, John Wallace Gillies, Illustrator and Photographer, 1912.*
John Wallace Gillies, "The Significance of Design in Picture Making," *The Photo-Miniature* 15, no. 176 (September 1919), 330–52. Author Collection.

[Fig. 23d] *Anne Tracy Morgan House, 3 Sutton Place, New York, New York, Mott Brooshouft Schmidt, Architect, Nellie Beatrice Osborn Allen, Landscape Architect, View from Garden to Queensboro Bridge, Spring 1926.* 9¾- by 7¾-inch gelatin silver print. Ann Morgan, through her secretary, wrote FBJ on receipt of Sutton Place photographs. "[I] have never seen anything more enchanting than the pictures … The big beautiful picture of the Bridge is also a lovely thing, for which I am very grateful." The photograph reproduced here is one of two photographs of the bridge.
Letter from Daisy Rogers to FBJ, August 30, 1926, LOCFBJ reel 9. For the second version, see LOCFBJphot LOT 12637-4. (LC-DIG-ppmsca-31675)

[Fig. 24a] *Landscape "Enframement" Diagram for Designing a Garden with a Mountain View, Illustration, Henry Vincent Hubbard and Theodora Kimball, 1917.* Henry Vincent Hubbard and Theodora Kimball, *An Introduction to the Study of Landscape Design* (New York: McMillan, 1917), 128. (LC-DIG-ppmsca-31752)

[Fig. 24b] *Arcady, George Owen Knapp House, Montecito, California, Francis Townsend Underhill, Architect and Landscape Architect, 1914. Lower Garden, View to Santa Ynez Mountains, Spring 1917.* (LC-DIG-ppmsca-16097)

[Fig. 25a] *Biltmore, George Washington Vanderbilt House, Asheville, North Carolina, Richard Morris Hunt, Architect, Frederick Law Olmsted, Landscape Architect, 1888–95, FBJ with Camera, circa 1938. Photographer unknown.* 5- by 4-inch gelatin silver print. "Speaking of Pictures … These are by a U.S. 'Court Photographer,'" *Life* 26, no. 17 (April 25, 1949): 13. (LC-DIG-ppmsca-31666)

[Fig. 25b] *Biltmore, George Washington Vanderbilt House, Asheville, North Carolina, Richard Morris Hunt, Architect, Frederick Law Olmsted, Landscape Architect, 1888–95, FBJ Photographing the Garden, circa 1938. Photographer unknown.* 5- by 4-inch gelatin silver print. (LC-DIG-ppmsca-31665)

[Fig. 26a] *Villa Farnese, Caprarola, Italy, Giacomo Barozzi da Vignola, House and Landscape Architect, from 16th century, View to Casino, Summer 1925.* (LC-DIG-ppmsca-16495)

[Fig. 26b] *Las Tejas, Oakleigh Thorne House, Montecito, California, Francis William Wilson, Architect, Helen Stafford Thorne, Landscape Gardener, from 1918, View from Swimming Pool Pavilion to House, Spring 1923.* At its annual meeting in 1925, The Garden Club of America awarded this photograph first prize for a view or vista.
Helen S. Thorne, "When an Easterner Gardens in the Golden West," *The Garden Magazine* 34, no. 4 (December 1925): 178–80; Frances Benjamin Johnston, "Las Tejas," Estate of Mr. and Mrs. Oakleigh Thorne," LOCFBJ reel 21.
For coloring of this slide see LOCFBJphot LOT 11729-8, black and white print, verso, "Lovely variation of greens … warm creamy stucco house-blue-purple mountains…." For prize, see "A Garden Photographer," p. 23 and p. 341, note 56. (LC-DIG-ppmsca-16037)

[Fig. 27a] *Unidentified Artist Painting Lantern Slides, Slide Room, National Cash Register Company, Dayton, Ohio, Photographer unknown, January 25, 1903.* Black-and-white scan from 8- by 10-inch glass negative. The NCR Archive, Dayton History, Dayton, Ohio.

[Fig. 27b] *Advertisement for Roehrig-Bollenberg Lantern-Slide Paints, 1922. Pictorial Photography in America* (New York: Pictorial Photographers of America, 1922), n.p. For both lantern slides and print photographs, *Photo-Era* magazine recommended Japanese watercolors and the Roehrig and Meteor Photographic Oil Colors brands for "unsurpassed transparency, beauty and color." Wilfred A. French, "Our Illustrations," *Photo-Era Magazine* 49, 1 (August 1922): 272. (LC-DIG-ppmsca-31753)

[Figs. 28a–b] *Casa de Mariposa, Walter Franklin Cobb House, Montecito, California, Cary Fish Cobb, Landscape Gardener, circa 1916. Rock Garden Photograph, Verso and Recto, with FBJ Notes for Coloring, Spring 1917.* 7¾- by 9¾-inch gelatin silver print. (LOCFBJphot LOT 11729-8)

[Fig. 28c] *Casa de Mariposa, Walter Franklin Cobb House, Montecito, California, Cary Fish Cobb, Landscape Gardener, 1916. Rock Garden Slide, Spring 1917.* (LC-DIG-ppmsca-16047)

[Fig. 29a] *Près Choisis, Albert Herter House, East Hampton, New York, Grosvenor Atterbury, Architect, 1898–99, Albert and Adele McGinnis Herter, Landscape Gardeners, from 1898. Blue-and-White Garden Terrace, Fall 1913.* 8- by 10-inch gelatin silver print. (LC-DIG-ppmsca-31879)

[Fig. 29b] *Près Choisis, Albert Herter House, East Hampton, New York, Grosvenor Atterbury, Architect, 1898–99, Albert and Adele McGinnis Herter, Landscape Gardeners, from 1898. Blue-and-White Garden Terrace, Fall 1913.* Photo reproduction of autochrome. Agnes Rowe Fairman, "Furnishing and Decorating the Summer House," *The New Country Life* 32, no. 1 (May 1917): 36–7. (LC-DIG-ppmsca-31747)

[Fig. 29c] *Près Choisis, Albert Herter House, East Hampton, New York, Grosvenor Atterbury, Architect, 1898–99, Albert and Adele McGinnis Herter, Landscape Gardeners, from 1898. Blue-and-White Garden Terrace, Lantern Slide, Fall 1913.* (LC-DIG-ppmsca-16870)

[Fig. 30a] *Claude Monet,* Le Bassin aux Nymphéas, Harmonie Verte *("The Lily Pond, Green Harmony"), oil on canvas, 35.2 by 36.4 inches, 1899.* Musée d'Orsay, Paris, France.

[Fig. 30b] *Grey-Croft, Stephen Swete Cummins House, East Hampton, New York, Emma Woodhouse Cummins, Landscape Gardener, circa 1903, Lily Pool, July 1913.* Inspired by her husband's travels in Hawaii and the East, Emma W. Cummins planted a Japanese iris garden at her house near the Atlantic Ocean. More than 10,000 bulbs of Invisible Virtue (*Kigan-no-misao*), Girdle of Cobweb (*Kumo-no-obi*) and Voice of the Hero (*Sofu-no-koi*) bloomed from May until August. Magazine articles and club lectures by iris cultivator John Caspar Wister (1887–1952) made iris a prized American flower, ideal for bogs, summer bloom, and structure in flower borders.

"An Iris Garden and Its Gift to Blinded Soldiers," *Vogue* 48, no. 10 (May 15, 1918): 40, 70; Jessie Tarbox Beals, "Gardens in the East," *House & Garden* 46, no. 11 (August 1919): 91. (LC-DIG-ppmsca-16236)

[Fig. 30c] *Lilla Cabot Perry,* A Stream Beneath Poplars, Oil on Canvas, 25¾ by 32 inches, circa 1890–1900. Hunter Museum of American Art, Chattanooga, Tennessee. Encouraged by Claude Monet (1840–1926), the artist Lilla C. Perry (1848–1933) was influential in bringing Impressionism to American art circles. The writings of Ralph Waldo Emerson inspired Perry and her generation living in an industrial world.

Meredith Martindale, with Pamela Moffat, *Lilla Cabot Perry: An American Impressionist.* (Washington, D.C.: The National Museum of Women in the Arts, 1990.)

[Fig. 30d] *Michael Cochrane Armour House, Pasadena, California, Robert Gordon Fraser and/or Thomas Chisholm, Landscape Gardeners, from 1910, Native Plant Garden Pathway, Spring 1917.* For this garden, see plate 118 and p. 310. (LC-DIG-ppmsca-16012)

[Fig. 31] *"Garden Sentinels,"* Our Garden Journal, *September 1917, Photoreproduction of hand-tinted black-and-white photograph. Our Garden Journal 1, no. 1 (September 1917): frontispiece.* A 10- by 8-inch tinted photograph of the staircase is LOCFBJphot LOT 11729-2 and slide LC-DIG-ppmsca-16935. (LC-DIG-ppmsca-31751)

[Fig. 32a] *Villa Bel Riposo, George Gregory Smith House, San Domenico, Italy, Cedars of Lebanon, Summer 1925, Exhibition Print, Ferargil Gallery, New York, New York, 1926.* 9- by 13¼-inch gelatin silver print on 10¼- by 14-inch mount. (LC-DIG-ppmsca-31680)

[Fig. 32b] *Philipland, Philip Laird House, New Castle, Delaware, Robert Buist, Landscape Gardener, 1847, Grape Arbor, Spring 1928.* 10¾- by 8¼-inch gelatin silver print on 18¼- by 13-inch rice paper mount. This garden was at the historic George Read Jr. house, owned in the 1920s by Philip Laird, a Washington, D.C., stockbroker. (LC-DIG-ppmsca-31861)

[Fig. 33] *Auld Lang Syne, James Herndon Lightfoot House, Takoma Park, Maryland, Virginia Dorsey Lightfoot, Landscape Gardener, 1935. Frances Benjamin Johnston Under an Arbor, 1938.* Photographer unknown. 10- by 8-inch safety film negative. (LC-DIG-ppmsca-31737)

[Fig. 34a] *Beacon Hill, Arthur Curtiss James House, Newport, Rhode Island, Olmsted Brothers, Landscape Architects, 1908–13, 1915–16, Blue Garden, Gate, July 1917.* (LC-DIG-ppmsca-16750)

[Fig. 34b] *Enniscorthy, Albert Henry Morrill House, Green Mountain, Virginia, Birdbath, 1932.* (LC-DIG-ppmsca-16171)

[Fig. 34c] *Claverack, Colonel Thomas Henry Barber House, Southampton, New York, Frederick Law Olmsted, Landscape Architect, 1893–1894. Rustic Gate, circa 1915.* (LC-DIG-ppmsca-16231)

[Fig. 34d] *Vivian Spencer Town House, New York, New York, Marian Cruger Coffin, Landscape Architect, circa 1921, Garden in Two Seasons, Exhibition Display at The City Gardens Club of New York City, December 1922.* (LC-DIG-ppmsca-16301)

[Fig. 34e] *Daniel Elezer Pomeroy House, Englewood, New Jersey, Ruth Bramley Dean, Landscape Architect, circa 1915. Iris Pathway, Spring 1918.* (LC-DIG-ppmsca-16798)

[Fig. 34f] *Villa Lante, Bagnaia, Italy, Giacomo Barozzi da Vignola and Carlo Maderno, Landscape Architects, 1568–1600, Water Chain, Summer 1925.* (LC-DIG-ppmsca-16296)

[Fig. 35a] *El Fureidis, James Waldron Gillespie House, Montecito, California, Bertram Grosvenor Goodhue, Landscape Architect, 1902–06. Reservoir, Spring 1917.* (LC-DIG-ppmsca-16039)

[Fig. 35b] *El Fureidis, James Waldron Gillespie House, Montecito, California, Bertram Grosvenor Goodhue, Landscape Architect, 1902–06, Italian Cypress, Spring 1917.* (LC-DIG-ppmsca-16038)

[Fig. 35c] *El Fureidis, James Waldron Gillespie House, Montecito, California, Bertram Grosvenor Goodhue, Landscape Architect, 1902–06, Quarry Garden, Spring 1917.* (LC-DIG-ppmsca-16083)

[Fig. 36a] *Mrs. Leslie Williams,* A Garden in the Suburbs. *London & New York: John Lane, 1901. Front cover.* In the Collection of the LuEsther T. Mertz Library, New York Botanical Garden, Bronx, New York. Reproduced courtesy of the library.

[Fig. 36b, 36c] *Porter Garnett,* Stately Homes of California. *Boston: Little, Brown, 1915. Front Cover and Inside Cover with Frances Benjamin Johnston Bookplate.* In the Collection of the LuEsther T. Mertz Library, New York Botanical Garden, Bronx, New York. Reproduced courtesy of the library.

Plates

[FRONTISPIECE] MOUNT VERNON, GEORGE WASHINGTON HOUSE, MOUNT VERNON, VIRGINIA, GEORGE WASHINGTON, LANDSCAPE GARDENER, 18TH CENTURY WITH RESTORATIONS

Privy in Vegetable Garden, 1894. Frances Benjamin Johnston began her presentation "Our American Gardens" with this image. The house and garden of the first president reassured suburban house owners that America, like Europe, had a design heritage of its own. (LC-DIG-ppmsca-16335)

Gardens of the East

[FRONTISPIECE] THE APPLETREES, HENRY EUGENE COE HOUSE, SOUTHAMPTON, NEW YORK

View from Porch, 1914. Investor Henry E. Coe and his wife, Eva Johnston, daughter of the Central New Jersey railroad president John Taylor Johnston, purchased a 19th-century farmhouse. They remodeled it as a Colonial Revival mansion and decorated low-ceiling rooms with Americana. FBJ photographed the garden to show the transition from surrounding fields, through a boxwood flower parterre, to a porch along a new wing. In its consistent American theme, The Appletrees, wrote *House & Garden,* was an example of "fitting a house to its setting and fitting the setting to a house."

"The Residence of Mrs. Henry C. Coe, at Southampton, Long Island," *House & Garden* 29, no. 3 (March 1916): 37. (LC-DIG-ppmsca-16274)

PLATES 1–2 THE ELMS, EDWARD JULIUS BERWIND HOUSE, NEWPORT, RHODE ISLAND, HORACE TRUMBAUER, ARCHITECT, 1899–1901, 1911, HORACE TRUMBAUER, LANDSCAPE ARCHITECT, 1907–14

[1] *Boxwood Parterre, Summer 1914.* In a period of old-world inspiration, the coal millionaire and his wife, Sarah Williams, razed a 19th-century Classical Revival cottage and built their mansion modeled on the 18th-century Château d'Asnières outside Paris, France. Berwind superintendent Bruce Butterton wrote in 1915 that nurseries in Holland and France had sold out their stock of boxwood with the fashion for formal gardens. A Newport gardener, presumably himself, had imported 120,000 specimens the year before and yet was unable to fill his order.

Bruce Butterton, "The Boxwood and its enemies," *Annuaire of the Newport Garden Club* (1915): 38, with this photograph. (LC-DIG-ppmsca-16293)

[2] *Fountain Alley, Summer 1914.* Frances Benjamin Johnston stood in the court of the carriage house, built 1911, to photograph this vista of the sunken garden. "There are no trees which lend themselves to fanciful pruning so readily as do the box and the bay; well-planned planting and clipping of these trees give to this Newport garden an air of formality," wrote FBJ about this view. A decade before she studied and photographed European gardens, Johnston thought that the French Revival house and landscape were Italianate.

"The Influence of Italy Predominates in the Architecture...." *Vogue* 46, no. 4 (August 15 1915): 36. (LC-DIG-ppmsca-16728)

PLATE 3 THE BREAKERS, CORNELIUS VANDERBILT II HOUSE, NEWPORT, RHODE ISLAND, RICHARD MORRIS HUNT, ARCHITECT, ERNEST WILLIAM BOWDITCH AND JAMES HIGGINSON BOWDITCH, LANDSCAPE ARCHITECTS, 1892–96

Loggia Parterre, Summer 1914. The spectacle of a house owned by one of the super rich captivated Johnston's garden club audiences and reporters who consistently commented on her slides of The Breakers. Richard Morris Hunt designed the neo-Renaissance villa for a New York Central Railroad heir and his wife, Alice Gwynne Vanderbilt. Their daughter was Gertrude Vanderbilt Whitney, founder of the Whitney Museum in New York City and an FBJ client from 1911.

Ernest W. Bowditch first landscaped the estate's 13 acres in 1877 as a late Victorian park and then redesigned them for Cornelius Vanderbilt in the new French style, with clipped lawns and flower arabesques.

To transform a photographic positive into a painting, slide artists created form through color. Here, untinted areas convey the graying effects of light shadows against the limestone building, in the warm, summer light.

John R. Tschirch, "The Evolution of a Beaux Arts Landscape, The Breakers in Newport, Rhode Island," *Journal of the New England Garden History Society* 7 (Fall 1999): 1–14. For Whitney New York City Fifth Avenue house, see "A Handsome Town House," *Town & Country* 66, no. 3413 (October 14, 1911); 32–3. (LC-DIG-ppmsca-16771)

PLATES 4–6 HAMMERSMITH FARM, HUGH DUDLEY AUCHINCLOSS HOUSE, NEWPORT, RHODE ISLAND, OLMSTED BROTHERS, LANDSCAPE ARCHITECTS, 1909–10

[4] *Rock Garden, July 1917.* This walled retreat overlooking the sunken garden in the distance was known for its spring-to-summer color that Johnston described as "a thick carpet of pink, lavender, yellow, and creamy white fairy-bloom." Olmsted's Hans J. Koehler was impressed but hoped to do better at Beacon Hill where he was overseeing that estate's rockery.

[FBJ], "Hammersmith Farm," *Town & County*, 54, no. 7 (July 1919): 64; LOCOA reel 225, job 3974. (LC-DIG-ppmsca-16778)

[5] *Lily Pool in Sunken Garden, July 1917.* While working at nearby Beacon Hill, the Olmsted firm landscaped this 19th-century farm estate that overlooked fields to Narragansett Bay. New York investor Hugh D. Auchincloss was married to Emma Brewster Jennings, a Standard oil heir and sister of Walter Jennings, owner of Burrwood on Long Island, also landscaped by Olmsted Brothers and photographed by FBJ.

Hugh and Emma Auchincloss were actively involved in the planning and planting of their 75 acres, importing plants from Europe for their rock, rose, and sunken gardens. (LC-DIG-ppmsca-16739)

[6] *Pergola Overlooking the Sunken Garden, July 1917.* Pergolas bordered the sunken garden. (LC-DIG-ppmsca-16794)

PLATES 7–11 BEACON HILL, ARTHUR CURTISS JAMES HOUSE, NEWPORT, RHODE ISLAND, OLMSTED BROTHERS, LANDSCAPE ARCHITECTS, 1908–13, 1915–16

[7] *Blue Garden, View to Pergola, Summer 1914.* Beacon Hill house and garden were the triumph of a railroad and mining fortune over nature. High above Narragansett Bay, the site posed innumerable challenges to creating what the landscape firm called a "Plaisance." Beginning in 1910 James' staff blasted rock to level ground for this sheltered flower garden planted and replanted over six years.

LOCOA reel 208, job 3558. (LC-DIG-ppmsca-16756)

[8] *Blue Garden, Pergola, Summer 1914.* Wisteria, clematis, and morning glories provided continuous bloom. (LC-DIG-ppmsca-16755)

[9] *Blue Garden, View to Pergola, July 1917.* FBJ returned from California in 1917 to project her American garden slides at a Beacon Hill Red Cross fund-raiser. This view of the Blue Garden, taken at the time of her visit, shows that the Olmsted firm, by building a greenhouse, succeeded in providing Mrs. Arthur C. "Harriet"

James her "dazzling blue all summer long with a touch of white."

Garden authority Alice Morse Earle (1851–1911) associated blue with Mediterranean civilization, writing in 1901 that "the Persian art workers … accomplished the combining of varying blues most wonderfully and successfully." For the pools at her hilltop agora, James wanted "Persian" blue tiles and discovered the Durant Kilns in Bedford Village, New York. The art pottery firm, Johnston wrote, learned "the long-lost secret of the famous blue glass used by Egyptian potters" while working for Beacon Hill.

Alice Morse Earle, *Old World Gardens* (New York: Macmillan, 1901), 253; [FBJ], "A Newport Garden, A Color Symphony in Blue," *Vogue* 45, no. 12 (June 15, 1915): 54. (LC-DIG-ppmsca-16542)

[10] *Blue Garden, Flower Border, Summer July 1917*. In the color-conscious world of turn-of-the-century gardening, color themes assured harmonious borders. Garden club members cultivated larkspurs, violas, pansies, iris, catmint, and Canterbury bells for their tonal relation to sky, water, and grass. Here clematis and sweet pea climb slat fences sheltered by pine and cedar. (LC-DIG-ppmsca-16540)

[11] *Vegetable Garden, July 1917*. Estates were self-sustaining, with livestock and vegetable gardens for servants and owners. The photograph exemplified Johnston's adage that "cabbages hold beauty the same as roses."

"Backyard Preacher," *Cleveland Plain Dealer*, March 27, 1921. (LC-DIG-ppmsca-21928)

PLATE 12 SURPRISE VALLEY FARM, ARTHUR CURTISS JAMES ESTATE, NEWPORT, RHODE ISLAND, GROSVENOR ATTERBURY, ARCHITECT, 1914–16

Farmer Cottages, July 1917. With stone blasted from Beacon Hill, the architect created a rustic Swiss-Italian village for James' herd of prize-winning Guernsey cows and livestock. A staff of 100 oversaw the enterprise.

Peter Pennoyer and Anne Walker, *The Architecture of Grovesnor Atterbury* (New York: W. W. Norton, 2009), 92–9. (LC-DIG-ppmsca-16246)

PLATES 13–14 ARMSEA HALL, CHARLES FREDERICK HOFFMAN JR. HOUSE, NEWPORT, RHODE ISLAND, HOPPIN & KOEN, ARCHITECTS, COMPLETED 1901, OLMSTED BROTHERS, LANDSCAPE ARCHITECTS, 1911–18

[13] *Flower Garden Gate, Summer 1914*. Shortly after its completion in 1901, New York City real estate heir Charles F. Hoffman Jr. and his wife Zelia Krumbhaar acquired this estate with a Georgian Revival brick house designed by Francis Laurens Vinton Hoppin (1876–1941), architect of Edith Wharton's The Mount. It overlooked Narragansett Bay and bordered Hugh D. Auchincloss' Hammersmith Farm.

Mrs. Hoffman brought Frances Benjamin Johnston and Mattie Edwards Hewitt to Newport in 1914. They photographed Hoffman's famed roses and the gardens of her friends who belonged to the Newport Garden Club she helped found the same year.

Paul F. Miller, *Lost Newport* (Carlisle, MA: Applewood Books, 2009), 125–26. (LC-DIG-ppmsca-16228)

[14] *Flower Garden, Summer 1914*. Frances Benjamin Johnston opened her essay, "Rose Gardens of America," with this image. She wrote that the rose was America's flower, having grown in Northeastern gardens since British colonists introduced Sweet Bryer and Eglantine varieties "to brighten the garden plots they were to wrest so valiantly from the New England wilderness." A brick wall sheltered Hoffman's cascades of Dorothy Perkins roses.

FBJ, "Rose Gardens of America," *Art and Life* 10, no. 6 (June 1919): 303-07. (LC-DIG-ppmsca-16235)

PLATES 15–16 MARIEMONT, THOMAS JOSEPHUS EMERY HOUSE, MIDDLETOWN, RHODE ISLAND, RICHARD MORRIS HUNT, 1871, WITH CHANGES FOR THOMAS J. EMERY, CIRCA 1901, OLMSTED BROTHERS, LANDSCAPE ARCHITECTS, 1903–08

[15] *Rockery, Summer 1914*. Thomas and Mary Hopkins Emery came to Newport for the summer from Cincinnati, where they made a fortune manufacturing candles and developing real estate along the Ohio River. When Johnston visited the garden, Mrs. Emery was a widow and progressive philanthropist. Working with John Charles Olmsted, Henry Vincent Hubbard, and John Frederick Dawson over several years, she added formal gardens to an existing 19th-century naturalized landscape that included a rockery and pathways.

Millard F. Rogers Jr. "The Lost Gardens of Mariemont, Rhode Island," *Journal of the New England Garden History Society* 10 (Fall 2002): 1-10. (LC-DIG-ppmsca-16243)

[16] *Flower Garden, Summer 1914*. This lantern-slide view to the long axis of the formal garden was colored from an autochrome that Louise Shelton published in her 1915 book, *Beautiful Gardens in America*. On reviewing the book Gertrude Jekyll wrote that "seriously good gardening" was being practiced in America, and

she particularly admired the Johnston-Hewitt "pictures" of Mariemont because they, and a few others, had "the inestimable advantage of mature tree growth, either in main feature or background." FBJ composed her photographs to show this growth.

"Letter from Miss Jekyll," *Bulletin of The Garden Club of America* 14 (May 1916): n.p. (LC-DIG-ppmsca-16801)

PLATES 17–18 KENARDEN LODGE, JOHN STEWART KENNEDY HOUSE, BAR HARBOR, MAINE, ROWE & BAKER, HOUSE AND PROBABLE LANDSCAPE ARCHITECTS, 1892; BEATRIX JONES FARRAND, LANDSCAPE ARCHITECT, BEFORE 1914

[17] *Italian Garden, View from Pergola, Summer 1920.* At the time of his death in 1909, John S. Kennedy, noted a reporter, was one of America's "little known rich men." He made a fortune in coal, iron, and railroads that he left to his wife and progressive causes, including Booker T. Washington's Tuskegee Normal and Industrial Institute.

The Maine seaside resort must have appealed to the Scottish native. "The cool, even temperature of this region and the sea moisture afford a climate much like that of the English coast," observed FBJ. These conditions made for continuous bloom in the Kennedy garden, likely designed at the end of the 19th century by the estate's house architects, Rowe & Baker, and replanted by Farrand in the teens.

"Record Will This," *Montreal Gazette,* November 6, 1909; FBJ, "A Garden Set by the Sea," *Vogue* 58, 1 (July 1, 1921): 65, 98; Judith B. Tankard, *Beatrix Farrand, Private Gardens, Public Landscapes* (New York: The Monacelli Press, 2009), 104. (LC-DIG-ppmsca-16551)

[18] *Italian Garden, View to Pergola and Champlain Mountain, Summer 1920.* Kennedy's Norman-Tudor stone and half-beamed mansion, seen here in the distance, looked over a mowed field to the sunken garden. Snapdragons, sweet peas, poppies, larkspur, and the garden's "famous stock of penstemon," wrote FBJ, made this an exceptional flower garden.

FBJ, "A Garden Set," 65. For Kenarden Lodge, G. W. Helfrich and Gladys O'Neil, *Lost Bar Harbor* (Camden, Maine: Down East Books, 1983), 58. (LC-DIG-ppmsca-16937)

PLATES 19–20 REEF POINT, BEATRIX JONES FARRAND HOUSE, BAR HARBOR, MAINE, ROTCH & TILDEN, ARCHITECTS, 1883, BEATRIX JONES FARRAND, LANDSCAPE ARCHITECT, FROM 1917

[19] *Pathway to House, Summer 1920.* Farrand was one of America's first women landscape architects and was elected a garden consultant at the founding of The Garden Club of America in 1913.

At Reef Point, Farrand left native shrubs and ground covers to integrate her 6-acre garden into the craggy coastline. A fieldstone pathway led to a shingled cottage designed for Farrand's parents. This Maine landscape was a counterpoint to Johnston's slides of Italianate terrace gardens.

Tankard, *Beatrix Farrand,* 101–2. (LC-DIG-ppmsca-16695)

[20] *Stone Pathway, Summer 1920.* The woodland garden was a summer retreat for Farrand and her husband, Max Farrand (1869–1945), the first director of the rare book library Henry E. Huntington built on his estate in San Marino, California. (LC-DIG-ppmsca-16693)

PLATE 21 ROOKWOOD, EVELYN RUSSELL STURGIS HOUSE, MANCHESTER, MASSACHUSETTS

View to Atlantic Ocean, Summer 1924. This scenic view exemplified the garden vistas from houses along the coast that Johnston photographed in the 1920s. Sturgis was a daughter of Boston architect John Hubbard Sturgis (1834–88) and the cousin of Edith Wharton collaborator, Ogden Codman Jr. (1863–1951). (LC-DIG-ppmsca-16775)

PLATE 22 CHAILEY, CHARLES WILLIAM MOSLEY HOUSE, NEWBURYPORT, MASSACHUSETTS, CHARLES WILLIAM MOSELEY, LANDSCAPE GARDENER, FROM CIRCA 1915

Flower Garden, Summer 1920. The heir to a Boston mercantile fortune, Moseley lived in a farmhouse overlooking the historic Merrimack River, walked by nature writer Henry David Thoreau. It was on land contiguous with Maudesleigh, the estate of Moseley's brother, Frederick Strong Moseley, also photographed by FBJ. Pansies, mignonettes, alyssum, candytuft, and lady slippers evoked "the memory of a grandmother's garden," wrote Johnston of this enclosure.

FBJ, "The Mellow Charm of an Old-Fashioned Garden." *Vogue* 58, no. 7 (October 1, 1921): 73, 100. (LC-DIG-ppmsca-16753)

PLATE 23 DR. CHARLES WILLIAM RICHARDSON HOUSE, DUXBURY, MASSACHUSETTS, AMY SMART RICHARDSON, LANDSCAPE GARDENER

[23] *Native Plant Garden, August 1927.* While photographing New England estates and art collections, experiencing "nearly three weeks of rain, mostly in deluge…," FBJ stayed with Amy Richardson, a Washington friend with shared interests. She was a fellow D.A.R. member, Y.M.C.A. philanthropist and preservationist, a descendent of horticulturists, and sister of Johnston's client, landscape architect John H. Small III.

With precedent in 17th-century Native American gardens, picket-fence yards, wrote Frank A. Waugh, were appropriate for Cape Cod cottages. Richardson honored this history and planted her garden with regional plants.

Letter from FBJ to Nellie B. Allen, August 24, 1927, LOCFBJ reel 10; Charles Moore, "In Memoriam, Mrs. Amy Elizabeth Richardson," *Records of the Columbia Historical Society* 39 (1938): 101–03; Frank A. Waugh, "Picketed Gardens from Cape Cod," *House & Garden* 56, no. 1 (July 1929): 87. (LC-DIG-ppmsca-16973)

PLATES 24–25 DUDLEY LEAVITT PICKMAN JR. HOUSE, BEVERLY, MASSA-CHUSETTS, LITTLE & BROWNE, LANDSCAPE ARCHITECTS, 1899–1900

[24] *Fountain Basin, 1926.* Attorney and descendent of an 18th century Salem, Massachusetts merchant family, Dudley L. Pickman Jr. was a Henry James Bostonian. In 1899 he hired his Commonwealth Avenue neighbor, architect Arthur Little, to renovate and enlarge his Beverly country house and garden in the Colonial Revival style. This lily pool was at the center of a sunken terrace.

Little & Browne Archives, Account Book, Historic New England Library and Archives, Boston, Massachusetts. For a plan of this garden see "A Garden at Beverly, Massachusetts," *American Gardens,* ed. Guy Lowell (Boston: Bates & Guild, 1902), n.p. (LC-DIG-ppmsca-16788)

[25] *View from House, 1926.* Little & Browne aligned the brick-walled sunken terrace with Pickman's white-shingled house. For lecture audiences this was the new American formal garden derived from English and colonial precedents. "Every condition of climate and growth make for opulence of bloom with richness of color in these gardens of the North Shore," Johnston wrote. "Sheltered by dense woods … the flower masses reach a perfection seldom surpassed even in the garden spots of Bar Harbor and Long Island."

FBJ, "Captions. *Town and Country.* Garden of Mrs. Dudley Pickman, Beverly Cove, Massachusetts," LOCFBJ reel 23. (LC-DIG-ppmsca-16790)

PLATE 26 HOLM LEA, CHARLES SPRAGUE SARGENT HOUSE, BROOKLINE, MASSACHUSETTS, THOMAS LEE AND CHARLES SPRAGUE SARGENT, LANDSCAPE GARDENERS, 1845–1927

Crab Apple (Malus), *circa 1914.* Holm Lea was the 130-acre family estate of Charles Sprague Sargent, first director of the Arnold Arboretum, author of *The Silva of North America* (1891–1902), and early supporter of the garden club movement.

The crab apple was symbolically a portrait of the noted dendrologist who prized the flowering genus. Sargent's colleague and plant collector for the Arboretum, botanist Ernest Henry Wilson, wrote that the tree's bloom "had the delicate odor of violets…"

This slide established Johnston's credentials as a photographer of America's garden aristocracy.

Stephane Barry Sutton, *Charles Sargent Sprague and the Arnold Arboretum* (Cambridge: Harvard University Press, 1970); Ernest Henry Wilson, *Aristocrats of the Garden,* vol. 2 (Boston, The Stratford Company, 1932), 238. (LC-DIG-ppmsca-16685)

PLATES 27–33 WELD, LARZ ANDERSON HOUSE, BROOKLINE, MASSACHU-SETTS, CHARLES ADAMS PLATT, LANDSCAPE ARCHITECT, LATE 1899 OR 1900–01; LITTLE & BROWNE, TEMPLE ARCHITECTS, 1911

[27] *Herms at Pathway from House Lawn, the Bowling Green, to Italian Garden, circa 1914.* Platt influenced Johnston's photographic composition and her lectures. His Italian Garden, also known as the Formal Garden, was already famous in 1914 as a model of integrated house and garden design. (LC-DIG-ppmsca-16730; for landscape plan, see 16455)

[28–29] *Italian Garden Stairway and Terrace, circa 1914.* Larz Anderson, American ambassador to Japan (1912–13), and his wife landscaped their 60-acre estate with English, Italian, and Japanese gardens that reminded them of their travels and their guests of the Andersons' culture and wealth. Platt's design of this garden was inspired by Italian gardens he visited in 1892. (LC-DIG-ppmsca-16805 and 16294)

[30–31] *Italian Garden, View from Terrace to Cupid Fountain, View from Cupid Fountain to Terrace, circa 1914.* This 200-foot square garden was aligned with the house, screened from view by pines and hemlocks above the terrace.

Isabel Perkins Anderson inherited a clipper ship fortune and was an active garden club member. Supporting progressive causes, she hosted settlement house children at Weld. On the Italian Garden green in May 1916, boys and girls performed Anderson's play, *The Witch of the Woods,* a fairy tale with a nature message.

Richard G. Kenworthy, "Bringing the world to Brookline: the gardens of Larz and Isabel Anderson," *Journal of Garden History* 11, no. 4 (October–December 1991): 224–40; *Larz Anderson, Letters and Journals of a Diplomat,* edited by Isabel Anderson (New York: Fleming H. Revell, 1940), 113; *Bulletin of The Garden Club of America* 7, new series (December 1920): 20. (LC-DIG-ppmsca-16295 and 16796)

[32] *Willow Alley from the Rond Point to Temple, circa 1914.* At the bottom of the hillside property in the water garden, a circular enclosure by an unidentified architect "served as an outdoor theater for many a play, pageant, and ballet, a double row of willows providing entrance for the actors," wrote Larz Anderson. Outdoor performances were high-art culture in the American industrial renaissance.

Larz Anderson, Letters, 213. (LC-DIG-ppmsca-16561)

[33] *Temple in Water Garden, circa 1914.* The Boston firm of Little & Browne designed the Andersons' Washington, D.C., mansion, their renovated house at Weld, and this temple which introduced the English Picturesque to the hillside estate. Temples, at once decorative and practical, were ubiquitous in gardens photographed by Johnston. (LC-DIG-ppmsca-16751)

PLATES 34–35 BROOKSIDE, WILLIAM HALL WALKER HOUSE, GREAT BARRINGTON, MASSACHUSETTS, WALTER BRADNEE KIRBY, BOAT LANDING ARCHITECT, FERRUCCIO VITALE, LANDSCAPE ARCHITECT, 1912–18

[34] *Boat Landing, circa 1916.* Walker contributed to the invention of the flexible film roller and was a major shareholder in the Eastman Kodak Company, founded by George Eastman. The lake was in a landscape that included a walled garden and flower terrace. Johnston likely photographed this estate in June 1916, while attending the annual meeting of The Garden Club of America at nearby Lenox. At the event she projected her recently assembled "Our American Gardens" lecture slides. (LC-DIG-ppmsca-16780, crack in plate)

[35] *Perennial Garden Fountain, circa 1916.* Writing in 1922 about the more than 50 varieties of phlox, aster, columbine, alyssum, and water plants *Acorus* and *Cyperus* in this garden, Alfred Geiffert Jr. (1890–1957), then Vitale's partner, explained that "intricacy gives interest to landscape composition—it surprises with a series of successive pictures."

Country Life in America 41, no. 4 (February 1922): 52; R. Terry Schnadelbach, *Ferruccio Vitale, Landscape Architect of the Country Place Era* (New York: Princeton Architectural Press, 2001), 79–83. (LC-DIG-ppmsca-16288)

PLATES 36–37 WAVENY, LEWIS HENRY LAPHAM HOUSE, NEW CANAAN, CONNECTICUT, WILLIAM BUNKER TUBBY, ARCHITECT, 1911–12, OLMSTED BROTHERS, LANDSCAPE ARCHITECTS, 1907, 1911–15

[36] *View From House Terrace, circa 1915.* A tannery entrepreneur and founder of the Texas Company, which became Texaco Oil, Lapham converted a 300-acre farm into a modern country estate. The businessman's intentions reflected the aspirations of wealthy Americans in the country house era. "I understand that as long as the place is satisfactory to your taste, and is admired by your friends, or at any rate, not disagreeably criticized, and so long as you obtain from it such table supplies as can be raised on the place, satisfactorily and with reasonable economy, you will be in the main content," wrote John Charles Olmsted to Lapham in 1907.

LOCOA reel 195, job B237; Lois Bayles, Mary Louise King and F. David Lapham, *The Story of Waveny* (New Canaan Historical Society, 1969). (LC-DIG-ppmsca-16292)

[37] *Fountain, circa 1915.* The Tudor Revival house overlooked fields cleared of century-old trees. In a series of slides, Johnston walked her garden audience from the house. The fountain was at the center of a cruciform perennial garden. (LC-DIG-ppmsca-16786)

PLATES 38–39 ARNOLD SCHLAET HOUSE, SAUGATUCK, CONNECTICUT, WILLIAM BUNKER TUBBY, ARCHITECT, BEGUN 1911, OLMSTED BROTHERS, LANDSCAPE ARCHITECTS, 1907–11

[38] *View from House to Sunken Garden, circa 1915.* Lewis H. Lapham, neighbor and partner in founding the Texas Company, introduced Schlaet to the Olmsted firm. The businessman, who emigrated from Germany in 1877, haggled over the design and cost of his garden along Long Island Sound. Reporting on a visit in 1911, John Charles Olmsted wrote that Schlaet "spoke of the problem of tying the formal garden to the house. He spoiled our design by doing the garden first and then shortening the house. I could see no way of doing it—at any rate not without tearing down the pergola and parapet or something radical like that." Johnston overcame this defect by photographing the garden from the house. LOCOA reel 170, job 3138. (LC-DIG-ppmsca-16737)

[39] *View from Pergola, circa 1915.* To show the scale of the garden and yet avoid the problematic house, Johnston focused on the Italian fountain in the curve of the pergola. (LC-DIG-ppmsca-16738)

PLATES 40–41 CHELMSFORD, ELON HUNTINGTON HOOKER HOUSE, GREEN-WICH, CONNECTICUT, WARREN HENRY MANNING, LANDSCAPE ARCHITECT, 1909–1914

[40] *Brook Garden, circa 1914.* Hooker pioneered hydroelectric power; his wife was Blanche Ferry, the daughter of Dexter Mason Ferry, a prominent American seed propagator. With his fortune from the Hooker Electrochemical Company, the manufacturer hired McKim, Mead & White to enlarge a Tudor-style manor overlooking wooded acres.

Landscape architect Charles F. Gillette memorialized his early professional years as supervisor at Chelmsford with "Ode to Hooker Brooke. "Its voice is soft and seems to soothe, The Weary mind at close of day. It seems somehow to dull care to move, And with the current drift away."

Junior League of Greenwich, *The Great Estates, Greenwich, Connecti-cut, 1880–1930* (Greenwich, CT, Phoenix Publishing, 1986), 102–05; George C. Longest, *Genius in the Garden, Charles E. Gillette & Landscape Architec-ture in Virginia* (Richmond: Virginia State Archives and Library, 1992), 11. (LC-DIG-ppmsca-16280)

[41] *Vegetable Garden, circa 1914.* FBJ photographed this Connecticut garden to show that vegetables could be as decorative as flowers. "Eastern Gardens in Color Slide," *The Morning Press,* Santa Barbara, May 3, 1917, LOCFBJ reel 29. (LC-DIG-ppmsca-16281)

PLATES 42–43 THE PAVILION, STEPHEN HYATT PELHAM PELL HOUSE, FORT TICONDEROGA, NEW YORK, ALFRED CHARLES BOSSOM, ARCHITECT, 1910, MARIAN CRUGER COFFIN, LANDSCAPE ARCHITECT, 1920–26

[42] *Pathway to Teahouse in Walled Garden, August 1927.* Pell's restoration of his family's 19th-century house and nearby fort at Lake Champlain exemplified the American enthusiasm for the colonial past that inspired FBJ to photograph historic houses in the late 1920s. Bossom designed the teahouse and 9-foot wall of a flower garden laid out by Marian C. Coffin. (LC-DIG-ppmsca-16731)

[43] *Pathway in Walled Garden, August 1927.* The plaque recorded that French soldiers planted the first garden on this site in 1757 and dedicated it "Le Jardin du Roi" (The King's Garden). When FBJ visited in 1927, the garden was considered the oldest in America.

Lucinda A. Brockway, *A Favorite Place of Resort for Strangers: The King's Garden at Fort Ticonderoga* (Ticonderoga: Fort Ticonderoga, 2001). (LC-DIG-ppmsca-16258)

PLATES 44–47 THORNEDALE, OAKLEIGH THORNE HOUSE, MILLBROOK, NEW YORK, HELEN STAFFORD THORNE, LANDSCAPE GARDENER, FROM 1908

[44] *Lawn Terrace and Pond, 1919.* Post-Civil War wealth brought aristocratic grandeur to the American country house. Thornedale, wrote Johnston, was "remodeled from a farmhouse in the ownership of the Thorne family for gen-erations." Since its building in 1849, the Federal Revival villa had "assumed the dignified proportions of a great manor, standing amid gardens, and terraced lawns and surrounded by stately trees."

Garden Club of America board member Helen S. Thorne developed the grounds over three decades with a family fortune from publishing and California banking.

Mac Griswold and Eleanor Weller, *The Golden Age of American Gardens* (New York: Harry N. Abrams, 1992), 83–5; [FBJ], "Thornedale, The Coun-try Estate of Mr. Oakleigh Thorne," *Harper's Bazar* 55, no. 6 (June 1920): 56. (LC-DIG-ppmsca-16266)

[45] *Pond at House Entrance, 1919.* A comparison of Johnston's 1925 photograph of the upper terrace fountain at the Villa Torlonia with this image makes clear the influence of Italian garden design at this New York estate. (LC-DIG-ppm-sca-16745; for Torlonia, see 16350.)

[46] *Sugar Maple Hedge Along Alley to Rose Garden, 1919.* This main alley ter-minated at a pond. (LC-DIG-ppmsca-16196)

[47] *Canal, 1919.* In the spirit of Italian gardens, water was a unifying element at Thornedale. The slide artist made this image an Impressionist harmony in blue, green, and ochre. (LC-DIG-ppmsca-16644)

EPIGRAM, OPPOSITE PLATE 48
"It is not what…," "Horticulturist Urges more Gardens for Akron," *The Akron Press,* March 8, 1923.

PLATE 48 CRAGSTON, JOHN PIERPONT MORGAN HOUSE, HIGHLAND FALLS, NEW YORK

Spring Bulbs, circa 1913. In 1871 J. Pierpont Morgan purchased a 368-acre working farm on the unfashionable west side of the Hudson River. By the end of the 19th century he had transformed his country retreat near West Point into an estate that included tennis courts, kennels, greenhouses, orchards and vineyards. He cleared woodlands and planted hillside lawns with daffodils and tulips. Planning to be in Europe and therefore missing the springtime bloom, Morgan commissioned FBJ to photograph Cragston's dazzling floral display.

Jean Strouse, Morgan, *American Financier* (New York: Random House, 1999), 147-48; "Famous Gardens in Slides," *The New York Times*, November 1, 1916. (LC-DIG-ppmsca-16265)

PLATE 49 BARTOW MANSION, INTERNATIONAL GARDEN CLUB HEADQUARTERS, PELHAM BAY, NEW YORK, DELANO & ALDRICH, ARCHITECTS AND LANDSCAPE ARCHITECTS, 1914

Terrace Fountain, Fall 1915. With the Royal Horticultural Society of Great Britain as their inspiration, New Yorker Zelia K. Hoffman and English gardener Alice Martineau founded this club to advance horticulture through cultural exchange. The terrace at the renovated historic house was a model of landscape design for club members planning new gardens. (LC-DIG-ppmsca-16838)

PLATE 50 SAMUEL KNOPF HOUSE, LAWRENCE, NEW YORK, CIRCA 1907

Flower Garden, circa 1913. Knopf, an advertising executive and father of book publisher, Alfred Abraham Knopf, built his Classical Revival three-story house circa 1907. The property had all the essentials of the businessman's country estate "35 minutes from town": tennis courts, vegetable gardens, "sanitary chicken house," "Italian gardens, lily pool and marble fountains," a garage for three cars, a stable for four horses, "dustless roads," apartments for a chauffeur and gardener, all on "50 city lots."

Sale advertisement, "Gentleman's All Year Country Home," *Country Life in America* 4, no. 5 (April 1914): 5. (LC-DIG-ppmsca-16844)

PLATES 51–52 WILLOWMERE, REAR ADMIRAL AARON WARD HOUSE, ROSLYN HARBOR, NEW YORK, REAR ADMIRAL AARON AND ELIZABETH CAIRNS WARD, LANDSCAPE GARDENERS, FROM 1900

[51] *Rear Admiral Aaron and Elizabeth Cairns Ward, circa 1914.* In a period of military campaigns, Aaron Ward (1851–1918) was a national hero from the Spanish American War. He and his wife lived in a 19th-century house built by her family in a town famous for Cedarmere, the home of poet William Cullen Bryant.

The J. Horace McFarland Company, Harrisburg, Pennsylvania, made this slide from a photograph taken by Johnston-Hewitt. It is the only portrait of owners in the Johnston slide collection. A print of the original photograph is in the Aaron Ward file, Mattie Edwards Hewitt Collection, Nassau County Museum, Roslyn Harbor, New York. (LC-DIG-ppmsca-16315)

[52] *Rose Garden, circa 1914.* FBJ searched for famous gardens, and this Long Island collection was renowned in a period of rose cultivation. After retiring in 1913, Ward devoted his life to cultivating more than 3,000 roses. He recorded each plant in a diary to track its progress and befriended French rose cultivator Joseph Pernet-Ducher (1859–1928) who named varieties after Ward family members. The Garden Club of America annually voted the yellow, hybrid tea "Mrs. Aaron Ward" among the five best American roses.

J. Horace McFarland, "The Passing of a Great Rosarian," *The American Rose Annual, 1919:* 53–8. (LC-DIG-ppmsca-16273)

PLATE 53 CLARABEN COURT, BENJAMIN STERN HOUSE, ROSLYN HARBOR, NEW YORK, ACHILLE DUCHÊNE, LANDSCAPE ARCHITECT, FROM 1906

Terracing to Harbor, circa 1914. Stern was a founder of Stern Brothers, the New York department store. He was a client of French landscape designer Achille Duchêne who, with his father, Henri, revived the French tradition of *parterres de broderie* and *treillage*. In Johnston lectures, the formality of the Stern garden, with hydrangea borders and lawns, was in contrast to the late 19th-century horticultural display of Stern's neighbor, Rear Admiral Aaron Ward. (LC-DIG-ppmsca-16863)

PLATE 54 FANNY A. MULFORD HOUSE, HEMPSTEAD, NEW YORK, RUTH BRAMLEY DEAN, LANDSCAPE ARCHITECT, CIRCA 1915

Arbor Seat, circa 1916. Johnston presented slides of this garden and its landscape plan to demonstrate what Dean herself promoted, that a designed garden was possible at any scale. In her suburban garden, Mulford planted domesticated flowers, but her avocation was collecting and recording native plants around Hempstead Lake. Her catalog contributed to Norman Taylor's classic 1915 *Flora of the Vicinity of New York.*

Eric Lamont, "Fanny Mulford's Orchid Collection from the Late 1890s," *Long Island Botanical Society Newsletter* 5, no. 2 (March–April 1992): 7–9. (LC-DIG-ppmsca-16260; landscape plan, 16314).

PLATES 55–56 MARSHFIELD, GEORGE WOODWARD WICKERSHAM HOUSE, CEDARHURST, NEW YORK, MARY RUTHERFORD JAY, LANDSCAPE ARCHITECT, 1914

[55] *Pond Before Landscaping, 1914*. Mary Rutherford Jay (1872–1953) was an avid traveler and lectured on the garden club circuit. For George W. Wickersham, recently retired as President William Howard Taft's attorney general, Jay designed a Japanese garden by draining a pond and laying concrete foundations for four islands. Johnston dramatized the garden's transformation by projecting this "before" photograph in black and white.
Cynthia Zaitzevsky, *Long Island Landscapes and the Women Who Designed Them* (New York and London: Society for the Preservation of Long Island Antiquities in association with W. W. Norton, 2009), 196–99. Photographer unknown. (LC-DIG-ppmsca-16200)

[56] *View from House to Japanese Garden, circa 1915*. The red bridge led to a Guest's Island where, according to tradition, visitors gathered before proceeding to a Master's Island, also represented in the Wickersham garden. Evergreens, rhododendrons, iris, and bamboo grew along banks secured by wood posts. Johnston photographed strategically to avoid the road at the far side of the pond. (LC-DIG-ppmsca-16158)

PLATE 57 BARBERRYS, NELSON DOUBLEDAY HOUSE, MILL NECK, NEW YORK, HARRIE THOMAS LINDEBERG, ARCHITECT, BUILT 1916, OLMSTED BROTHERS AND OTHERS, LANDSCAPE ARCHITECTS, 1919–24

Garden Gate, 1921. Walls sheltered this garden from nearby Long Island Sound. Olmsted Brothers laid out the grounds for the scion and business heir of Frank Nelson Doubleday (1862–1934), publisher of *Country Life in America, The Garden Magazine*, and garden books. His mother was author Neltje Blanchan de Graff (1865–1918), a celebrity in garden club circles for her lyrical scientific writing on flowers and bird life. She gave prizes to children who worked in gardens and organized plant donations to public schools.
Bulletin of The Garden Club of America 25 (May 1918): n.p. (LC-DIG-ppmsca-16901)

PLATE 58 OLD ACRES, ROBERT LOW BACON HOUSE, OLD WESTBURY, NEW YORK, MARTHA BROOKES BROWN HUTCHESON, LANDSCAPE ARCHITECT, 1904–10

Steps from Rose Garden to Wild Flower Sanctuary, April 1921. At the urgent request of Mrs. Robert L. "Virginia" Bacon, FBJ rushed by train to photograph the azaleas and dogwoods in bloom. This path, with white rock cress, phlox, and primroses, led downhill to a wildflower garden that combined preservation and education. Mrs. Bacon, married to a New York banker and soon-to-be United States congressman, labeled the plants, "to have the children learn about the flowers." Landscape architect Isabella Pendleton (1891–1965) observed after a tour that Hutcheson had designed the garden to lead guests from a grass terrace at the house "through formal gardens to semiformal gardens and on to wilder parts; and … a pond."
Isabella Pendleton, "Some Lessons to Be Learned from a Long Island Garden," *Country Life* 63, no. 5 (March 1923): 39. (LC-DIG-ppmsca-16282)

PLATES 59–60 WELWYN, HAROLD IRVING PRATT HOUSE, GLEN COVE, NEW YORK, MARTHA BROOKES BROWN HUTCHESON AND JAMES LEAL GREENLEAF, 1911–13, HARRIET BARNES PRATT, LANDSCAPE GARDENER, FROM 1906

[59] *Sundial, "The Fruit Bearer," by Edward Francis McCartan, circa 1918*. The City Beautiful movement brought an American sculpture renaissance, with commissions for McCartan and his generation trained in Paris. The New York-based artist was sympathetic to importing 18th-century statues and decorative vases to new gardens but wrote that "estate owners should be more adventurous," choosing sculpture "with the architecture of a garden in mind." FBJ's close-focus photograph showed the circular form of the garden terrace in relation to the sculpture.
Augusta Owen Patterson, "Edward McCartan, Sculptor," *International Studio* 83, no. 345 (January 1926): 27. (LC-DIG-ppmsca-16811)

[60] *View from Living Room to Sunken Garden, 1915*. Harriet B. Pratt was a leader in the garden club movement, elected in the teens to both her local North Country Garden Club and The Garden Club of America. She was one of FBJ's first clients and in 1916 personally presented FBJ's "Our American Gardens" slides at Welwyn. Her extensive garden had borders planted by cultivator John C. Wister, naturalized bulb plantings, and an enclosed rose garden Pratt maintained following the recommendations of Rear Admiral Aaron Ward.
"Many Gardens in One, *House & Garden* 77, no. 3 (March 1940): 25–6; Harriet

Barnes Pratt, "Hybrid Teas, The Routine of the Rose Garden at Welwyn," *Bulletin of The Garden Club of America* 16 (September 1916): n.p. (LC-DIG-ppmsca-16868)

PLATES 61–62 KILLENWORTH, GEORGE DUPONT PRATT HOUSE, GLEN COVE, NEW YORK, TROWBRIDGE & ACKERMAN, ARCHITECTS, COMPLETED 1913, OLMSTED BROTHERS AND JAMES LEAL GREENLEAF, LANDSCAPE ARCHITECTS, 1906–13

[61] *View to Tea House from Swimming Pool, circa 1915.* In a period of academic design, the Standard Oil heir razed his eclectic Queen Anne cottage and built a granite, Jacobean Revival manor on a terrace facing south to a swimming pool and north to Long Island Sound. For this work, Pratt hired his brother-in-law, Frederick Lee Ackerman (1878–1950), trained at Cornell University and at the École des Beaux-Arts.

Killenworth, with house and landscape conceived together, represented in FBJ's lecture, "Our American Gardens," an ideal estate for the aspiring country house owner and gardener. (LC-DIG-ppmsca-16841)

[62] *View from Terrace to Swimming Pool, circa 1918.* In 1914, *County Life in America* named Killenworth "Best House of the Year," noting that prevailing winds and the swimming pool had determined the orientation of the stone mansion. At once ornamental and practical, the Pratt pool was an American synthesis of modern convenience and Old World design.

George D. Pratt was conservation commissioner for the State of New York, 1915–17, and a patron of art photography. His interest in American forests guided the planning of his 39½ acres in the Pratt family compound, Dosoris. To Pratt's once barren site, Lewis & Valentine, known for moving mature specimens, imported arborvitae, spruce, and pine.

In this painterly slide, FBJ's artist composed a vision of azure, violet, and cerulean, glazing the coping green and painting rhododendron blooms pink-white to harmonize with a neoclassical statue of Hebe, the goddess of youth.

"The Best House of the Year," *Country Life in America* 26, no. 6 (October 1914): 35-40, with site plan. (LC-DIG-ppmsca-21914; for slide of same view, circa 1915, see 16869)

PLATES 63–66 BURRWOOD, WALTER JENNINGS HOUSE, COLD SPRING HARBOR, NEW YORK, FREDERICK LAW OLMSTED AND OLMSTED BROTHERS, LANDSCAPE ARCHITECTS, FROM 1895, 1915–16

[63] *View from Drive to Sunken Garden, 1916.* "I have a piece of property at Cold Springs Harbor, Long Island, consisting of 110 acres," wrote Walter Jennings, nephew of William Avery Rockefeller, to Frederick Law Olmsted in 1895. "I am anxious to develop it in a moderate way in order to make the best use of the natural beauty." The letter initiated a 30-year relationship with the Olmsted firm as it designed the original rose garden in this ravine circa 1898–1900 and then redesigned it 15 years later for perennial borders.

Mrs. Walter "Jean" Jennings was active in The Garden Club of America and relied on Rear Admiral Aaron Ward for her roses. Her husband participated as a collector and painter of lantern slides. In 1922 he gave the club a stereopticon (lantern slide projector) for its 644 slides.

LOCOA reel 296, job 6287; *Bulletin of The Garden Club of America,* no. 6 (July, 1922): 345. (LC-DIG-ppmsca-16221)

[64] *Sunken Garden, Fountain, 1916.* Like Harriet B. Pratt nearby, Jennings stayed with the times by adding contemporary sculpture to his collection of antiquities. *The Dogwood Lady* by Janet Scudder was at the center of the sunken garden and on alignment with the entrance to the house designed by Carrère & Hastings.

Town & Country, when publishing this photograph, observed that the installation was particularly noteworthy, because the "usual fashion in America has been to acquire something good in the way of sculpture and then to set it out quite coldly."

Town & Country 71, no. 3643 (October 1, 1916): 28. (LC-DIG-ppmsca-16212)

[65] *Sunken Garden, Evergreens, 1916.* In 1915 the Olmsted firm replanted the borders along the faux-ruin, retaining walls they built circa 1900. New steps and garden ramps were made from rubble stone excavated to build the New York City subway. (LC-DIG-ppmsca-16230)

[66] *Sunken Garden, Pathway, 1916.* This slide was the final in a walking sequence through the newly landscaped American flower garden. (LC-DIG-ppmsca-16210)

PLATE 67 PLANTING FIELDS, WILLIAM ROBERTSON COE HOUSE, OYSTER BAY, NEW YORK, TEA HOUSE AND LANDSCAPE ARCHITECTS, GUY LOWELL AND ANDREW ROBESON SARGENT, 1914–16, OLMSTED BROTHERS, FROM 1918

View to Blue Pool Garden and Tea House, Spring 1926. The insurance millionaire and his wife, Mary R. Coe, a daughter of Standard Oil industrialist Henry Huttleston Rogers, built from 1918 to 1921 a Tudor Revival manor designed by

Walker & Gillette on over 350 acres landscaped with specimen trees and plants. This garden room was a collaboration of Charles Sprague Sargent's son and his son-in-law, architect and garden-book author Guy Lowell. Its plan, a rectangular pool in a flower garden aligned with a house, was a convention in landscape design across America. Johnston photographed Planting Fields for its bulb supplier, John Scheepers. (LC-DIG-ppmsca-16975; for view from teahouse, see 16976)

PLATE 68 LAURELTON HALL, LOUIS TIFFANY FOUNDATION, COLD SPRING HARBOR, NEW YORK, LOUIS COMFORT TIFFANY, ARCHITECT AND LANDSCAPE GARDENER, BEGUN 1902

Octagonal Garden, circa 1918. In an era when Americans promoted beauty through education, the decorator and glass designer, Louis C. Tiffany, donated in 1918 his Persian-inspired villa and 60 landscaped acres to a foundation for art students. The plan of this sunken garden echoed the octagonal court of the house above. "In greater or lesser degree, beauty is within the reach of everybody," Tiffany explained. He found his neighbors building Tudor manors and French châteaux "extravagant people living extravagant lives," and in a Ruskinian voice urged "a more restrained and reasonable decoration, with nature as a stimulus, a harmonizer."
    Louis C. Tiffany, "The Quest for Beauty," *Harper's Bazar* 52, no. 12 (December 1917): 43. (LC-DIG-ppmsca-21922)

PLATE 69 CLAVERACK, COLONEL THOMAS HENRY BARBER HOUSE, SOUTHAMPTON, NEW YORK, ROBERT HENDERSON ROBERTSON, ARCHITECT, BUILT 1892, FREDERICK LAW OLMSTED, LANDSCAPE ARCHITECT, 1893–94

View to House from Garden, circa 1915. To reflect her establishment heritage, Harriet Townsend Barber instructed Robertson to model her house on the 18th-century Albany, New York, stone manor of her grandfather, Stephen van Rensselaer. Hedges framed garden rooms with Colonial Revival flower beds edged in boxwood. The finished house and garden, concluded the local magazine, was "a palatable blend of the past and present, of Dutch, English, and American … of plain green grass and brilliantly blooming flowers." Slides of Claverack were Johnston's only images of a garden by Frederick Law Olmsted, a fact she recounted in lectures.
    "Claverack," *Southampton Magazine* 1, no. 2 (Summer 1912): 30-3. (LC-DIG-ppmsca-16834)

PLATE 70 MILLEFIORI, ALBERT BARNES BOARDMAN HOUSE, SOUTHAMPTON, NEW YORK, POLHEMUS & COFFIN, LANDSCAPE ARCHITECTS, DESIGNED 1910

Garden Gate, Summer 1914. Georgina Bonner Boardman supported women artists. She hired landscape architect Marian Cruger Coffin to design her Southampton garden and encouraged Long Island club members to commission the photographers Frances Benjamin Johnston and Mattie Edwards Hewitt to document their Hamptons estates.
    The imposing gate in the flower garden at Millefiori was in keeping with the house, a close adaptation by architects Hill & Stout of the 16th-century Villa Medici in Rome by Annibale Lippi. (LC-DIG-ppmsca-16188)

PLATES 71–72 WOOLDON MANOR, DR. PETER BROWN WYCKOFF HOUSE, SOUTHAMPTON, NEW YORK, BARNEY & CHAPMAN, ARCHITECTS, HICKS NURSERIES, LANDSCAPE GARDENERS, BUILT AND PLANTED, CIRCA 1900

[71] *View from East Terrace, 1914.* The autochrome of this photograph was the frontispiece to the illustrated book by Louise Shelton, *Beautiful Gardens in America,* 1915. A comparison reveals that the lantern-slide artist heightened contrasts for pictorial depth and dimension. (LC-DIG-ppmsca-16563, crack in plate)

[72] *View to East Terrace, 1914.* The daughter of Sidney Dillon, a builder and president of the Union Pacific Railroad, Cora Dillon Wyckoff built a massive Tudor Revival house on 16 oceanfront acres. In September 1915, FBJ presented a slide lecture here at a luncheon for local club members whose gardens she photographed. (LC-DIG-ppmsca-16850)

PLATE 73 THE STEPPINGSTONES, ANNIE MAY HEGEMAN HOUSE, SOUTHAMPTON, NEW YORK, CIRCA 1900

Sunken Garden, circa 1915. Communities founded utopian art colonies as a response to industrialization. Hegeman was an artist and her house was in the Southampton "Art Village" organized in 1891 by a committee that included architect Grosvenor Atterbury, museum founder and real estate developer Samuel Longstreth Parrish, and Hegeman's mother, artist Annie de Camp Hegeman Porter. They persuaded American Impressionist painter William Merritt Chase (1849–1916) to live in Southampton and direct the Shinnecock Summer School of Art.

For correspondence relating to the founding and ownership in the colony, see Art Colony Archive, Southampton Historical Museum, Southampton, New York. (LC-DIG-ppmsca-16887)

PLATE 74 BLACK POINT, COLONEL HENRY HUTTLESTON ROGERS JR. HOUSE, SOUTHAMPTON, NEW YORK, WALKER & GILLETTE, ARCHITECTS, OLMSTED BROTHERS, LANDSCAPE ARCHITECTS, 1914–15

Children's Garden, circa 1916. Small buildings served diverse purposes in the new American garden, with professional design making the functional beautiful. This cottage, in the Italianate style of the main house, was for both flower arranging and educating children through play about nature and domestic life. Its "attractive exterior," an editor wrote, hid its "practical purposes."

Propinquity and social conformity characterized the society Johnston served. Oil millionaire Henry H. Rogers was the brother of Mary R. Coe living at Planting Fields. Both commissioned Walker & Gillette and Olmsted Brothers to design their Long Island estates.

Roger B. Whitman, "Hobby Houses," *The House Beautiful* 56, no. 1 (July 1924): 38. (LC-DIG-ppmsca-16877)

PLATE 75 GARDENSIDE, FREDERICK AUGUSTUS SNOW HOUSE, SOUTHAMP-TON, NEW YORK, CLARENCE FOWLER, LANDSCAPE ARCHITECT, CIRCA 1913

View North to Flower Garden, circa 1914. Johnston's frequent client Clarence Fowler designed an axial garden for this house sited close to its eastern boundary. This walkway led north to the street and south to a vegetable garden. The flower borders were examples of continuous bloom, from May to November, planted along a brick walk that was easily groomed. "The material for the walks depends to a great extent on the surroundings," wrote the landscape architect. "Grass is the least desir-able … If the low growing flowers fall over on the sides, a bare spit will surely be left or the lawn mower will cut them off the plants and make them unsightly…."

Clarence Fowler, "Making the Most of the Herbaceous Border, Its Design and Care," *The Garden Magazine* 34, no. 1 (September 1921): 18, illustrated with FBJ photographs. (LC-DIG-ppmsca-16884; landscape plan 16446)

PLATES 76–79 THE ORCHARD, JAMES LAWRENCE BREESE HOUSE, SOUTH-AMPTON, NEW YORK, MCKIM, MEAD & WHITE, ARCHITECTS AND LAND-SCAPE ARCHITECTS, 1898–1907

[76] *Entrance Drive, 1912.* For art collector, stockbroker, and amateur art photogra-pher James L. Breese, Stanford White designed a Colonial Revival house in an Itali-anate garden, making the 30-acre property uniquely modern. "Once upon a time, a small farm house stood in the midst of the fertile fields on which now stands this great estate…. This low, broad, beautiful home, set in the flower garden is surely what we may call an ideal American home," wrote editors of *The Touchstone.*

"One of the Loveliest of Long Island Modern Homes Belongs to James L. Breese," *The Touchstone* 3, no. 1 (April 1918): 21–7. (LC-DIG-ppmsca-16564)

[77–79, gatefold] *Pergola Garden Pathway, Herms Along Pathway, Fountain, 1912.* Johnston walked her viewer along a path between pergolas to the center bay of the house. At the end, boxwood moved from 19th-century gardens framed the fountain, *The Frogs,* by American sculptor Janet Scudder. Wilhelm Miller wrote that the "charm of the Breese house is partly due to these old specimens of box, because box is the one plant that commonly survives a century in gardens … Mr. Breese must have spent a small fortune on box, for it leads you up the long path to his house, humanizes the portico, flanks the garden, and helps tie the whole to the landscape."

When painting this slide, the artist glazed the white shingles to add depth to the composition.

Burdette Crane Maercklein, "Old Boxwood in New Garden," *House & Garden* 28, no. 2 (August 1915): 28. (LC-DIG-ppmsca-16816, 16812, 16560; landscape plan 16445)

PLATE 80 PRÈS CHOISIS, ALBERT HERTER HOUSE, EAST HAMPTON, NEW YORK, GROSVENOR ATTERBURY, ARCHITECT, 1898–99, ALBERT AND ADELE MCGINNIS HERTER, LANDSCAPE GARDENERS, FROM 1898

View to House from Orange-and-Yellow Garden, Fall 1913. The artist Albert Herter was an heir to the Herter Brothers furniture fortune. With his wife Adele McGinnis, also an artist and heir, he built a pink stucco villa overlooking a pond flowing out to the Atlantic Ocean. When asked why his house and garden were reminiscent of Sicily, Albert Herter answered, "It is perhaps the sea; and I am sure our three Sicilian workmen are also responsible." The house had color-themed gardens: a blue and white terrace, and this orange-and-yellow court with continu-ous bloom; tulips and crocus in April, climbing yellow roses in May and June, fol-lowed by yellow phlox and orange-yellow Sweet William, dahlias, trumpet vine, and zinnias.

A gray fog softened the floral brilliance when Johnston photographed the house in the early fall. She considered it to have the "the loveliest and most consistently developed waterside garden I know in this country."

"Three Sicilian Gardeners: What They Have Accomplished With the Help of Two Artists and Nature," *The Craftsman* 26, no. 3 (June 1914): 292–302, illustrated with FBJ's photographs; FBJ, "Small Long Island Gardens," LOCFBJ reel 28. (LC-DIG-ppmsca-16820)

PLATE 81 BALLYSHEAR, CHARLES BLAIR MACDONALD HOUSE, SOUTHAMPTON, NEW YORK, FRANCIS BURRALL HOFFMAN JR., ARCHITECT, SETH JAY RAYNOR AND ROSE STANDISH NICHOLS, LANDSCAPE ARCHITECTS, COMPLETED 1913

Flower Garden, circa 1915. For MacDonald, a stockbroker and amateur golfer, Nichols designed a terraced flower garden on axis with a Georgian Revival house overlooking Peconic Bay. (LC-DIG-ppmsca-16880)

PLATES 82–84 GRAY GARDENS, ROBERT CARMER HILL HOUSE, EAST HAMPTON, NEW YORK, ANNA GILMAN HILL, LANDSCAPE GARDENER, FROM 1913

[82] *Plan, 1914.* In 1913 Consolidation Coal Company executive Robert C. Hill purchased a shingle cottage on 4½ acres. His wife designed this much-published garden with concrete walls to protect the 40- by 70-foot flower garden from ocean wind. The garden's fame continued after Edie Bouvier Beal acquired the house in 1924.

This plan is one of 14 landscape plans in the FBJ slide collection, 11 of which are from the 1913 publication, *Monograph of the Work of Charles A. Platt.* Johnston photographed from direct experience of gardens and wrote in poetical, not landscape terms. She stressed in lectures the importance of conceiving house and garden together.

Cynthia Zaitzevsky notes: "The Hill garden in East Hampton is sometimes incorrectly attributed to Dean." Editors of *The Touchstone* wrote that the garden was "designed and created by Mrs. Robert C. Hill." Dean did not credit herself as its designer when publishing the Johnston-Hewitt Gray Gardens photographs in her book, *The Livable House.* A 1921 magazine caption for a version of the slide *View from House* was: "A Happy Example of Landscaping by Miss Ruth B. Dean." In the accompanying article Dean discussed changes in the garden made by Hill. A print of the garden gate (LC-DIG-ppmsca-16220) in the collection of the Nassau County Museum of Art is annotated in an unidentified hand, "Ruth

Dean, Landscape archt." Attribution of this plan to Hill is based on a drawing in the same hand of Hill's Englewood, New Jersey, garden.

Hill, at a time when American writers adopted the English "grey," spelled her house "Gray Gardens."

"Garden Photography as a Fine Art: Illustrated by Rare Photographs of Beautiful Gardens, *The Touchstone* 2, no. 3 (December 1917): 280; *The Livable House, Its Garden* (New York: Moffat, Yard and Company, 1917), 125; Ruth Dean, "In the Country Garden," *The Garden Magazine* 33 no. 7 (July 1921): 46; *The Garden Magazine* 33, no. 7 (July 1921): 46; Mattie Edwards Hewitt Collection, Robert C. Hill file, Nassau County Museum of Art, Roslyn Harbor, New York; Zaitzevsky, 283 n. 24; Anna Gilman Hill, *Forty Years of Gardening* (New York: Frederick A. Stokes, 1938), 127–35. For Beechgate, see here, Plate 183–184 and p. 318. (LC-DIG-ppmsca-16270)

[83] *View from House, 1914.* Johnston photographed this garden from its planting in 1914 until 1917. The "garden architecture repudiates that of the house altogether and yet it is not inharmonious, for the reason that it loses itself delightfully in the low sand hills of the surrounding country," wrote landscape architect Ruth Dean.

Ruth B. Dean, "Garden Shelters," *The New Country Life* 34, no. 2 (June 1918): 48. For Hill and Johnston, see here "The Garden Photograph,"p. 45 and p. 348, note 76. (LC-DIG-ppmsca-16217)

[84] *View West to Pergola, 1914.* On receiving a black-and-white print of this photograph, Hill wrote, "it was taken the first year before the roses were up on the pergola and oak branches were used to shade the pergola which looks badly." Slide coloring further enhanced this early view of the garden before mature growth.

Robert C. Hill file, recto of corresponding photograph, Mattie Edwards Hewitt Collection, Nassau County Museum of Art, Roslyn Harbor, New York. (LC-DIG-ppmsca-16215)

PLATE 85 GREY-CROFT, STEPHEN SWETE CUMMINS HOUSE, EAST HAMPTON, NEW YORK, EMMA WOODHOUSE CUMMINS, LANDSCAPE GARDENER, CIRCA 1903

Rustic Bridge in Japanese Iris Garden, July 1913. In composition and theme, both the garden itself and FBJ's photographs of Grey-Croft are reminiscent of Claude Monet's paintings of Giverny, France. Emma Woodhouse cut alders and wild cherries growing in a marsh near her house to make pathways to a grass-roofed tea pavilion overlooking this pond. Native wild aster, Joe Pye weed, Meadow Rue and fern grew along its banks.

For this garden and Impressionism, see Figs. 30a, b, p. 42 and p. 292. (LC-DIG-ppmsca-16223; for pavilion, see LC-DIG-ppmsca-16807)

PLATES 86–88 GEORGE FISHER BAKER HOUSE, TUXEDO PARK, NEW YORK, CLARENCE FOWLER, LANDSCAPE ARCHITECT, CIRCA 1913

[86] *Rockery Pool, circa 1913.* A founder of the First National Bank of the City of New York and Harvard University philanthropist, George F. Baker purchased his house in 1895 from the wife of Tuxedo Park's founder, Pierre Lorillard. The pool was in a naturalized garden on a slope leading down to Tuxedo Lake.

Tuxedo Park, The Historic Houses, edited by Christian R. Sonne and Chiu Yin Hempel (Tuxedo Park: Tuxedo Historical Society, 2007), 98–101. (LC-DIG-ppmsca-16252)

[87] *Bridge, circa 1913.* Fletcher Steele wrote that the "true garden is a work of art, and the place and character of all garden furniture should be carefully studied when the skeleton plan of beds, walks, fountains, and lawns is studied…." If not, "the object, no matter how beautiful in itself, is almost certain to look … like a lace fan with a tailored gown." He illustrated the successful placement of an object with this view of the Baker Japanesque bridge, planted with yellow and purple iris.

Fletcher Steele, "The Secrets of Garden Furnishings," *Vogue* 45, no. 9 (May 1, 1915): 47. (LC-DIG-ppmsca-16799)

[88] *Rhododendron, circa 1913.* Johnston promoted herself as an avid horticulturist with slides of specimen plants and wildflowers. (LC-DIG-ppmsca-16740)

PLATES 89–90 DRUMTHWACKET, MOSES TAYLOR PYNE HOUSE, PRINCETON, NEW JERSEY, RALEIGH COLSTON GILDERSLEEVE, ARCHITECT FOR ADDITIONS TO 1833 HOUSE, 1893 AND 1900, DANIEL WEBSTER LANGTON, LANDSCAPE ARCHITECT, FROM 1893

[89] *House Overlooking the Italian Garden, 1911.* A National City Bank of New York and railroad heir, Pyne enlarged an existing Greek Revival house and built a garden inspired by the Villa Gamberaia in Italy. For Johnston the over 600-acre estate was ideal, combining the best of Europe and America. Princeton had "the finished charm and restfulness of an English landscape," the garden "so perfect in plan and execution that it might have been transported bodily from the setting of some Roman or Florentine villa." The house was more than a country residence, it was "a home." At the time, Americans wanted houses that impressed while offering bourgeois comfort.

Frances Benjamin Johnston, "The Country Seat of Mr. Moses Taylor Pyne," *Town & Country* no. 3409 (September 16, 1911): 26, photograph credited to FBJ only; the same photograph in Louise Shelton, *Beautiful Gardens in America* (New York: Charles Scribner's Sons, 1915), is credited to Miss Johnston–Mrs. Hewitt, likely because the image was in the partners' inventory by 1915. William K. Selden, *Drumthwacket* (Princeton: The Drumthwacket Foundation, 2005), 35–48. (LC-DIG-ppmsca-16782)

[90] *Italian Garden Stairway, 1911.* Two garden terraces stepped down from the house to this staircase above a spring in a rocky grotto. On seeing this photograph and two others of Drumthwacket in Louise Shelton's 1915 *Beautiful Gardens in America,* Gertrude Jekyll wrote: "A very capable architect has been at work on Drumthwacket, and has reproduced some genuine Italian feeling…. The success … is that of the artist although it is fairly far north."

"Letter from Miss Jekyll," n.p. (LC-DIG-ppmsca-16742)

PLATES 91–92 ANDORRA, WILLIAM WARNER HARPER HOUSE, WYNDMOOR, PENNSYLVANIA, OLMSTED BROTHERS AND DUHRING & HOWE, LANDSCAPE ARCHITECTS, 1912–13

[91] *Garden Bench, Spring 1919.* In a region of nurseries, the Andorra company was known for its ornamental trees and shrubs that owner William W. Harper promoted to garden club members who owned estates he supplied. They were "a good investment, for grounds so adorned increase rapidly in value, and there is a minimum of expense in caring for [them]…."

When Harper built a house on his 350 acres in 1912, Olmsted Brothers laid out the grounds, following the client's instructions that a "forest must have lots of Pines, Hemlocks, Oaks, Beeches, and Dogwoods. Locate lots of mysterious walks and benches for lovers, plenty of rhododendrons and azaleas to come suddenly into the view of the lovers…." Duhring & Howe designed a topiary garden immediately west of the new manor house.

"Andorra," *Country Life in America* 1, no. 2 (December 1901): back cover; "The Nurseries of Philadelphia," *The National Nurseryman* 16, 6 (November 2, 1903): 188; letter from William Warren Harper to James Frederick Dawson, June 20, 1912, LOCOA reel 258, job 5517; James B. Garrison, *Houses of Philadelphia: Chestnut Hill and the Wissahickon Valley, 1880–1930* (New York: Acanthus Press, 2008), 126–29. (LC-DIG-ppmsca-16253)

[92] *Fountain, Spring 1919.* The house garden was three interconnected rooms. (LC-DIG-ppmsca-16565)

PLATES 93–94 ALLGATES, HORATIO GATES LLOYD HOUSE, HAVERFORD, PENNSYLVANIA, WILSON EYRE, ARCHITECT, OLMSTED BROTHERS WITH MARY HELEN WINGATE LLOYD, LANDSCAPE ARCHITECTS, 1910–15

[93] *View to House, Spring 1919.* After Mary W. Lloyd died in 1934 at age 65, The Garden Club of America published a memorial *Bulletin* recounting the diverse activities of this wealthy modern woman: painter, book collector, suffragette, birth control advocate, and gardener. She and her banker husband, a partner with Johnston client Edward T. Stotesbury at Drexel & Company in Philadelphia, began in 1910 with 25 farmland acres and by the 1930s had 75 landscaped acres with flower gardens and naturalized stands of trees. The herbaceous borders in the flower garden were in keeping with Lloyd's Arts and Crafts house finished in cream-colored stucco.

Bulletin in Memory of Mary Helen Wingate Lloyd, The Garden Club of America (February 1936); William Morrison. *The Main Line, Country Houses, 1870–1930* (New York: Acanthus Press, 2002), 122–29. (LC-DIG-ppmsca-16279)

[94] *View from House, Spring 1919.* Johnston took this photograph shortly before Mary W. Lloyd transformed the open fields into a terraced garden. (LC-DIG-ppmsca-16255)

PLATE 95 BOXLEY, FREDERICK WINSLOW TAYLOR HOUSE, CHESTNUT HILL, PENNSYLVANIA, OLMSTED BROTHERS, LANDSCAPE ARCHITECTS, 1902–04

Boxwood Path, Spring 1919. Taylor studied at Phillips Exeter Academy and trained as an engineer at the Stevens Institute of Technology. He pursued the progressive cause of engineered labor but when he built his house, he kept the status quo. A white Colonial Revival manor with a columned portico overlooked garden rooms edged with old boxwood that Taylor moved to his suburban lot. (LC-DIG-ppmsca-16642)

PLATE 96 THE CAUSEWAY, JAMES PARMELEE HOUSE, WASHINGTON, D.C., CHARLES ADAMS PLATT AND ELLEN BIDDLE SHIPMAN, LANDSCAPE ARCHITECTS, FROM 1912

[96] *Walkway, 1919.* In 1912, on 20 acres in northwest Washington, the Cleveland industrialist built a Georgian Revival house designed by Charles A. Platt. It looked over a ravine to the new National Cathedral. This pathway was in an enclosed flower garden laid out by Shipman after a general landscape plan by Platt.

"They turned out well and Mrs. Parmelee and I were much pleased with them," wrote the owner to FBJ on receiving prints of her photographs before Christmas, 1919.

Penelope F. Heavner, "The Woodland Garden at Tregaron: An Ellen Biddle Shipman Garden Revealed," *Magnolia* 23, no. 2 (Spring 2010): 6–8. Letter from James Parmelee to FBJ, December 24, 1919, LOCFBJ reel 9. (LC-DIG-ppmsca-16321)

PLATE 97 LOB'S WOOD, CARL H. KRIPPENDORF HOUSE, PERINTOWN, OHIO, CARL H. AND MARY GREENE KRIPPENDORF, LANDSCAPE GARDENERS, FROM 1898

Woodland Daffodils, circa 1920. At the turn of the century photographs of William Robinson's Gravetye Manor and William Wordsworth's Grasmere inspired daffodil planting in the American naturalized garden. Commenting on this photograph indebted to Pierre-August Renoir (1841–1919) and followers, garden writer Grace Willard wrote that "it is possible that the American scenery, the American spirit, both bolder and more prodigal" than England's, "touch the imagination with a magic curiosity all of their own."

Carl H. Krippendorf was a friend of garden writer Louise Beebe Wilder and became a legend as the second gardener in Elizabeth Lawrence's *The Little Bulbs: A Tale of Two Gardens* (1957). On 175 acres of farmland and woods, he planted an estimated 150 varieties of snowdrops, windflowers, winter aconite, snow crocus, tulips, narcissus, glory-of-the-snow, and squill. Lawrence thought that Krippendorf had "the same purity of conception" for the natural American garden as Jens Jensen (1860–1951).

Grace Willard, "The Pageant of the Daffodil," *Vogue* 57, no. 7 (April 1, 1921): 55; "Krippendorf Estate," *National Register of Historic Places Registration Form,* [2011], www.ohiohistory.org/resource/histpres/docs/nr/krp_media.pdf; Elizabeth Lawrence, *Lob's Wood* (Cincinnati: Cincinnati Nature Center, 1971); Elizabeth Lawrence, *The Little Bulbs: A Tale of Two Gardens* (New York: Criterion Books, 1957), 1. (LC-DIG-ppmsca-16691)

PLATE 98 LAKE TERRACE, JOHN STOUGHTON NEWBERRY JR. HOUSE, GROSSE POINTE FARMS, MICHIGAN, ALFRED BEAVER YEOMANS, LANDSCAPE ARCHITECT, CIRCA 1911

Pergola Garden, Summer 1917. The Newberrys were establishment Detroit, with a family fortune from railroads and manufacturing. Edith Stanton Newberry was twice president of the Garden Club of Michigan.

When Johnston stopped here on her return from California, she photographed the clouds characteristic of the Lake St. Clair setting. The enclosed garden near John Newberry's 1911 Georgian Revival house, designed by Albert Kahn, was blooming with lemon lilies, columbine, candytuft, and foxglove. *House & Garden* editor Richardson L. Wright used this photograph to illustrate that pathways organized flower gardens, with birdbaths or sundials marking center points.

Tonnancour: Life in Grosse Pointe and Along the Shores of Lake St. Clair, edited by Arthur M. Woodford (Detroit: Omnigraphics, 1984), 133–34; Mrs. Francis King, *In a New Garden* (New York: Alfred A. Knopf, 1930), 157–59; [FBJ], "Summer in the Garden of Mrs. John S. Newberry," *Vogue* 54, no. 1 (July 15, 1919): 46; *House & Garden's Book of Gardens*, edited by Richardson Wright (New York: Condé Nast, 1921), 59. Wright's book includes other photographs by FBJ, but does not credit any photographer. (LC-DIG-ppmsca-16177)

Gardens of the West

[FRONTISPIECE] SANTA BARBARA MISSION, SANTA BARBARA, CALIFORNIA, BUILT FOR FATHER ANTONIO PATERNA, 18TH CENTURY, REBUILT 1815

Friar in the Garden Court, Spring 1917. FBJ's sunny views of the mission were romantic mementos of California's colonial past, which she used to distinguish the state from the East Coast represented by colonial Mount Vernon. Compositionally, this image and others of the mission by Johnston conformed to photographs produced by railroads and chambers of commerce.

Elizabeth Kryder-Reid, " 'Perennially New,' Santa Barbara Mission and the Origins of the California Mission Garden," *Journal of the Society of Architectural Historians* 69, no. 3 (September 2010): 378–405. (LC-DIG-ppmsca-16051)

PLATES 99–100 JOHN HENRY FISHER ADOBE, REDLANDS, CALIFORNIA, JOHN HENRY FISHER, BUILDER AND LANDSCAPE GARDENER, CIRCA 1915

[99] *Water Garden, Spring 1917.* The romance of rural life and the rise of nationalism spurred regional architecture inspired by an agrarian past. Fisher, a power and electric executive, participated in the Pueblo Revival with his two-story adobe built behind his Redlands villa. "No hillside garden in California is complete without its arroyo or rocky cañon," wrote FBJ. "It is in just such a tiny gorge, hardly more than a gully, lying at the edge of the garden proper, that Mr. Fisher reproduced in miniature some of the rugged picturesqueness of primitive living."

David Gebhart, "The Myth and Power of Place: Historic Revivalism in the American Southwest," *Architectural Regionalism, Collected Writings on Place, Identity, Modernity, and Tradition*, edited by Vincent B. Canizaro (New York: Princeton Architectural Press, 2007), 194–203; FBJ, "A'dobe Trophy House," *Country Life in America* 36, no. 4 (August 1919): 54–5. (LC-DIG-ppmsca-16076)

[100] *Trophy Room, Spring 1917.* Fisher's den, wrote FBJ, was in a "typical house of the mesas," built in "a small patch of the primeval wild ... an inspiration to those who seek originality in their planning."

FBJ, "A'dobe Trophy House," 54. (LC-DIG-ppmsca-16109)

PLATE 101 KIMBERLY CREST, JOHN ALFRED KIMBERLY HOUSE, REDLANDS, CALIFORNIA, GEORGE EDWIN BERGSTROM, LANDSCAPE ARCHITECT, AFTER 1905

Italian Garden, Spring 1917. The cofounder of the Kimberly-Clark Corporation and his wife, Helen Cheney, hired their son-in-law, a Los Angeles architect, to create this water terrace for the hillside garden of their 19th-century, French Revival château. (LC-DIG-ppmsca-16016)

PLATE 102 MYRON HUNT HOUSE, PASADENA, CALIFORNIA, MYRON HUNT, ARCHITECT AND LANDSCAPE ARCHITECT, FROM 1905

View to House, Spring 1917. Myron Hunt, son of a nurseryman and MIT graduate trained to integrate house and garden design, explained in an interview that his Pasadena garden "helped to convince clients that it is possible for an architect to think in terms of three dimensions in planting as well as in building material."

Johnston personally thought that "Myron Hunt's backyard garden" retained all "the homey quality and beauty a true garden should have." She photographed this high view from a ladder or platform placed at the rear of the suburban lot.

Henry Higgins, "Homes of Well-Known Architects," *The House Beautiful* 39, no. 4 (March 1916): 101; Myra Nye, "Federation of Clubs to Meet," *Los Angeles Times*, April 29, 1923; FBJ, "Myron Hunt's Backyard," *Country Life in America* 18, 3 (March 1918): 50–1. (LC-DIG-ppmsca-16090)

PLATES 103–106 MRS. ELDRIDGE MERICK FOWLER HOUSE, PASADENA, CALIFORNIA, MYRON HUNT WITH PAUL JOSEPH HOWARD, LANDSCAPE ARCHITECT, 1915

[103–104] *Terrace Wall and Terrace Wall Steps, Spring 1917.* Like Johnston, Margaret Brewer Fowler was a New Woman. Educated at New York University, she worked as a missionary and arts instructor before marrying a Minnesota industrialist with mining, lumber, and railroad interests. For her Pasadena garden, she and Myron Hunt turned to the Italian Renaissance. (LC-DIG-ppmsca-16002 and 16003)

[105–106] *Wall Fountain and Fountain in Flower Garden, Spring 1917.* Hunt studied and made measured drawings of Italian architecture while traveling in the Old World as a graduate student. He thought Renaissance traditions were appropriate and affordable in Southern California, with its hilly terrain and Mediterranean climate. "To be sure, elaborate architectural gardens are today being built in Lennox [*sic*], Tuxedo, on Long Island, and at Brookline, but this is not wholly a natural development. Only great wealth can produce practical results under their [weather] conditions."

Myron Hunt, "Scenic Gardens in a Favored Clime," *Los Angeles Express,* December 19, 1903. (LC-DIG-ppmsca-16009 and 16077)

PLATES 107–111 MRS. FRANCIS LEMOINE LORING HOUSE, PASADENA, CALIFORNIA, MYRON HUNT, LANDSCAPE ARCHITECT, COMPLETED 1917

[107] *View to Staircase Landing, Spring 1917.* Hunt had recently completed this terraced garden for a New York grain merchant's widow when FBJ arrived to photograph California gardens. Hunt was well acquainted with California-based photographers but thought she produced the "finest slides of American gardens." With landscapes "necessarily ephemeral by nature," he wrote, photography was essential. "Each year there is a month, a day, an hour, when the garden is at its very best. It is at this moment that the photographer makes us our record of achievement. Without the appreciative, painstaking, and expert photographer, the results of our best efforts are soon forgotten, even by ourselves."

FBJ, undated press release [circa 1924], LOCFBJ reel 21; Winifred Starr Dobyns, *California Gardens,* foreword by Myron Hunt (New York: Macmillan, 1930), 11. (LC-DIG-ppmsca-16103)

[108] *Staircase Landing, Spring 1917.* The garden stepped down the west slope of Pasadena's Arroyo Seco ("dry riverbed"). Johnston reflected its sequential design by walking her viewer from a bench at the bottom of the garden up to the landing, and then to a flower terrace below the house.

For a plan of this garden, with FBJ's photographs, see "Portfolio of Current Architecture," *Architectural Record* 43, no. 1 (January 1918): 65.

(LC-DIG-ppmsca-16102; for third slide in sequence see 16078)

[109] *Staircase from Landing, Replanted, Spring 1917.* Between takes, Hunt and Johnston replaced dwarf orange trees with smaller specimens and added clay pots. These changes made the photograph dimensional, highlighting the architecture and depth of the stairs. (LC-DIG-ppmsca-16022)

[110] *Flower Garden, Spring 1917.* Shaded by live oaks and cooled by the sound of a fountain, this colorful terrace was an outdoor living room in a Los Angeles suburb. (LC-DIG-ppmsca-16001)

[111] *Bougainvillea Pergola, from Flower Garden to House, Spring 1917.* The pergola shaded the steps from the flower terrace to the house and lawn above. (LC-DIG-ppmsca-16004)

PLATES 112–113 MI SUEÑO, HERBERT COPPELL HOUSE, PASADENA, CALIFORNIA, BERTRAM GROSVENOR GOODHUE, ARCHITECT, PAUL GEORGE THIENE, LANDSCAPE ARCHITECT, BUILT 1916

[112] *Pergola, from House to Flower Garden, Spring 1917.* For Wall Street investor Herbert Coppell, Goodhue was an ideal architect. He was a fellow New Yorker and was known for his work at the 1915–17 Panama-California Exposition at San Diego, California. Critics considered the Coppell Mediterranean Revival, pink, stucco house on the east side of the Arroyo Seco appropriate for Southern California, a region promoted by city boosters as America's own Italy.

Sam Watters, *Houses of Los Angeles, 1885–1919* (New York: Acanthus Press, 2007), 304–11. (LC-DIG-ppmsca-16207)

[113] *Water Rill, Spring 1917.* At this house, sited between an orange grove at the east entrance drive and a terrace facing west over a lawn to the Arroyo Seco, Johnston focused on architectural garden features. This Moorish rill was exotically Californian to East Coast gardeners. (LC-DIG-ppmsca-16107)

PLATES 114–116 IL PARADISO, MRS. DUDLEY PETER ALLEN HOUSE, PASADENA, CALIFORNIA, GREENE & GREENE, ARCHITECTS AND LANDSCAPE ARCHITECTS, 1911–13

[114] *Loggia, Spring 1917.* Originally designed for lumber heir Cordelia Culbertson, this Arts and Crafts house was in a development on former San Gabriel

Mission land. The slide artist, assuming that Il Paradiso was in the Mediterranean Revival style, painted the roof tiles terra-cotta. In reality they were glazed green, intermixed with red, to suggest a Chinese influence. This slide showed audiences the second of the site's three terrace levels. (LC-DIG-ppmsca-16014)

[115–116] *Ornamental Pool and Lower Garden Stairs, Spring 1917.* On seeing this sun-dappled photograph of the stairs stepping downhill from the loggia level, journalist Charles Alma Byers wrote that "having a somewhat aged appearance, it might easily be imagined as belonging to some old romance-laden garden of Italy." Charles Sumner Greene had in fact toured Italian gardens on his honeymoon in 1901; visits to the Fountain of the Dragons at the Villa d'Este and water channels at the Villa Aldobrandini may have inspired this Pasadena fountain.

Johnston photographed the ornamental pool to demonstrate, as she wrote, "a classic instance where architectural and landscape treatment are so perfectly adapted to one of the small arroyos or canyons so characteristic of this section" of California.

Charles Alma Byers, "On Garden Stairways," *The House Beautiful* 47, no. 3 (March 1920): 198; Edward R. Bosley, *Greene & Greene*, (London: Phaidon, 2000), 159; Henry Hawley, "An Italianate Garden by Greene and Greene," *Journal of Decorative and Propaganda Arts* 2 (Fall/Summer 1986): 32–45; [FBJ], "Garden Pools of California," *Harper's Bazar* 53, no. 1 (January 1918), 30. (LC-DIG-ppmsca-16935 and 16936)

PLATE 117 DAVID BERRY GAMBLE HOUSE, PASADENA, CALIFORNIA, GREENE & GREENE, HOUSE AND LANDSCAPE ARCHITECTS, 1908–09

Water Terrace, Spring 1917. The Japanesque garden of the Arts and Crafts bungalow looked west over the Arroyo Seco to the San Rafael Hills. The hazy pink and violet slide presented California romantica. (LD-DIG-ppmsca-16011)

PLATE 118 MICHAEL COCHRANE ARMOUR HOUSE, PASADENA, CALIFORNIA, ROBERT GORDON FRASER AND/OR THOMAS CHISHOLM, LANDSCAPE GARDENERS, FROM 1910

Lily Pool, Spring 1917. The president of the Iroquois Iron Company in Chicago and his gardener wife, Minnie Tomlinson Armour, built a modest bungalow designed by J. Constantine Hillman. They were leaders in the Pasadena Garden Club and supported the replanting of the Arroyo Seco at the base of their west-facing, hillside site. At the invitation of the couple, California naturalists Charles

Francis Saunders (1859–1941) and Theodore Payne (1872–1963) spoke to children about the Armours' wildflower garden.

Bulletin of The Garden Club of America 23, no. 9 (January 1917): n.p.; 7, new series (December 1920): 35; 5, new series (May 1922): 261. (LC-DIG-ppmsca-16013)

PLATE 119 JOHN CONSTANTINE HILLMAN HOUSE, PASADENA, CALIFORNIA, LOUIS BYRON EASTON AND JOHN CONSTANTINE HILLMAN, BUILDER AND ARCHITECT, 1907

Pergola Porch, Spring 1917. The Arts and Crafts builder and architect Louis B. Easton (1865–1921) was married to the sister of FBJ's friend, Roycroft community founder Elbert Green Hubbard (1856–1915). When photographing this hand-crafted house, FBJ followed the tradition of photographers for magazines, postcards, and promotional brochures to picture California arbors and pergolas covered with wisteria, roses, and bougainvillea to convey the bloom possible in America's paradise.

Tim Anderson, "Louis B. Easton," *Towards a Simpler Way of Life, The Arts & Crafts Architects of California*, edited by Robert Winter (Berkeley, Los Angeles, and London: University of California Press, 1997), 149, 155–56. (LC-DIG-ppmsca-16082)

PLATE 120 WELLINGTON STANLEY MORSE HOUSE, PASADENA, CALIFORNIA, REGINALD DAVIS JOHNSON, ARCHITECT, PAUL GEORGE THIENE, LANDSCAPE ARCHITECT, BUILT 1919

Terrace Gate, Spring 1923. Paul G. Thiene designed this garden for a Mediterranean Revival house on the west bank of the Arroyo Seco, built by mining and lumber heir, Cora Dorr Morse. The closed gate, suggesting a *hortus conclusus* ("enclosed garden"), was a poetic photography trope. Johnston included slides of medieval walled gardens in her slide lectures. (LD-DIG-ppmsca-16932)

PLATE 121 GLENN-ORR, WILLIAM MEADE ORR HOUSE, ALHAMBRA, CALIFORNIA, HUNT, EAGER & BURNS, ARCHITECTS, 1910–11, CHARLES GIBBS ADAMS, LANDSCAPE ARCHITECT, CIRCA 1920

The Secret Garden, Spring 1923. Adams redesigned this terrace garden, first planted in 1911, for Pittsburgh, Pennsylvania, paper manufacturer and Los Angeles Occidental College benefactor William M. Orr. A native plant advocate, Adams removed paved paths and replaced topiary with Mexican sage (*Salvia leucantha*).

In 1926 the landscape architect urgently wrote FBJ: "Am collecting an exhibition set of pictures. The requisite are speed and uniformity of print. I especially want your lovely one of the Orr garden with Spanish irises in foreground, around a pool."

"Fine Alhambra Home Finished," *Los Angeles Times*, February 12, 1911; "Residence of William Mead Orr," *Architectural Record* 48, no. 4 (October 1920): 335–39; letter from Charles Gibbs Adams to FBJ, January 3, 1926, LOCFBJ reel 9. (LC-DIG-ppmsca-16112)

PLATE 122 WILLIAM ALEXANDER SPINKS JR. RANCH, DUARTE, CALIFORNIA, WILLIAM ALEXANDER SPINKS JR., LANDSCAPE GARDENER, FROM 1908

Fish Pond, Spring 1917. Billy Spinks, a Southland oilman, national billiards champion, and coinventor of the game's cue chalk, acquired his ranch overlooking the San Gabriel Valley in 1908. He was an early competitor in avocado hybridizing, raising the Spinks cultivar. At the crest of his property he built this pool stocked with black bass from the East. In Johnston's slide presentations, the ranch was an example of integrated agricultural and ornamental planting.

"Avocado Growers Meet at Famous Mountain Estate," *The Los Angeles Times*, February 12, 1922. (LC-DIG-ppmsca-16545)

PLATE 123 HENRY EDWARDS HUNTINGTON HOUSE, SAN MARINO, CALIFORNIA, WILLIAM HERTRICH, LANDSCAPE GARDENER, 1911

Drum Bridge in the Japanese Garden, Spring 1923. In 1911 the real estate developer purchased a teahouse, built in 1903 by Japanese craftsmen for dealer George Turner Marsh, as a commercial venture. Huntington moved the Pasadena house and its plantings to a ravine at his 500-acre hillside ranch. His gardener, William Hertrich (1878–1966), added this bridge and lily pool to the picturesque setting.

In FBJ's lectures, the Huntington, Stephen S. Cummins, and George W. Wickersham slides showed East and West coast interpretations of Asian traditions.

Sam Watters, *Houses of Los Angeles, 1920–1935* (New York: Acanthus Press, 2007), 213–14. (LC-DIG-ppmsca-16159)

PLATE 124 CASA DE MARIPOSA, WALTER FRANKLIN COBB HOUSE, MONTECITO, CALIFORNIA, CARRIE FISH COBB, LANDSCAPE GARDENER, CIRCA 1916

Garden Gate, Spring 1917. The Chicago grain merchant Walter Cobb named his Italiante villa after the Monarch butterfly that migrated across his estate. "I am quite daring in some of my fancies," Carrie Fish Cobb told Mrs. Francis King, "but

California seems to call for bold effects...." To this end she painted trellis and gates a "beautiful indescribable blue-green." Johnston too was impressed with the color, focusing on the gate and centering its circular opening on the mountain beyond. She delivered her lecture "Our American Gardens" at Casa de Mariposa while in Santa Barbara to photograph neighboring estates.

Mrs. Francis King, *Chronicles of the Garden* (New York and London: Charles Scribner's Sons, 1925), 167. (LC-DIG-ppmsca-16046)

PLATES 125–126 INELLAN, WALTER DOUGLAS HOUSE, MONTECITO, CALIFORNIA, FRANCIS TOWNSEND UNDERHILL, ARCHITECT AND LANDSCAPE ARCHITECT, 1902, HOUSE ADDITIONS FROM 1906

[125] *Garden Facade, Spring 1917.* In 1906 Phelps Dodge mining heir Walter Douglas purchased this house from Underhill, who had built the bungalow at his oceanside estate, La Chiquita. The architect moved the house and transformed it into a rose-covered cottage for Douglas' wife, Edith Bell, a Scotland native.

In 1917 FBJ stayed here as the guest of New Yorkers Helen and Oakleigh Thorne, who rented the cottage before building Las Tejas. Inellan was "a place so quaint," wrote Johnston, as "to remind one of Shakespeare's home at Stratford-on-Avon."

[FBJ] "The Sea and the Mountain Form an Elemental Setting for Inellan...," *Vogue* 54, no. 4 (August 15, 1919): 59. (LC-DIG-ppmsca-16060)

[126] *Pergola at the Pacific Ocean, Spring 1917.* Johnston discovered in gardens along this coast, as fine as the "Côte d'Azur, the Riviera, Sorrento, or Capri...," the promise of a unique "heritage, which all the gods of beauty have lavished upon this favored region."

FBJ, "The Gardens of a Garden Spot," *Santa Barbara Community Life* 1, no. 9 (September 1923): 3. (LC-DIG-ppmsca-16091)

QUOTATION, OPPOSITE PLATE 127
"Many of those...," FBJ, "The Gardens of a Garden Spot," 4.

PLATES 127–130 GLENDESSARY, ROBERT CAMERON ROGERS HOUSE, SANTA BARBARA, CALIFORNIA, PETER AND THOMAS POOLE, STONE MASON AND LANDSCAPE GARDENER, FROM 1900

[127] *Shaded Terrace, Spring 1917.* Gardeners and house owners preserved California live oaks that dotted the fields of former California mission lands. (LC-DIG-ppmsca-16031)

[128–130, *gatefold*] *Walk from Terrace to Fountain, Along the Fountain Walk, Fountain, Spring 1917.* FBJ used sequential photography to create a virtual experience of this terraced garden of a Tudor Revival manor. "Much skill must be expended to get the old cared-for casualness that this garden expresses," FBJ wrote. "It is composed of terraces and enclosed in hedges of Monterey cypresses. The graceful tall sentinels guard the long path to the pool. But before one comes upon this walk, there runs a low ivy-covered wall, broken at intervals by terracotta bowls, overflowing with pink geraniums."

Johnston thought this garden, in a town where "romance lurks," was one of "the loveliest and most romantic." Her literary description was appropriate. Rogers was a poet in the genteel tradition and author of the ode for the Buffalo Pan-American Exposition, where FBJ took the last photograph of President McKinley before his assassination.

[FBJ], "Glimpses into the Enchanting Romance and Beauty of a Garden in Santa Barbara," *Vogue* 53, no. 8 (April 15, 1919): 77; Santa Barbara Conservancy, *Stone Architecture in Santa Barbara* (Santa Barbara: Arcadia Publishing, Charleston, 2009), 50–1; Obituary, *New York Times*, October 21, 1912. (LC-DIG-ppmsca-16007, 16093, 16006)

PLATES 131–134 SOLANA, FREDERICK FORREST PEABODY HOUSE, MONTECITO, CALIFORNIA, FRANCIS UNDERHILL, ARCHITECT, BUILT 1913–14, CHARLES FREDERICK EATON, LANDSCAPE GARDENER, FROM 1906

[131–133] *Entrance Drive, View to Interior Court, Interior Court, Spring 1917.* From the drive, through the door, and into the interior court with Pompeian-red walls, the visitor, in life and at Johnston's slide presentation, entered the neoclassical world of Arrow Shirt manufacturer Frederick F. Peabody. The 150- by 100-foot white stucco house was on 60 acres landscaped with 7,000 eucalyptus and oak trees that transformed a barren hilltop into an American acropolis in the California Mediterranean.

David F. Myrick, *Montecito and Santa Barbara*, vol. 2 (Glendale: Trans-Anglo Books, 1991), 334–39. (LC-DIG-ppmsca-16105, 16054, 16053)

[134] *Terrace, Spring 1917.* This terrace above the house suggested a modern-day ruin. (LC-DIG-ppmsca-16084)

PLATES 135–140 EL FUREIDIS, JAMES WALDRON GILLESPIE HOUSE, MONTECITO, CALIFORNIA, BERTRAM GROSVENOR GOODHUE, ARCHITECT AND LANDSCAPE ARCHITECT, 1902–06

[135] *Interior Court, Spring 1917.* Following a seven-month tour of India, Persia, and Italy with his client, New York real estate heir James W. Gillespie, Bertram Grosvenor Goodhue designed a house and garden on Gillespie's 30-acre hillside site that combined Moorish and Italian traditions.

Country Life editor Henry H. Saylor selected the Gillespie villa as one of the 12 best country houses in America, writing that this patio "belongs to California as Colonial Architecture belongs to New England."

Henry Saylor, "Best 12 Country Houses in America: El Fureidis, The Home of James Waldron Gillespie at Montecito, California," *Country Life in America* 28, no. 6 (October 1915): 28. (LC-DIG-ppmsca-16043)

[136] *Banksia Roses (Rosa banksiae) Along Terrace, Spring 1917.* Johnston wrote that, "save for the rectitude of Monterey Cypresses, we might be looking across this riot of roses toward the Berkshires or even the far foothills of Italy…." El Fureidis was miles from the East, but for FBJ, it showed the promise of a civilized garden.

With captions by Frances Benjamin Johnston, Waldron Gillespie, "Why Palms Belong in Southern California," *The Garden Magazine* 22, no. 12 (December 1922): 190. (LC-DIG-ppmsca-16045)

[137] *View from Casino to House, Spring 1917.* "As one hardly imagines a Mediterranean landscape without Palms," observed Gillespie, "so one may feel about California." At the top of his neo-Persian water walk, he planted specimen *Roystoneae*. They were "grande dames presiding over an assemblage of minor folk," Johnston wrote about this view.

Waldron Gillespie, "Why Palms Belong in Southern California," *The Garden Magazine* 22, no. 12 (December 1922): 187. (LC-DIG-ppmsca-16144)

[138–140] *View from House to Casino, Water Terrace on Stairs to Casino, Stairs at Water Terrace, Spring 1917.* Johnston paused her downhill walk to show audiences that, as in Mediterranean gardens, El Fureidis combined "utility and beauty." The pools were ornamental and serviceable as reservoirs.

Johnston included slides of the water terrace gardens of Fin-nahë at Kashan, Iran, Shalimar Bagh in Lahore, Pakistan, and of Abdul Baha at Acre, Syria, to show audiences the Middle-Eastern traditions that inspired Goodhue.

"The Photographic Inventory of the Garden's Fleeting Beauty," *Christian Science Monitor*, June 8, 1923. (LC-DIG-ppmsca-16307, 16042, and 16080; for slides of Persian gardens, see LC-DIG-ppmsca-16410, 16413, 16972)

PLATES 141–143 PIRANHURST, HENRY ERNEST BOTHIN HOUSE, MONTE-CITO, CALIFORNIA, JOHN J. WHIPPLE AND JAMES WILKINSON ELLIOTT, LANDSCAPE ARCHITECTS FOR OUTDOOR THEATER, 1901–10

(left to right) View to Outdoor Theater Boxes, Wings, and Stage, Spring 1917. At a time when America aspired to Italian Renaissance culture, the outdoor theater, associated with classical drama, became a feature of public parks, universities, and estate gardens.

The landscape architects at Piranhurst modeled this room on the 17th-century theater at the Villa Gori (La Palazzina) in Siena, Italy. Sheldon Cheney, writing for *The Craftsman* magazine, thought the Bothin theater and others in private gardens defeated the progressive cause to bring high art to the public. Only if estate owners opened their gardens to guests could they be of "great value in the development of a healthy civic consciousness."

As she had in her image of the gate at Casa de Mariposa, Johnston aligned the theater stairs with the mountain peak in the distance. She included a white urn as a focal point to orient the viewer as she turned her camera toward the stage.

"Seeing Our Plays Out-of-Doors," *The Craftsman* 30, no. 5 (August 1916): 519; David F. Myrick, *Montecito and Santa Barbara*, vol. 2 (Glendale: Trans-Anglo Books, 1991), 294–97; Sheldon Cheney, *The Open-Air Theater* (New York: Mitchell Kennerley, 1918), 99–100. (LC-DIG-ppmsca-16071, 16933 and 16028)

PLATES 144–148 ARCADY, GEORGE OWEN KNAPP HOUSE, MONTECITO, CALIFORNIA, FRANCIS UNDERHILL, ARCHITECT AND LANDSCAPE ARCHI-TECT, POOL HOUSE AND LOWER GARDEN, COMPLETED 1916; CARLETON MONROE WINSLOW AND CHARLES GIBBS ADAMS, LANDSCAPE ARCHI-TECTS, UPPER GARDEN, CIRCA 1913

[144–145] *Lower Garden, Pool House and View to Swimming Pool, Spring 1917.* The cofounder of Union Carbide was among the "Hill Barons" who transformed Montecito and Santa Barbara into a garden mecca rivaling East Coast enclaves. Over two decades Knapp aggregated 160 acres and built rustic lodges and a teahouse from a hollowed redwood, reflecting Western heritage. His Roman pool house had indoor and outdoor swimming pools.

David F. Myrick, *Montecito and Santa Barbara*, vol. 2, 309–23. (LC-DIG-ppm-sca-16085 and 16086)

[146] *Lower Garden, View to Santa Ynez Mountains, Spring 1917.* Johnston did not include swimmers in photographs of swimming pools. Landscape design, not exercise, was her subject. (LC-DIG-ppmsca-16097)

[147] *Lower Garden, Marble Seat at Terminus, Spring 1917.* Underhill continued the Greco-Roman theme of the pool house with an Italianate garden walk to this seat shaded by a California live oak (*Quercus agrifolia*). (LC-DIG-ppmsca-16111)

[148] *Yellow Garden in Upper Garden, Spring 1917.* Pride of ownership drove gardeners to spectacular feats. For The Garden Club of America tour of Arcady in 1926, Knapp self-published a guide to his estate with landscape architect Neville Richardson Stephens (1891–1977), listing more than 200 flower varieties in Knapp's iris, rose, blue, and yellow gardens. Here California poppies, geraniums, birds of paradise, and primrose grew in borders below the Green Terrace, planted with acanthus, jasmine, and evergreen grape.

"Arcady," Montecito, Santa Barbara, California (Montecito, privately printed, 1926). (LC-DIG-ppmsca-16070)

PLATES 149–150 VILLA ROSE, JOSEPH DONOHOE GRANT HOUSE, HILLS-BOROUGH, CALIFORNIA, LEWIS PARSONS HOBART, ARCHITECT, LEWIS PARSONS HOBART WITH EDITH MACLEAY GRANT, LANDSCAPE ARCHITECT, COMPLETED 1912

[149] *Garden Gate, Spring 1917.* Grant inherited ownership in the San Francisco mercantile firm Murphy-Grant Company and then made a fortune in real estate, oil, steel, hydroelectricity, and banking. He assumed leadership in California red-wood preservation and, when building his Renaissance Revival house in a canyon, preserved his own forest of bay and buckeye trees above a terrace garden. This path along the ravine led to the house and pool beyond.

Porter Garnett, *Stately Homes of California* (Boston: Little, Brown, 1915), 16–8. (LC-DIG-ppmsca-16017)

[150] *View from House Library to Swimming Pool, Spring 1917.* The pool pavilion and main house were finished in Tuscan pink stucco. The conception of California as an American Italy guided the design of northern, as well as southern, California estates. (LC-DIG-ppmsca-16074)

PLATES 151–152 NEW PLACE, WILLIAM HENRY CROCKER HOUSE, HILL-SBOROUGH, CALIFORNIA, BRUCE PORTER, LANDSCAPE ARCHITECT, COMPLETED 1910

[151] *Exedra, Spring 1917.* William H. Crocker, bank president and Central Pacific Railroad heir, and his wife, Ethel Sperry Crocker, collected and exhibited Impressionist paintings. Bruce Porter (1865–1953) brought to their 600-acre estate a lyrical informality in keeping with their art collection. (LC-DIG-ppmsca-16020)

[152] *Reflecting Pool, Spring 1917.* The pool was at the end of a grass walk aligned with the house, designed by Lewis Parsons Hobart. (LC-DIG-ppmsca-16072)

PLATES 153–154 UPLANDS, CHARLES TEMPLETON CROCKER HOUSE, HILL-SBOROUGH, CALIFORNIA, WILLIS JEFFERSON POLK, ARCHITECT AND LAND-SCAPE ARCHITECT, 1913–15

[153] *View to Porte Cochere Terrace, Spring 1917.* An explorer and lantern-slide lecturer, Crocker was a Central Pacific Railroad heir and nephew of William H. Crocker. He hired San Francisco architect Willis J. Polk to design a Beaux-Arts house and garden on 160 acres that Crocker inherited from his father, Charles Frederick Crocker. The entrance overlooked a French water terrace with pools. Though the terrace had an open view to hills, Johnston focused on the relationship of the garden to the house entrance.
    Donald DeNevi and Thomas Moulin, *Gabriel Moulin's San Francisco Peninsula, Town & Country Homes 1910–1930* (Sausalito, California: Windgate Press, 1985): n.p; notes from Ward Hill, author of *Houses of the San Francisco Peninsula, 1865–1940,* forthcoming from Acanthus Press. (LC-DIG-ppmsca-16063)

[154] *View to Porte Cochere Terrace with Herbaceous Border, Spring 1917.* This pair of slides offered garden club audiences a comparison of the entrance view with and without trees, shrubs, and herbaceous plantings. The flower borders were unexpected in an otherwise rigorous Beaux-Arts design. (LC-DIG-ppmsca-16106)

PLATES 155–156 NEWMAR, SENATOR GEORGE ALMER NEWHALL HOUSE, HILLSBOROUGH, CALIFORNIA, LEWIS PARSONS HOBART, HOUSE AND LANDSCAPE ARCHITECT, COMPLETED 1913

[155] *Rose Garden, Spring 1917.* This slide of a formal flower garden contrasted with FBJ's images of Italianate and Persian water gardens in Southern California. (LC-DIG-ppmsca-16094)

[156] *House Terrace, Spring 1917.* The California land development heir built a two-story French Classical Revival house on 20 acres. Symmetrical arcades and pavilions framed the terrace overlooking the flower garden. (LC-DIG-ppmsca-16073)

PLATES 157–158 JAMES KENNEDY MOFFITT HOUSE, PIEDMONT, CALIFORNIA, WILLIS JEFFERSON POLK, ARCHITECT AND PROBABLE LANDSCAPE ARCHITECT, BUILT 1912

View from House to Water Terrace and Steps from Water Terrace, Spring 1917. A Crocker Bank president, bibliophile, and University of California, Berkeley, benefactor, James K. Moffitt built a Mediterranean Revival house that looked east to the Oakland Hills. Johnston photographed the defining elements of the garden, its terrace and staircase that stepped down the hillside site. (LC-DIG-ppmsca-16034 and 16036)

PLATE 159 THORNEWOOD, CHESTER THORNE HOUSE, LAKEWOOD, WASHINGTON, KIRTLAND KELSEY CUTTER, ARCHITECT, 1909–11, OLMSTED BROTHERS, LANDSCAPE ARCHITECTS, 1908–13

[159] *View to House from Flower Garden, Spring 1923.* The president of the National Bank of Commerce acquired land in a new subdivision associated with a nearby country club. With guidance form Mrs. Chester "Annie" Thorne and their experience at Portland's 1905 Lewis and Clark Centennial Exposition where they framed a view to Mount Saint Helens, Olmsted Brothers angled the walled flower garden southwest to center on Mount Rainier. In a period of parallel and perpendicular alignment of gardens to houses, this plan, reflected in FBJ's photograph, was exceptional.
    LOCOA reel 203, job 3494; Samuel Howe, "The Estate of Mr. Chester Thorne at Tacoma," *Town & Country* 64, no. 18 (July 19, 1913): 17–19. (LC-DIG-ppmsca-16329)

Gardens for City and Suburb

[FRONTISPIECE] DEMONSTRATION GARDEN, BRYANT PARK, NEW YORK, NEW YORK, NATIONAL WAR GARDEN COMMISSION, LANDSCAPE ARCHITECT, SUMMER 1918

Visitors Studying Gardening Notices, August 1918. Vegetable plantings, tips on gardening, and a display of poison ivy showed New Yorkers what to plant and what to avoid in city yards during World War I. New gardens, explained commissioner Charles L. Pack, transformed vacant lots that had been "ugly ash-heaps and piles of litter" into beautiful yards, bringing "material prosperity" and "civic progress" to cities. Experiences learned in "food for the people" gardens informed urban renewal planting in the 1920s.

Charles Lathrop Pack, *The War Garden Victorious* (Philadelphia: J. P. Lippincott, 1919), 100; "What You May See in City War Garden," *New York Times,* August 17, 1919. (LC-DIG-ppmsca-16152)

PLATE 160 THE TOUCHSTONE GARDEN, NEW YORK, NEW YORK, ELOISE ROORBACH, LANDSCAPE GARDENER, FROM 1917

Sculpture Exhibition, Summer 1918. The *Touchstone* magazine offices, located in two adjoining town houses at 118 East 30th Street, overlooked this garden. Founded by former editors of *The Craftsman* magazine, the Arts and Crafts enterprise held exhibitions of contemporary art to further holistic design. "This tiny garden might be a bit of Italy or along the Sicily coast or close to the heart of Florence, back of one of her lovely dingy palaces," wrote publisher Mary Fanton Roberts. Garden editor Eloise Roorbach transformed "the dreariest backyard in all New York … not a hint that children have ever played in it…. I am confident that the average New York house can have its own delightful garden with not nearly the cost of the usual sartorial outfitting for a summer in the country."

In 1917 Johnston exhibited her photographs of California and East Coast gardens in a gallery that overlooked this garden, seen here with sculptures by Florence Lucius and Harriet Frishmuth.

Mary Fanton Roberts, "The Touchstone Garden: A Lesson in Making Over Backyards," *The Touchstone* 1, no. 4 (August 1917): 496–98; "Sculpture for a Garden Setting," *Vogue* 54, 4 (April 15, 1919): 58. (LC-DIG-ppmsca-16504)

PLATES 161–163 TURTLE BAY GARDENS, NEW YORK, NEW YORK, WILLIAM LAWRENCE BOTTOMLEY AND EDWARD CLARENCE DEAN, ARCHITECTS AND LANDSCAPE ARCHITECTS, 1919–20

[161] *View East to Common Garden, Fall 1920.* Critic Arthur Willis Colton wrote that before town-house renovation in the 1920s brought light and air to row-house gardens, city backyards were "the staring example of the unloveliness of the unblended…. The whole block's meager space of possible sunlight, grass and garden is marked off in harsh little squares of mutual dislike, barren, neglected and discouraged, or littered with rubbish, or decorated with clothes lines for the family wash."

Creating common gardens to overcome these conditions was already a model in England and America when socialite Charlotte Hunnewell Sorchan purchased and renovated 21 town houses between East 48th and 49th Streets. She joined their backyard lots and created a 100- by 200-foot common garden, where Social Register elite owning houses and artists and writers renting them mixed for Christmas caroling and summer entertainments. Architect Edward C. Dean, author E. B. White, and Justice Learned Hand lived in Turtle Bay Gardens during Johnston's lifetime. For his glowing review of the new development, Colton published FBJ's photographs, taken with Dean's permission in the fall of 1920.

Arthur Willis Colton, "Turtle Bay Gardens, New York City," *Architectural Record,* 48, no. 6 (December 1920): 466–93; Andrew Dolkart, *The Row House Reborn, Architecture and Neighborhoods in New York City, 1908–1929* (Baltimore: The Johns Hopkins University Press, 2009), 87–97; Mabel Detmold, *The Brownstones of Turtle Bay Gardens* (New York: The East 49th Street Association, 1964); letter from Edward C. Dean to FBJ, October 2, 1920, LOCFBJ reel 9. For plants in the common garden, see Walter F. Wheeler, "A Prized Oasis in the Heart of the City," *The House Beautiful* 62, no. 5 (November 1922): 582. (LC-DIG-ppmsca-16118)

[162] *Charlotte Hunnewell Sorchan House Garden, Fall 1920.* The developer lived in a double house at the northwest corner of the common garden with a loggia that overlooked this terrace and fountain. Johnston wrote that houses in Italian, English, and Spanish Revival styles gave Turtle Bay Gardens "unity without monotony."

"Turtle Bay," *Vogue* 57, no. 7 (April 1921): 54. (LC-DIG-ppmsca-16676)

[163] *Charlotte Hunnewell Sorchan House, Loggia, Fall 1920.* Italy was never far from the minds of wealthy Americans civilizing 19th-century houses and gardens in the 1920s. (LC-DIG-ppmsca-16101)

PLATES 164–165 JONES WOOD, NEW YORK, NEW YORK, EDWARD SHEPARD HEWITT AND WILLIAM EMERSON, ARCHITECTS AND LANDSCAPE ARCHITECTS, FROM 1919

[164] *North Terrace Fountain, 1921.* Johnston and her generation advocated nature study in backyards for keeping children off streets. The communal garden here and at Turtle Bay achieved both goals, benefiting children and adults.
   (LC-DIG-ppmsca-16195)

[165] *View to North Terrace, 1921.* As Charlotte H. Sorchan was creating Turtle Bay Gardens, real estate agent James van Alst Jr. and a syndicate including Edward S. Hewitt were renovating 12 town houses between East 65th and 66th Streets. The architects accommodated a gentle slope with a terraced communal garden.
   Dolkart, *The Row House*, 96–8. (LC-DIG-ppmsca-16686)

QUOTATION, OPPOSITE PLATE 166
"The most ardent and enthusiastic horticulturist…," FBJ, "In Yesterday's Garden," [1926], 1, LOCFBJ reel 21.

PLATE 166 JANITOR APARTMENT, NEW YORK, NEW YORK, THE JANITOR, LANDSCAPE GARDENER, CIRCA 1922

Stairwell Garden, circa 1922. A city garden club, wrote landscape architect Arthur Herchel Helder, was responsible for encouraging gardening among "the working classes" so their children would enter "life's battlefields with stronger minds and sturdier bodies…." In this spirit, the New York City Gardens Club in 1922 awarded the janitor's garden at 137 East 30th Street honorable mention at the club's photography exhibition. In the status-conscious club world, the janitor remained unidentified, his name irrelevant to members.
   Johnston frequently presented this slide in her "Gardens for City and Suburb" lecture to show that money alone did not build a garden. "Gardens are not made by saying 'Oh, how beautiful,' and sitting in the shade," she forewarned women in Akron, Ohio.
   Arthur Helder, "What a City Garden Club May Do," *The American City* 16, no. 3 (January-June 1916): 265; *The City Gardens Club Bulletin* 1, no. 3 (Fall and Winter 1922): 4; "Horticulturist Urges More Gardens for Akron," *The Akron Press*, March 8, 1923. Research in voting and census records did not yield the janitor's name. (LC-DIGppmsca-16187)

PLATES 167–168 GEORGE HOADLY INGALLS HOUSE, NEW YORK, NEW YORK

View from Garden to Terrace, View from Terrace to Garden, 1921. At The City Gardens Club exhibition, Katherine Hinkle Ingalls won a mention for her "beautiful little pool in the center for goldfish and aquatic plants, its gravel paths leading to the Little Pan playing on his pipes … its attractive tables and chairs, inviting to tea in so lovely a surrounding, and its verdure of Forsythia covering the walls."
   The City Gardens Club Bulletin 1: 4. (LC-DIG-ppmsca-16670 and 16666)

PLATES 169–170 DR. ALEXANDER MURRAY JR. HOUSE, NEW YORK, NEW YORK, CLARENCE FOWLER, LANDSCAPE ARCHITECT, CIRCA 1922

View to Terrace from Garden and View from Terrace to Sandbox, 1922. Beginning in the 1880s, educators, settlement house managers, and psychologists urged city planners to install sand lots in new parks, believing that safe outdoor play would bring moral improvement. Murray, an American psychologist trained in both Jungian and Freudian analysis and brother of estate owner Mrs. Robert Low Bacon, participated in this movement, building a sandbox in his town-house yard. His conception, reconciling social ideals and personal privacy, reflected progressivism amongst the rich.
   This garden won second prize for a city backyard garden at the 1922 New York City Gardens Club exhibition, but its designer, Clarence Fowler, wrote Johnston that he preferred his elegant garden for decorator Mrs. George "Dorothy" Draper.
   The City Gardens Club Bulletin 1: 3; letter from Clarence Fowler to FBJ, December 22, 1922, LOCFBJ reel 9. For the George Draper garden photographed by FBJ, "The Magic of Landscape Architecture," *Vogue* 60, 2 (July 15, 1922): 54 and Dolkart, 83, Fig. 3.14. (LC-DIG-ppmsca-16660 and 16663)

PLATES 171–173 FLAGSTONES, CHARLES CLINTON MARSHALL HOUSE, NEW YORK, NEW YORK, ABBY STORY MARSHALL, LANDSCAPE GARDENER, CIRCA 1921

[171–172] *Porch and Laundry, 1922.* At her house on West 55th Street, Abby S. Marshall built a porch that hid the daily wash. Urban planners at the time considered laundry hung on clotheslines between buildings a blight in city yards. (LS-DIG-ppmsca-16659 and 16662)

[173] *Tea House/Sleeping Porch, 1922.* New York City Gardens Club member Abby S. Marshall won a "Special Medal … for her enclosed garden developed from three

typical unsightly backyards" at the club's 1922 exhibition. The pavilion doubled as a sleeping porch, an amenity considered restorative by health-conscious progressives.

The City Gardens Club Bulletin I: 3; "The Garden of Mrs. C. C. Marshall," *The House Beautiful* 64, no. 5 (December 3, 1922): 549. (LC-DIG-ppmsca-16138)

PLATES 174–175 QUIET CORNER, JOHN WESLEY BAXTER HOUSE, GREEN-WICH, CONNECTICUT, BENJAMIN WILLIAM MORRIS, ARCHITECT, CIRCA 1903

[174] *View from Terrace, Winter 1920.* Landscape architects purchased photo-graphs to study gardens in all seasons. (LC-DIG-ppmsca-16164)

[175] *Macaws on Terrace, Summer 1920.* Broadway playwright William Clyde Fitch (1865–1909) built this house as a country retreat in 1903 and furnished it with the help of Johnston client, Elsie de Wolfe. After his death in 1909, the Baxter family pur-chased the cottage and transformed it into a suburban mansion with a brick terrace and formal garden that FBJ thought was a creatively conceived "outdoor living room."

Montrose J. Moses, *Clyde Fitch and His Letters* (Boston: Little, Brown: 1924), 191–241; "Their Gorgeous Feathers on the Open Terrace," *Vogue* 55, no. 11 (June 1, 1920): 78–9. (LC-DIG-ppmsca-16343)

PLATE 176 AXARIAN PLEASURE GARDEN (PROSPECTUS HORTI DELICIARUM AXARIANI), SAINT PETERSBURG, RUSSIA

View to Trellis, copper plate engraving from the workshop of Giovanni Antonio Remondini (1634–1711), Bassano, Italy, 1780. FBJ likely photographed the engrav-ing while at the Colgate house. Unlike her slides of other historic images made from books, this photograph is directly from a print, without its identifying inscription.

The background mountains, not associated with St. Petersburg gardens, sug-gest that the Italian artist never visited the pleasance. Axarian may be a mis-translation of "Azarian," the root of Lazareff, a prominent Persian-Armenian family who moved to Russia in the 17th century.

Per author correspondence with Elena Grant and Paul Micio, and research by Boris Sokolov. (LC-DIG-ppmsca-16355)

PLATE 177 LATHROP COLGATE HOUSE, BEDFORD VILLAGE, NEW YORK, EDITH LEONARD COLGATE, PROBABLE LANDSCAPE GARDENER, CIRCA 1920

View to Garden Trellis, 1921. For landscape architects and house owners, period paintings and illustrations suggested scale and motifs for revivalist gardens. To design her backyard in an American colonial town, Edith Leonard Colgate turned to the Italian Axarian engraving for inspiration.

Married to a toothpaste-manufacturing heir, Colgate was prominent in the founding and development of the Bedford Garden Club. (LC-DIG-ppmsca-16347)

PLATES 178–179 FENIMORE, JAMES STETSON METCALFE HOUSE, BEDFORD HILLS, NEW YORK, ELIZABETH TYREE METCALFE, PROBABLE LANDSCAPE GARDENER, CIRCA 1920

[178] *Portrait of Gardener, 1922.* By the 1920s Johnston, with few exceptions, no longer pictured garden owners but continued to photograph gardeners. Anecdotal stories about the "*Maître Jardinier*" at Elsie de Wolfe's Villa Trianon outside Paris, and Jeffreys, the 78-year-old gardener at Cliveden, added to Johnston's lectures a quaint, literary tone that entertained wealthy house owners. This slide was a pic-turesque portrait inspired by Vincent van Gogh (1853–90) and Camille Pissarro (1830–1903).

For gardeners, see FBJ, "In Yesterday's Gardens," Introduction and sections on France and England, LOCFBJ reel 21. (LC-DIG-ppmsca-16309)

[179] *View to Lake Marie from Terraced Garden, 1922.* Married to a *Wall Street Journal* and *Life* magazine theater critic, Virginia-born actor "Bessie" Metcalfe was a Broadway star and dedicated gardener. She was an active "farmerette" during World War I, planting food for the troops, and produced a movie on roadside van-dalism for the Bedford Garden Club. Always searching for famous owners, Johnston pursued Metcalfe, a fellow board member of The City Gardens Club of New York City. In 1922 she finally photographed the actor's naturalized garden.

Elaine F. Weiss, *Fruits of Victory, The Woman's Land Army in the Great War* (Washington, D.C. Potomac Books, 2008), 90–1; *Bulletin of The Garden Club of America* 12, new series (November 1926): 79; letter from Frances Peter to Frances Benjamin Johnston, October 1 [1921] LOCFBJ reel 18. (LC-DIG-ppmsca-16733)

PLATES 180–182 WILLIAM SAMUEL KIES HOUSE, SCARBOROUGH, NEW YORK, CLARENCE FOWLER, LANDSCAPE ARCHITECT, CIRCA 1920

(left to right) Pergola, Walkway to Vegetable Garden, Further Along Walkway, 1922. Insurance executive William S. Kies acquired land circa 1916 in a subdivision planned by Olmsted Brothers for neighbor Frank A. Vanderlip. The landscape firm, which advised Kies briefly, thought that architects Patterson & Dula had awkwardly sited Kies' Colonial Revival house on the triangular lot bordered by roads on two

sides. Clarence Fowler designed a pergola to screen the white manor from public view and from a vegetable garden along a stone path.

Johnston pictured the walk from house to flower-bordered pathway with three slides in the clear palette of American Impressionism.

LOCOA, Box B346, Reel 302; "Garden of Mrs. W. S. Kies at Scarborough, N.Y.," *The Garden Magazine* 37, no. 4 (June 1923): 262–64, with a plan. (LC-DIG-ppmsca-16234, 16760, 17746)

PLATES 183–184 BEECHGATE, ROBERT CARMER HILL HOUSE, ENGLEWOOD, NEW JERSEY, ANNA GILMAN HILL, LANDSCAPE GARDENER, CIRCA 1911

[183] *View from Flower Garden to House, 1918.* When not at Gray Gardens in East Hampton in the 1910s and 1920s, Anna Gilman Hill lived at this house on four hillside acres. She planted her flower garden with peonies from expert Alice Howard Harding, blue geraniums from Mrs. Francis King, and irises from Mary Helen Wingate Lloyd. Hill encouraged gardeners to "acquire the swapping habit early in their career."

Anna Gilman Hill, *Forty Years of Gardening* (New York: Frederick A. Stokes, 1938), 126. (LC-DIG-ppmsca-16797)

[184] *Flower Garden Gate, 1918.* Three semicircular grass terraces, planted with *Pallida dalmatica* and Rhein Nixon irises that thrived in the rocky soil, led to a gate opening to a 40- by 72-foot enclosure framed with privet. The dimensions were almost identical to those of Hill's walled East Hampton garden.

An editor wrote that Beechgate's suburban garden, composed of hardy perennials, was practical. "A few hours a week spent in it by its mistress is all it needs to keep it neat and the dead flowers cut. It is distinctly a spring garden, for the owner is away from June until autumn."

"The Glories of a Spring Garden," *Vogue* 53, no. 6 (March 15, 1919): 56–7, illustrated with photographs by FBJ and a plan by Anna G. Hill. (LC-DIG-ppmsca-16752)

PLATES 185–186 WILLOWBANK, JOSEPH COLEMAN BRIGHT HOUSE, BRYN MAWR, PENNSYLVANIA, JOHN IRWIN BRIGHT, ARCHITECT, ANN LINN BRIGHT, LANDSCAPE GARDENER, 1911

[185] *Pathway to House, Spring 1919.* Joseph C. Bright made a fortune building a chain of hardware stores in eastern Pennsylvania and became a director of the Reading Railroad. His son and daughter collaborated to design his Arts and Crafts

house and garden. Having "wandered through the gardens of Surrey and Kent," Ann L. Bright agreed in principal with Wilhelm Miller's regard for majestic, slow-growing trees in English parks. But in America, with estates lasting only one generation before subdivision, she thought gardeners should not wait for an effect. "So we return to the maligned poplar and privet—God bless them!" Willowbank was a model Anglo-American garden in FBJ's city and suburb collection.

A. L. Bright, "A Three-Year-Old Garden of Quick Growers," *The Garden Magazine* 14, no. 12 (December 1914): 161–63. For a plan, see Ralph Adams Cram, *American Country Houses of Today* (New York: The Architectural Book Publishing Company, 1913), 12. (LC-DIG-ppmsca-16247)

[186] *Pathway to Fountain, Spring 1919.* Viburnum and a fast-growing willow framed a pathway in the garden composed of rooms parallel to the house on a rectangular suburban lot. (LC-DIG-ppmsca-16682)

PLATE 187 THE WHITE HOUSE, WASHINGTON, D.C., JAMES HOBAN AND OTHERS, ARCHITECTS, BUILT FROM 1792, BEATRIX JONES FARRAND, LANDSCAPE ARCHITECT, 1913

Southeast Garden, Spring 1921. President T. Woodrow Wilson's first wife, artist and garden designer, Ellen Axson Wilson, transformed what had been the boxwood colonial parterres of Edith Carow Roosevelt into urban outdoor rooms. Beginning in fall 1913, White House gardener Charles Henlock planted this southeast garden, designed by Farrand, and the Wilson southwest rose garden, designed by George E. Burnap. He was inspired by Charles A. Platt's Augusta Slade garden in Cornish, New Hampshire.

"Here, throughout the warm weather…," wrote Johnston after photographing the two gardens in 1921, "President and Mrs. Harding received on Thursday of each week … preferring the background of massed shrubbery and brilliant flowers to the formal setting of the White House."

"The White House Gardens, Washington, D.C.," *The Gardener's Chronicle* 18, no. 3 (July 1914): 81–3; Ulysses Grant Dietz and Sam Watters, *Dream House: The White House as an American Home* (New York: Acanthus Press, 2009): 166; [FBJ], "The Colonial Gardens of the White House," *Harper's Bazar* 56, no. 5 (May 1921): 63. (LC-DIG-ppmsca-16125; Southwest garden 16899)

PLATE 188 WEST POTOMAC PARK, WASHINGTON, D.C., FREDERICK LAW OLMSTED JR., JAMES LEAL GREENLEAF, AND ARMY CORPS OF ENGINEERS, LANDSCAPE ARCHITECTS, 1907–22

[188] *Irises Along the Embankment, 1921.* This slide showed the beauty possible through government City Beautiful programs. The McMillan Commission, supported by Johnston's ally President Theodore Roosevelt, designated the land a public park in 1902. Work was completed in May 1922. (LC-DIG-ppmsca-16318)

PLATES 189–190 EDGAR THEODORE WHERRY HOUSE, CHEVY CHASE, MARYLAND, EDGAR THEODORE AND GERTRUDE SMITH WHERRY, LANDSCAPE GARDENERS, FROM 1914

[189] *Bull Frog in the Native Plant Garden, July 1921.* After mulching his garden with rocks, pine needles, wood, and plant mold, the noted pteridologist raised 20 varieties of *Phlox subulata,* rare *Shortia,* box huckleberry, rhododendrons, *Arbutus,* and partridge berries. He added sawdust each year to his peaty mix and recommended acid control for native flower cultivation. (LC-DIG-ppmsca-16275)

[190] *The Wherrys in Their Native Plant Garden, July 1921.* Mineralogist with the United States National Museum and United States Department of Agriculture, institutions where Johnston studied wildflowers and photography, the indefatigable Edgar T. Wherry (1885–1982) wrote books and lectured at garden club meetings on wildflower gardening and ferns. After he and his wife, Gertrude Smith, moved to their newly built house in 1914, Wherry developed a woodland garden for endangered plants. He sought out species for commercial propagation and was an active member of the Wildflower Preservation Society, founded in Washington, D.C., in 1925.

George Phair, "Memorial of Edgar Theodore Wherry," *American Mineralogist* 69 (1984): 580–85; "Dr. Wherry's Garden," *Bulletin of The Garden Club of America* 8, new series (November 1922): 34. (LC-DIG-ppmsca-16667)

PLATE 191 WILLIAM CORCORAN EUSTIS HOUSE, WASHINGTON, D.C., FEDERAL REVIVAL HOUSE REMODELED BY JAMES FENWICK, AFTER 1848

Courtyard Gate, circa 1895–1900. Johnston prepared slides with images from her early career as a photojournalist, including this one of the Renaissance Revival house Eustis inherited from his grandfather, Washington banker and founder of the Corcoran Gallery of Art, William Wilson Corcoran.

Johnston needed a decade of experience with professional design to compose photographs showing the dimensionality of gardens and architecture.

James W. Goode, *Capital Losses: A Cultural History of Washington's Destroyed Buildings,* 2nd edition (Washington and New York: Smithsonian Books, 2003), 64–5. (LC-DIG-ppmsca-16677)

PLATE 192 SAMUEL HILLS TAFT HOUSE, CLIFTON, OHIO, JOHN HAMILTON DELANEY WAREHAM AND MABEL DUNBAR TAFT, LANDSCAPE GARDENERS, FROM CIRCA 1915

Walkway to Lily Pool from Drive, April 1922. Through the 1920s Johnston toured the Midwest. She lectured in Cincinnati, Ohio, where that city's garden club chair, urban progressive, and dahlia expert, Mabel D. Taft, was her host.

Taft and her relative, Rookwood Pottery president John H. D. Wareham (1871–1954), landscaped her suburban garden on three sloping acres. They placed Arts and Crafts pots and tiles in a naturalized garden with spring-blooming fruit trees and bulbs.

This image is likely the photograph "Pergola or porch with blooming wisteria, with a vista of irregular stone path leading to the street" that won Taft fourth prize for "vista or view" at the 1925 Garden Club of America photographic exhibition in Detroit. Helen S. Thorne won first prize for FBJ's photograph of Las Tejas, reproduced here, see Fig. 26b, p. 29 and p. 291.

Bulletin of The Garden Club of America no. 4, 3rd series (July 1925): 30 and 33; Beth Sullebarger, "History of Walter F. Sheblessy House," www.cincinnatimodern.com/blog/tag/midcentury-modern-architecture. (LC-DIG-ppmsca-16759)

Gardens of the Old World

[FRONTISPIECE] PAVILLON COLOMBE, EDITH JONES WHARTON HOUSE, ST. BRICE-SOUS-FORÊT, FRANCE, LAWRENCE JOHNSTON, LANDSCAPE GARDENER, 1918–19

Terrace, Summer 1925. Edith Wharton was an arbiter of Old World beauty suitable for New World houses and gardens. For slide lectures FBJ chose this view of the author's garden at her "small country house" north of Paris. "The shaded gravel terrace," she wrote, "placed near the house, screened by orange trees, gay with flower vases, provided with comfortable chaises longues, cushioned settees and tables, and opening on some lovely garden vistas…" was an "out-door living room…."

Like Edith Wharton, Lawrence Johnston (1871–1956) was an expatriate American, born in New York and educated at Cambridge University in England. After serving in the Boer War, Johnston devoted his life to landscape gardening, most notably at Hidcote Manor in Gloucestershire, where he lived from 1907, perfecting his Arts and Crafts garden.

FBJ, "Pavillon Colombe," LOCFBJ reel 21; [FBJ], "Pavilion Colombe at

Saint-Brice-sous-Forêt," *Town & Country* 82, no. 3963 (July 1, 1927): 34–7; Allan Ruff, *An Author and a Gardener: The Gardens and Friendship of Edith Wharton and Lawrence Johnston* (Chichester: Packard Publishing, 2009). (LC-DIG-ppm-sca-16469; see also view to house, 16967)

PLATES 193–194 VILLA D'ESTE, TIVOLI, ITALY, PIRRO LIGORIO, HOUSE AND LANDSCAPE ARCHITECT, 1560–75

[193] *View to Sabine Mountains from Villa, Summer 1925.* "Such pictures of the mountain slopes melting in effable colors into the hazy Roman *campagna* below are framed in the deep green velvet of the towering cypress," wrote Johnston poetically about this view. A painting of the same vista by Charles A. Platt inspired this photograph.

FBJ, "In Yesterday's Gardens," Italy;" Charles Adams Platt, *Italian Gardens,* with an overview by Keith Morgan (Portland: Sagapress/Timber Press, 1993 reprint of 1894 edition), 52. (LC-DIG-ppmsca-16524)

[194] *View to Villa, Summer 1925.* The retreat of Cardinal Ippolito II d'Este had a "majestic beauty all its own, a quality of dignity, charm and mystery almost inde-scribable, but wholly in keeping with its history and traditions," wrote Johnston.

FBJ, "In Yesterday's Gardens," 14. (LC-DIG-ppmsca-16471)

PLATE 195 VILLA BORGHESE, ROME, ITALY, FLAMINIO PONZIO AND GIOVANNI VASANZIO, ARCHITECTS AND LANDSCAPE ARCHITECTS, 1609–21

Piazza di Siena, Summer 1925. Johnston photographed old-world gardens to illus-trate ideals defined in 20th-century garden writing. She wrote that in Italy, "the favored land, utility and beauty unite," with strong contrasts of green and sunlight. "Trees of incomparable beauty most characteristic of the Italian landscape"—stone pines and cypress—shaded this outdoor amphitheater in the Borghese gardens.

FBJ, "In Yesterday's Gardens," Italy. (LC-DIG-ppmsca-16516)

PLATE 196 VILLA TORLONIA, FRASCATI, ITALY, GIROLAMO FONTANA, CARLO MADERNO, AND FLAMINIO PONZIO, LANDSCAPE ARCHITECTS, 17TH CENTURY

Water Theater, Summer 1925. Waterfalls and fountains distinguished the Ital-ian garden for American visitors. From the water theater at Torlonia, wrote FBJ, "moss-grown crumbling steps lead up to a series of cascades … in a succession of circular marble basins, fairly melting down the slope. This cascade … constitutes

one of the most beautiful examples of fountain architecture in Italy."

FBJ, "In Yesterday's Garden," 10. (LC-DIG-ppmsca-16523)

PLATES 197–198 VILLA GAMBERAIA, BARONESS CLEMENS AUGUST FREI-HERR VON KETTELER HOUSE, SETTIGNANO, ITALY, ANDREA DE COSIMO LAPI AND OTHERS, LANDSCAPE ARCHITECTS, FROM 17TH CENTURY AND PRINCESS JEANNE GHYKA AND MARTINO PORCINAI, LANDSCAPE GARDEN-ERS, FROM 1896

[197] *Grotto, Summer 1925.* Echoing Edith Wharton and Cecil Pinsent, Johnston noted that the modest villa overlooking the Arno Valley had a variety of elements "remarkable for producing the effect of spaciousness in a plot less than three acres." The Baroness owner was American Maud Cass Ledyard, heir of Henry Brockholst Ledyard, general manager of the Michigan Central Railroad that con-trolled the line from Chicago to Detroit.

FBJ, "In Yesterday's Gardens," Introduction. (LC-DIG-ppmsca-16475)

[198] *Water Terrace, Summer 1925.* "A single majestic pine tree is brought into the composition with fine effect," wrote Johnston of this water terrace created by a Serbian princess when she owned the villa at the turn of the century. FBJ framed her photograph to reflect this harmonious design.

FBJ, "In Yesterday's Gardens" Italy. (LC-DIG-ppmsca-16515)

PLATES 199–200 VILLA I TATTI, BERNARD BERENSON HOUSE, SETTIGNANO, ITALY, CECIL ROSS PINSENT, RESTORATION ARCHITECT, FROM 1906, CECIL ROSS PINSENT, FROM 1909, AND WITH GEOFFREY SCOTT, FROM 1914, LANDSCAPE ARCHITECTS

[199] *View to Villa, Summer 1925.* While industrialists in America were building Long Island estates, the American-born scholar and art dealer Bernard Berenson (1865–1959) was becoming an Italo-American aristocrat at the villa he purchased in 1906 and continued to landscape until his death. In June 1925, his wife, art his-torian Mary Smith (1864–1945), wrote Johnston that if she wished, while visiting nearby Villa Gamberaia, FBJ was welcome to stop and see her garden, noting that "of course it couldn't compare with Gamberaia, as it is only 15 years old. Still it shows what could be done in a short time." Pinsent created a Renaissance Revival garden with clipped, geometric hedges and topiary. In its exactitude, the garden was distinctly American.

Francesca Romana Liserre, *Giardini anglo-fiorentini, Il Rinascimento all'inglese di Cecil Pinsent* (Florence: Angelo Pontecorboli, 2008), 53–66; letter from Mary Berenson to FBJ, June 8, 1925, LOCFBJ reel 8. (LC-DIG-ppmsca-16498)

[200] *View from Villa, Summer 1925.* Johnston made a pair of views to show the direct relationship between the house and its garden. (LC-DIG-ppmsca-16497)

PLATES 201–202 VILLA LA PIETRA, ARTHUR ACTON HOUSE, FLORENCE, ITALY, BUILT FOR FRANCESCO SASSETTI, FIRST HALF, 16TH CENTURY, ARTHUR AND HORTENSE MITCHELL ACTON, LANDSCAPE GARDENERS, FROM 1908

[201] *Entrance Drive, Summer 1925.* At the time Johnston visited La Pietra, Arthur Acton and his wife, a Chicago banking heir, had restored the villa built for a Medici banker. They had purchased the 57-acre estate in 1907. FBJ wrote that its gated drive was a "typical formal entrance to the grounds of a Florentine villa…. The main grille opens directly from the public road, passing through the clustered buildings of a small village."
FBJ, "In Yesterday's Gardens," Italy. (LC-DIG-ppmsca-16458)

[202] *Stairway to Lower Terrace, Summer 1925.* The green of Italian gardens was foreign to garden club audiences. Echoing Edith Wharton, FBJ explained that "flowers, strangely as it may seem, were never the most important features of the old Italian gardens. On the contrary, they were simply incidental notes of color according to the season, like the rambler roses which here cascade in billows of pink and crimson over walls and balustrades."
FBJ, "In Yesterday's Gardens," Italy. (LC-DIG-ppmsca-16489)

PLATES 203–204 VILLA ALDOBRANDINI, FRASCATI, ITALY, GIACOMO DELLA PORTA AND CARLO MADERNO, ARCHITECTS AND LANDSCAPE ARCHITECTS, 1598–1603

[203] *Water Theater, Summer 1925.* Paraphrasing Guy Lowell, Johnston considered the achievement of Italian landscape design the "perfect relation" of garden to house architecture. In Italy, the "aim was primarily for the more permanent effects, and one cannot but marvel at the endless variety and sheer beauty achieved by use of the three elements of garden composition, stone or marble, perennial verdure and water." From the villa at the top of a hill, water flowed down to this Atlas fountain.
FBJ, "In Yesterday's Gardens," Italy. (LC-DIG-ppmsca-16492)

[204] *Steps to Water Theater, Summer 1925.* The design of this garden likely influenced Charles S. Greene's California hillside garden at Il Paradiso, the Elisabeth S. Allen house photographed by Johnston in 1917. (LC-DIG-ppmsca-16493; for Il Paradiso, see plate 115 and p. 310, slide 16935)

QUOTATION, OPPOSITE PLATE 205
"It is really difficult to forgive…," FBJ, "In Yesterday's Gardens," Italy.

PLATE 205 VILLA BORROMEO, ISOLA BELLA, LAKE MAGGIORE, ITALY, GIOVANNI ANGELO CRIVELLI AND OTHERS, ARCHITECTS AND LANDSCAPE ARCHITECTS, FROM CIRCA 1630

Terrace Garden, Summer 1925. Johnston compared this slide of Isola Bella with a slide of its sister island, Isola Madre. There, at a Borromeo botanical garden, she discovered that "much of the natural beauty remains to salve the lacerated feelings of the visitor who has fled the tragedy of Isola Bella" and its "intrusion of the Baroque." For FBJ and her generation, restrained Renaissance classicism, not 17th-century exuberance, was good taste.
FBJ, "In Yesterday's Gardens," Italy. (LC-DIG-ppmsca-16527; Isola Madre, 16474)

PLATES 206–207 VILLA TORRE CLEMENTINA, LOUIS ANTOINE STERN HOUSE, ROQUEBRUN-CAP-MARTIN, FRANCE, LUCIEN HESSE, ARCHITECT, RAFFAELE MAINELLA, LANDSCAPE GARDENER, FROM 1904

View to Ruins; Pansy Ribbon, Summer 1925. "Black and white can never express the miracles of color particular to the Côte d'Azur, which seems to emerge from a sea of incredible turquoise blue," Johnston wrote. Edward van Altena produced FBJ's Maxfield Parrish vision in these slides of a neo-Romanesque garden designed by an Italian landscape painter for a French banker and his wife, author Ernesta Stern.
FBJ, "In Yesterday's Gardens," France. (LC-DIG-ppmsca-16172 and 16363)

PLATE 208 CHÂTEAU D'USSÉ, COMTE LOUIS DE BLACAS CASTLE, RIGNY-USSÉ, FRANCE, ARCHITECTURE, 15TH AND 16TH CENTURIES, POSSIBLY ANDRÉ LE NÔTRE, LANDSCAPE ARCHITECT, 17TH CENTURY

Parterre, Summer 1925. Johnston distinguished French and Italian gardens by types of formality. "All French gardens, however small or unpretentious, may be said to be based on the style created by Le Nôtre, or at least its chief elements: the parterre, the allées, graveled walks, the shaded terraces, the bosquets, the pools…." This garden in northwest Provence had these features and was known as the inspiration for the castle in Charles Perrault's 1697 tale, *La Belle au bois dormant* (*Sleeping Beauty*).

FBJ, "In Yesterday's Gardens," France. "Château d'Ussé, near Tours," *Town & Country* 81, no. 3436 (August 15, 1926): 56–9. (LC-DIG-ppmsca-16529)

PLATES 209–210 CHÂTEAU DE COURANCES, MARQUIS JEAN DE GANAY CASTLE, COURANCES, FRANCE, GILLES LE BRETON, ARCHITECT, BUILT FROM 1682, HENRI AND ACHILLE DUCHÊNE, LANDSCAPE ARCHITECTS, EARLY 20TH CENTURY

[209] *View to Castle from Canal, July 1925*. At Courances, Johnston wrote, two "etaings [*sic*] or long lateral canals fed by the moat stream, extend the length of the broad terrace drive. Avenues of giant plane trees border the canals, soaring to majestic heights and trailing their branches in the still waters which mirror the picturesque silhouette of the ancient chateau." The Marquis de Ganay, Charles Anne Jean Ridgway, descended from the colonial Philadelphia family of John Jacob Ridgway.

FBJ, "In Yesterday's Gardens," France. (LC-DIG-ppmsca-16478)

[210] *Plane Trees Along Canal, July 1925*. The alley was through the beech forest that surrounded the house. (LC-DIG-ppmsca-16479)

PLATE 211 CHÂTEAU DE BRÉAU, WALTER GAY CASTLE, DAMMARIE-LÈS-LYS, FRANCE, ARCHITECT UNKNOWN, MEDIEVAL BUILDING REBUILT IN 1663 AND 1667

Alley, July 1925. In 1905 Walter Gay (1856–1937), the American painter of upper-class domestic interiors, and his American heiress wife, Matilda Travers (1855–1943), leased this country castle. It was, wrote FBJ, "on the road to Barbizon, which is a part of that romantic country so long the delight and inspiration of artists," including Johnston herself.

[FBJ], "Château de Bréau, *Walter Gay House*, Dammarie-lès-Lys." *Town & Country* 82, no. 3958 (April 1, 1927): 74–7. (LC-DIG-ppmsca-16491)

PLATE 212 CHÂTEAU DE VAUX-LE-VICOMTE, EDME SOMMIER CASTLE, MAINCY, FRANCE, LOUIS LE VAU, ARCHITECT, BUILT FROM 1656, ANDRÉ LE NÔTRE, LANDSCAPE ARCHITECT, 1653–54, ÉLIE LAINÉ AND ACHILLE DUCHÊNE, LANDSCAPE ARCHITECTS, 19TH CENTURY AND 1911–23

[212] *View from Château, July 1925*. The inimitable story of this château's creation by Louis XIV's finance minister, Nicolas Fouquet, and his imprisonment by the jealous king ,was inseparable from Johnston's appreciation of the garden itself.

This vista was of the "noble parterre of the historic gardens … where the genius of Le Nôtre first found untrammeled expression…." FBJ failed to tell *Town & Country* readers that the castle's owner, sugar-refining heir, Edme Sommier, and Achille Duchêne had recently transformed the terrace into a *parterre de broderie*. Americans wanted to see authentic aristocratic gardens, not 20th-century restorations.

Le Style Duchêne, Architectes Paysagistes 1841–1947, Claire Frange et al., editor (Paris: Editions du Labyrinthe, 1998). FBJ, "Vaux-le-Vicomte, near Melun," *Town & Country* 82, no. 3974 (December 15, 1927): 74–7. (LC-DIG-ppmsca-16481)

PLATES 213–214 WELLSBRIDGE COTTAGE, PHILIP HERBERT MARTINEAU HOUSE, WELLSBRIDGE, ENGLAND, ALICE VAUGHAN-WILLIAMS MARTINEAU, LANDSCAPE GARDENER, FROM CIRCA 1920

[213] *Entrance Walk, August 1925*. "I should esteem it a great privilege to be able to visit *any* garden with Mrs. Martineau, whose works are so well and favorably known in America, and I will make all my plans for England subject to her convenience, as we regard her as an authority on gardening in England," wrote Johnston while planning her Old World tour. An author of books on herbaceous borders, gardens in California, and designer of both English and American gardens, Mrs. Martineau was, for Americans enthralled with English gardening, a celebrity with Gertrude Jekyll and William Robinson.

Johnston spent the night in this recently restored cottage, visiting nearby gardens designed by her host. In writing about its entrance pathway, FBJ commented that the "mushrooms" were not "strays from some Japanese gardens, but … old stone cores of regional haystacks."

Letter from FBJ to Captain Peter Beeman, July 29, 1925, LOCFBJ reel 9; FBJ, "A Famous Wayside English Garden," *Arts & Decoration* 25, no. 2 (June 1926): 32–3. (LC-DIG-ppmsca-16202)

[214] *Garden Doorway, August 1925*. For Frances Benjamin Johnston, the Italian garden was the garden of architecture; France, the country of parks and parterres; and across the channel were "the gardens of the cottage and hamlet of the English country-side, that the present day garden amateur may find the greatest inspiration." Martineau's Wellsbridge was exemplary, with a vegetable garden, an orchard in a meadow, a stream through a wild garden, and a wooded hillside.

FBJ, "In Yesterday's Gardens," England. (LC-DIG-ppmsca-16480)

PLATES 215–216 CLIVEDEN, VISCOUNT WALDORF ASTOR HOUSE, TAPLOW, ENGLAND, WILLIAM WALDORF ASTOR AND NORAH LINDSAY, LANDSCAPE GARDENERS, FROM 1893 AND FROM 1924

[215] *Water Garden, August 1925*. At Cliveden, wrote Johnston, one finds "the Naturalistic style, which shows its Oriental inspiration in the fantastic little pavilion…. In the 18th century, the ardent followers of the cult of Naturalistic gardening, or rather landscaping, were delightfully inconsistent in their actual practice, introducing mounds, pyramids, spiral walks, temples, and other artificialities." She concluded wrongfully, as did many in her generation, that Alexander Pope "with unconscious humor" described his grotto at Twickenham, "in the natural taste!" The pagoda was not Georgian chinoiserie, but from the 1867 Paris Exposition Universelle, acquired by William Waldorf Astor in 1900 from the Bagatelle sale of Lord Hertford. The camera lens made the human-scale pavilion appear diminutive.

FBJ, "In Yesterday's Gardens," England; James Crathorne, *Cliveden: The Place and the People* (London: Collins and Brown, 1995): 191. (LC-DIG-ppmsca-16490)

[216] *Long Garden, August 1925*. Echoing the sentiments of Wilhelm Miller, Johnston wrote of this view that "the serene beauty of these old English gardens is always enhanced by their noble trees…." Lindsay introduced topiary and box-bordered flower beds to this garden, originally known as the Main Formal Garden, planted by William W. Astor.

FBJ, "In Yesterday's Gardens," England, identified as the Long Garden; Allyson Hayward, *Norah Lindsay, The Art and Life of a Garden Designer* (London: Frances Lincoln, 2007), 125–31. (LC-DIG-ppmsca 16535)

Gardens of the South

[FRONTISPIECE] TUCKAHOE, NEHEMIAH ADDISON BAKER HOUSE, RICHMOND, VIRGINIA, THOMAS RANDOLPH, BUILDER, CIRCA 1720

View from Thomas Jefferson's Schoolhouse to Boxwood Maze, April 1936. The third president lived at Tuckahoe until he was nine. For garden club members, Johnston conjured up a vision of what Jefferson might have seen from the plantation schoolhouse. Boxwood in the background screened the Ghost Walk.

FBJ, "Notes and Captions, Tuckahoe," LOCFBJ reel 21. (LC-DIG-ppmsca-16341)

PLATES 217–218 HAMPTON, JOHN RIDGLEY HOUSE, TOWSON, MARYLAND, CAPTAIN CHARLES RIDGLEY AND JEHU HALL, ARCHITECT AND MASTER CARPENTER, FROM 1783, CHARLES CARNON RIDGLEY, LANDSCAPE GARDENER, BOXWOOD PARTERRES, 1795–1810

[217] *House Facing South to Hillside Parterre Garden, circa 1915*. Hampton was the first private southern house and garden that Frances Benjamin Johnston photographed, possibly when men and women associated with The Garden Club of America visited the estate in May 1915, for the club's third annual meeting. Descendants of the tobacco plantation builder still lived in the Georgian house when more than 200 guests walked down three terraces, each with boxwood parterres.

Ann Milkovich McKee, *Hampton National Historic Site* (Charleston: Arcadia Publishing, 2007), 8, 23. *Bulletin of The Garden Club of America* 8 (April 1915): n.p. (LC-DIG-ppmsca-16578)

[218] *First Parterre, circa 1915*. At the time Johnston visited Hampton, this terrace below the house was the only part of the hillside garden that retained its original late-18th- to early-19th-century design. (LC-DIG-ppmsca-16577)

PLATES 219–225 CHATHAM, COLONEL DANIEL BRADFORD DEVORE HOUSE, FREDERICKSBURG, VIRGINIA, ORIGINALLY BUILT 1771, OLIVER H. CLARK, RESTORATION ARCHITECT FOR DANIEL AND HELEN STEWART DEVORE, FROM 1920, ELLEN BIDDLE SHIPMAN, LANDSCAPE ARCHITECT, FROM 1922

[219] *West Garden, 1927*. Shipman excelled at re-creating the irregularity of old American gardens. At Chatham, clumps of boxwood grew on the west side of the house, facing the Rappahannock River and colonial Fredericksburg. The restoration architect contributed to the Old South feeling of this country retreat by scraping and whitewashing the manor's 18th-century brick.

Adaline D. Piper, "The Charm of Chatham," *The House Beautiful* 59, no. 4 (April 1926): 437. (LC-DIG-ppmsca-16348)

[220–221] *Porch and Service Court, 1927*. Without a porch on the 18th-century house, Helen S. Devore built this pavilion in a garden of its own.

Johnston posed the picturesque photograph of the garage as a genre painting, with no cars and a hay rake in the wheelbarrow. (LC-DIG-ppmsca-16204 and 16205)

[222–223] *East Garden Gate and East Flower Garden, 1927.* Trained at Annapolis, Colonel Devore served in the Spanish-American War, the Panama Canal Zone, the Philippines, and World War I. His wife was a lumber heir and the sister of Mary Stewart, who lived in Montecito, California, at Il Brolino. Like their friends Larz and Isabel Anderson, the Devores traveled extensively and had a town house in Washington, D.C., designed by Johnston client William Lawrence Bottomley. When they restored their 18th-century house at Fredericksburg, Helen S. Devore hired Ellen B. Shipman. Influenced by New Englander Alice Morse Earle, whose books Johnston collected, Shipman designed new Colonial Revival gardens.

(LC-DIG-ppmsca-16339 and 16334)

[224–225] *View to Kitchen from East Flower Garden and East Flower Garden Pergola, 1927.* Informally trained by Charles A. Platt, who designed the 1901 Larz Anderson garden, Weld, Shipman built walls and pergolas to relate Chatham house to its garden.

Judith B. Tankard, "Ellen Biddle Shipman's Colonial Revival Garden Style," *Recreating the American Past,* edited by Richard Guy Wilson, Shaun Eyring, and Kenny Marotta (Charlottesville and London: University of Virginia Press, 2006), 67–82. (LC-DIG-ppmsca-16349 and 16345)

PLATE 226 THOMAS R. BOGGS HOUSE, FREDERICKSBURG, VIRGINIA, BUILT CIRCA 1718, WITH LATER ADDITIONS, KATE DOGGETT BOGGS, LANDSCAPE GARDENER, CIRCA 1926

Terrace at The Quarters, 1927. A leader in the Garden Club of Virginia, Kate Doggett Boggs, author of *Prints and Plants of Old Gardens* (1932), inherited an historic Fredericksburg house from her father. Her antiques business, The Quarters, was in a former slave's house on the property. Fredericksburg neighbor Gari Melchers advised on architectural changes to the building and Frances Benjamin Johnston suggested "the arrangement of the garden and brick borders" of its shady court. The house and dependencies maintained an "air of dignity and simple elegance," wrote Johnston.

Letter from Kate Doggett Boggs to FBJ, January 10, 1928, LOCFBJ reel 10; FBJ, "Notes-Town & Country, Scenic Wallpaper in an Old Virginia Mansion," reel 21. (LC-DIG-ppmsca-16336)

PLATE 227 BELMONT, GARI MELCHERS HOUSE, FREDERICKSBURG, VIRGINIA, CORINNE MACKALL MELCHERS, LANDSCAPE GARDENER, FROM 1916

[227] *Arbor at the Long Walk, 1927.* Johnston photographed the defining axis of this garden designed and planted by the American Post-Impressionist painter and his artist wife.

Belmont, wrote Johnston, "was on terraces dropping from level to level into the valley, providing enchanting vistas to the rock gorge of the Rappahannock. A long walk, hedged with ancient box and a rose garden set on the edge of a woody ravine, give the necessary formality to link the spacious old Mansion with a landscape, which in many ways, suggests the beauty and romantic charm of the Scottish Lake country." FBJ and her garden audiences measured success in American gardens against Old World beauty.

FBJ, "Gari Melchers, Town and Country captions," LOCFBJ reel 21; Margaret Page Bemiss, *Historic Virginia Gardens: Preservation Work of the Garden Club of Virginia, 1975–2007* (Charlottesville: University of Virginia Press, 2009), 23–32. (LC-DIG-ppmsca-16161)

PLATE 228 REVEILLE, ELMER MULFORD CRUTCHFIELD HOUSE, RICHMOND, VIRGINIA, BUILT FROM 1720, ELIZABETH PATTERSON CRUTCHFIELD, LANDSCAPE GARDENER, CIRCA 1920S

Servant's Cottage, 1929. Converted from slaves' quarters, the clapboard house overlooked a Colonial Revival garden planted with peonies, damask roses, foxgloves, phlox, and poppies. Garden club member and historic preservationist Elizabeth P. Crutchfield, who inherited the property from her father, wrote that "Reveille is beautiful because of its simplicity…," a quality admired in the Colonial Revival and evoked by Johnston in her photographs of Virginia houses and gardens.

Elizabeth P. Crutchfield, "Reveille," *Homes and Gardens of Virginia,* edited by Susanne Williams Massie and Frances Archer Christian (Richmond: Garrett & Massie, 1932), 109. (LC-DIG-ppmsca-16344)

PLATE 229 MARY BALL WASHINGTON HOUSE, FREDERICKSBURG, VIRGINIA, BUILT 1761, WITH LATER ADDITIONS

View to Flower Garden, 1927. George Washington acquired this house for his mother in 1772. The Association for the Preservation of Virginia Antiquities saved the clapboard building from destruction in 1891. Though never carried out, the organization considered plans to ship the house for exhibition at the 1893 Chicago World's Fair. The shaded backyard was an old-fashioned Grandmother's garden planted with hollyhock (*Alcea*).

Bemiss, *Historic Virginia Gardens,* 97–104. (LC-DIG-ppmsca-16162)

PLATES 230–231 YORK HOUSE, CAPTAIN GEORGE PRESTON BLOW HOUSE, YORKTOWN, VIRGINIA, GRIFFIN & WYNKOOP, RENOVATION ARCHITECTS, FROM 1914, CHARLES FREEMAN GILLETTE, LANDSCAPE ARCHITECT, FROM 1914

[230] *Guest House in Memory Garden, 1929.* In 1914 Indiana businessman Captain Blow purchased York House from descendants of its famous owner, Thomas Nelson Jr., a signer of the Declaration of Independence. Blow acquired additional lots to make an 8-acre property. Like Helen S. Devore, he renovated his brick house, converted existing buildings to new uses, and planted a Colonial Revival boxwood flower garden with pansies, snapdragons, alyssum, and roses. Gillette based his plan on a garden at Groombridge Place in Kent, England, reportedly an ancestral home of the Blow family.

"York Hall," *Landscape Architecture* 28, no. 2 (January 1928): 80–1. (LC-DIG-ppmsca-16337)

[231] *Gardener's Cottage in Memory Garden, 1929.* With these two views FBJ showed garden clubs the relationship of the garden to both guest and gardener houses. Gillette developed the palette for the flower garden from the rose-colored bricks and "dark, dull blue" window headers of the main house.

George C. Logest, *Genius in the Garden*, 63. (LC-DIG-ppmsca-16338)

PLATE 232 WILLIAM ALBERT SMOOT JR. HOUSE, RICHMOND, VIRGINIA, 18TH-CENTURY HOUSE WITH ADDITIONS

Rose Garden, 1920. In 1918, William A. Smoot, from a family of tanners and lumbermen, purchased his house on a corner lot along historic Washington Street in a city undergoing renewal. In the conversion of existing buildings, Smoot and his wife, an officer of the Daughters of the American Republic, made a walled Colonial Revival rose garden edged in boxwood.

Timothy J. Dennée, "A History of Lloyd House, Part II, History of the Structure: 1833–1918, "*Historic Alexandria*" (Spring/Summer 2004): 1–10. (LC-DIG-ppmsca-16655)

PLATES 233–234 HICKORY HILL, HENRY TAYLOR WICKHAM HOUSE, ASHLAND, VIRGINIA, WILLIAM FANNING AND ANN CARTER WICKHAM, LANDSCAPE GARDENERS, BEGUN 1820

Elise W. B. Wickham at End of Boxwood Walk and with Henry T. Wickham at the Entrance Gate to Boxwood Walk, 1927. When Johnston photographed this historic garden, Wickham descendants still lived at Hickory Hill, once part of Robert Carter's Shirley Plantation. Henry T. Wickham, a Virginia state senator, wrote to Johnston that "the box walk is an avenue of Sempervirens boxwood, the trees varying in height from 30 to 40 feet and extending in a double line for over 400 feet from the terrace gate to the lower terrace…. At every season, at every hour, and in every kind of weather, there is beauty, majestic beauty. The legend is that the small box bushes were passed through General Wickham, then an infant, by his mother, the creator of the garden." In keeping with photographic conventions, Johnston included the Wickhams to show dimensions. The photo of the end of the walk was of "a lateral hedge where the trees reach 25 to 30 feet, present mistress of the garden giving scale to the picture." The couple appears in a photograph "made at a distance of some 300 feet."

FBJ, "Captions and Notes, Town and Country," LOCFBJ reel 21. See also Elsie W. B. Wickham on Hickory Hill in *Homes and Gardens of Virginia*, edited by Susanne Williams Massie and Frances Archer Christian (Richmond: Garrett & Massie, 1932), 119. (LC-DIG-ppmsca-16267 and 16163)

PLATE 235 PINE BARRENS NEAR WILMINGTON, NORTH CAROLINA

American Pitcher Plant (Sarracenia flava), *April 1929.* Johnston studied and photographed wild flowers for lectures on preserving the American countryside. (LC-DIG-ppmsca-16723)

LETTERS, OPPOSITE PLATE 235
"Bowling along I saw what…," letter from FBJ to Mrs. [Heningham Ellet] Smith, April 30, 1929, LOCFBJ reel 11.
"I have never seen…," letter from Heningham Ellett Smith to FBJ May 13 [1929], LOCFBJ reel 19.

PLATES 236–237 [GATEFOLD] MIDDLETON PLACE, JOHN JULIUS PRINGLE SMITH HOUSE, CHARLESTON, SOUTH CAROLINA, HENRY MIDDLETON, PLANTATION FOUNDER, 18TH CENTURY, JOHN JULIUS PRINGLE AND HENINGHAM ELLETT SMITH, LANDSCAPE GARDENERS, FROM 1920S

[236] *The Middleton Oak, March 1928.* The centuries-old live oak was a local landmark thought to be from the time of Christopher Columbus. Farmer and history writer Edward Terrie Hendrie Shaffer (1894–1997) wrote: "As one advances through enclosed paths, between the camellias, through the glory of ten thousand flaming azaleas, over open lawns, vistas of the great tree recur at intervals until

suddenly, it stands forth, fully revealed, beyond a rose garden and a sun dial, at the river's edge." FBJ included people in the photograph to convey the tree's 60-foot height and 190-foot diameter.

E. T. H. Shaffer, *Carolina Gardens*, Garden Club Edition (Raleigh: University of North Carolina Press, 1939), 72. (LC-DIG-ppmsca-16330)

[237] *Butterfly Lake, March 1928.* J. J. Pringle Smith was a direct descendant of Henry Middleton. Living in former guest quarters that survived a fire set by the Union Army in 1865, he and his wife restored and expanded one of America's earliest landscaped gardens. They opened Middleton Place to the public in 1925.

For the Smiths, FBJ was "the Lady with a Camera" who took "beautiful pictures," including this view of the terrace at the Ashley River. Johnston's gift of a pitcher plant was in honor of botanist André Michaux (1746–1802), whom Louis XVI sent to America in 1785 to collect plants of potential economic value to France. He lived between the Ashley and Cooper Rivers and reputedly introduced the *Camellia japonica* to Middleton Place from his nearby nursery. FBJ's gesture reflected her continuing garden interest and new fervor for historic preservation.

James R. Cothran, *Gardens of Historic Charleston* (Columbia: University of South Carolina Press, 1995), 41; letter from Heningham Ellett Smith to FBJ, December 2 [1928], LOCFBJ reel 11; George C. Rogers, "Gardens and Landscapes in Eighteenth-Century South Carolina," *British and American Gardens in the Eighteenth Century*, edited by Robert MacCubbin (Williamsburg: The Colonial Williamsburg Foundation, 1984), 150. (LC-DIG-ppmsca-16326)

PLATES 238–239 MAGNOLIA PLANTATION, CHARLESTON, SOUTH CARO-LINA, REVEREND JOHN GRIMKE DRAYTON, LANDSCAPE GARDENER, FROM 1840s

[238] *Azalea Reflections in Cypress Swamp, March 1928.* Gardeners knew the glow of the azaleas in the plantation's ink-black swamp through black-and-white photographs and magazine descriptions. FBJ's colored slides brought the spectacle alive. (LC-DIG-ppmsca-16325)

[239] *Azaleas Along Pathway, March 1928.* In 1870 the reverend opened his family plantation to the public as "Magnolia-on-the-Ashley." It was an early tourist attraction, and in 1928 Johnston traveled along the Ashley River to photograph the azalea bloom here and at neighboring Middleton Place. By the 1920s a spring trip to southern plantations was an annual garden club pilgrimage. (LC-DIG-ppmsca-16328)

PLATE 240 SMALLWOOD-WARD HOUSE, NEW BERN, NORTH CAROLINA, BUILT CIRCA 1812

Entrance, circa 1930. As the Depression settled over America and house owners struggled to maintain flower gardens, FBJ turned to photographing historic houses. This slide, in the documentary style FBJ adopted for her photographs for the Carnegie Survey of the Architecture of the South, is one of two color images of building exteriors in Johnston's lantern-slide collection at the Library of Congress. (LC-DIG-ppmsca-16643)

PLATE 241 TAVERN, RICHMOND, VIRGINIA

Children Pose for the Photographer, circa 1933 to 1935. Lantern Slide Reproduced to Scale, 3 ¼ by 4 inches. The sepia-toned slides FBJ produced for her lectures on southern buildings and gardens romanticized the poverty and cultural ruin that still remained in the post-restoration South. (LCDIG-ppmsca-16629-A)

[TAILPIECE] FRANCES BENJAMIN JOHNSTON PLACE CARD

William Mills Thompson, Place Card, 1896, watercolor on paper, 3 x 4½ inches. For a party that included young Washington, D.C., artists, musicians, and actors, illustrator Mills Thompson (1875–1944) drew portraits. He captured the essence of his close friend Frances Benjamin Johnston, who considered herself a fine artist pioneering photography, a new medium, to picture American life. (LC-DIG-ppmsca-23962 and ppmsc-04898)

"Our American Gardens"

Frances Benjamin Johnston created her first lantern-slide presentation with the photographs she and Mattie Edwards Hewitt produced from circa 1911 through 1916. She titled this talk "Our American Gardens," or, to capitalize on the status of wealthy owners, "Famous Gardens." Brief labels in Johnston's hand and newspaper reports make possible the identification of slides in this early collection. Though FBJ gave the talk and its corollary, "Gardens of the East," through the 1920s, the list that follows represents the slides she showed from 1915 until 1917. These are among the glass plates Johnston received as part of her March 1917 partnership settlement with Hewitt.

Johnston promoted her "Our American Gardens" lecture as presenting 75 to 150 slides. Intent on educating as well as entertaining, FBJ may have augmented this collection with slides of historical engravings and woodcuts. No slide lists remain for her garden lectures, and her labeling all but stopped after 1917.

The more-than 200 slides of 42 public and private gardens in this collection reflect the American landscape movement in the Northeast from 1900 until World War I, when servants maintained houses and elaborate ornamental gardens. Social and economic changes contributed to the end of the large-house era. Mrs. Walter "Jean" Jennings started her flower garden at Cold Spring Harbor on 110 acres in 1915 with a trained gardener overseeing a crew. By 1939, in the bottom of the Depression, she had no gardener and had been doing the work herself with two "laborers" for several years.[1]

Plate numbers for illustrated gardens appear in brackets

Weld, Larz Anderson house, Brookline, Massachusetts [27–33]

George Fisher Baker house, Tuxedo Park, New York [86-88]

Claverack, General Thomas Henry Barber house, Southampton, New York [69]

Bartow Mansion, International Garden Club, Pelham Bay Park, New York [49]

The Elms, Edward Julius Berwind house, Newport, Rhode Island [1–2]

Millefiori, Albert Barnes Boardman house, Southampton, New York [70]

The Orchard, James Lawrence Breese house, Southampton, New York [76–79]

The Appletrees, Henry Eugene Coe house, Southampton, New York
   [Frontispiece, Gardens of the East]

Grey-Croft, Stephen Swete Cummins house, East Hampton, New York [85]

George Washington Curtis house, Southampton, New York

The Reef, Theodore Montgomery Davis house, Newport, Rhode Island

Westlawn, Edward Tiffany Dyer house, East Hampton, New York

Mariemont, Thomas Josephus Emery house, Middletown, Rhode Island [15–16]

Darena, George Barton French house, Southampton, New York

The Steppingstones, Annie May Hegeman house, Southampton, New York [73]

Près Choisis, Albert Herter house, East Hampton, New York [80]

Gray Gardens, Robert Carmer Hill house, East Hampton, New York [82-84]

Francis Burrall Hoffman house, Southampton, New York

Chelmsford, Elon Huntington Hooker house, Greenwich, Connecticut [40–41]

Red Maples, Mrs. Rosina Sherman Hoyt house, Southampton, New York

Burrwood, Walter Jennings house, Cold Spring Harbor, New York [63–66]

Samuel Knopf house, Lawrence, New York [50]

Samuel Longstreth Parrish Art Museum, Southampton, New York

Waveny, Lewis Henry Lapham house, New Canaan, Connecticut [36–37]

Ballyshear, Charles Blair MacDonald house, Southampton, New York [81]

Cragston, John Pierpont Morgan house, Highland Falls, New York [48]

Fanny A. Mulford house, Hempstead, New York [54]

Killenworth, George Dupont Pratt house, Glen Cove, New York [61–62]

Welwyn, Harold Irving Pratt house, Glen Cove, New York [59–60]

Drumthwacket, Moses Taylor Pyne house, Princeton, New Jersey [89–90]

Hampton, John Ridgley house, Towson, Maryland [217–218]

Black Point, Colonel Henry Huttleston Rogers Jr. house, Southampton,
   New York [74]

Arnold Schlaet house, Saugatuck, Connecticut [38–39]

Lyndhurst, Finley Johnson Shepard house, Tarrytown, New York

Gardenside, Frederick Augustus Snow house, Southampton, New York [75]

Claraben Court, Benjamin Stern house, Roslyn Harbor, New York [53]

Oakland Farm, Alfred Gwynne Vanderbilt house, Portsmouth, Rhode Island

The Breakers, Cornelius Vanderbilt II house, Newport, Rhode Island [3]

Beechwood, Frank Arthur Vanderlip house, Scarborough, New York

Brookside, William Hall Walker house, Great Barrington, Massachusetts [34-35]

Willowmere, Rear Admiral Aaron Ward house, Roslyn Harbor, New York
   [51–52]

Marshfield, George Woodward Wickersham house, Cedarhurst, New York [56]

The Dunes, Frank Bestow Wiborg house, East Hampton, New York

Wooldon Manor, Dr. Peter Brown Wyckoff house, Southampton, New York
   [71–72]

"California Gardens"

FBJ did not write lectures about gardens but spoke extemporaneously from notes. The only slides she numbered were ones produced for her presentation, "California Gardens," a virtual recreation of her 1917 tour from Los Angeles to San Franciso. After her 1923 western trip, Johnston added slides to this lecture. She did not number the additions.

By the time FBJ reached the Golden State in 1917, magazine writer Kennedy Porter Garnett (1871–1951) had published *Stately Homes of California* (1915). Johnston owned a copy of this photo-illustrated book, and its selection of early 20th-century estates likely influenced her choice of gardens to photograph. Houses by architects Bertram Grosvenor Goodhue, Myron Hunt, Francis Townsend Underhill (1863–1929), Lewis Parsons Hobart (1873–1954), and Willis Jefferson Polk (1867–1924), featured in the volume, are in her slide and print collections.

Johnston's California lantern slides are representative of garden developments. Shaded terraces, water rills, groves of cypress, and water quarries present emerging Spanish Revival and California interpretations of the Italian, French, and English period garden. Her lectures presented California Beautiful, as civilized as New York, Massachusetts, Maryland, and New Jersey.

What impressed audiences about the California gardens in Johnston slides was their sunny brilliance. Compared to the green coolness of John Ridgley's Hampton in Towson, Maryland, Santa Barbara gardens were riotous. FBJ told members of the Butler Art Institute in Youngstown, Ohio, that these colorful havens presented a challenge. Every gardener, she said, should "beautify some spot whether it be a spacious plot, a window box or geranium in a pot … Let us continue to plant these 'lumps of leaven' until we shall put California to shame."[1]

01: missing

02: missing

03: Myron Hunt house, Pasadena, view from porch to garden path (16000)

04: Mrs. Francis Lemoine Loring house, Pasadena, view to staircase landing (16103)

05: missing

06: Mrs. Francis Lemoine Loring house, staircase to bench (16078)

07: missing

08: Mrs. Francis Lemoine Loring house, staircase landing (16102)

09: Mrs. Francis Lemoine Loring house, flower garden (16001)

10: Mrs. Francis Lemoine Loring house, bougainvillea pergola from flower garden to house (16004)

11: Mrs. Eldridge Merick Fowler house, Pasadena, terrace wall (16002)

12: Mrs. Eldridge Merick Fowler house, fountain in flower garden (16077)

13: Mrs. Eldridge Merick Fowler house, terrace wall steps (16003)

14: missing

15: Mrs. Eldridge Merick Fowler house, wall fountain (16009)

16: Il Paradiso, Mrs. Dudley Peter Allen house, Pasadena, pergola (16015)

17: Il Paradiso, loggia (16014)

18: missing

19: John Constantine Hillman house, Pasadena, pergola porch (16082)

20: Michael Cochrane Armour house, Pasadena, lily pool (16013)

21: Michael Cochrane Armour house, native plant garden pathway (16012)

22: David Berry Gamble house, Pasadena, water terrace (16011)

23: "Mi Sueño," Herbert Coppell house, Pasadena, west terrace (16010)

24: "Mi Sueño," water rill (16107)

25: "Mi Sueño," view from dining room to reflecting pool (16023)

26: William Alexander Spinks Jr. ranch, Duarte, fish pond (16545)

27: William Alexander Spinks Jr. ranch, lily pool (16026)

28: William Alexander Spinks Jr. ranch, pathway (16027)

29: John Henry Fisher adobe, Redlands, water garden (16076)

30: John Henry Fisher adobe, entrance door (16108)

31: John Henry Fisher adobe, trophy room (16109)

32: John Henry Fisher adobe, outdoor kitchen (16096)

33: Kimberly Crest, John Alfred Kimberly house, Redlands, Italian garden (16016)

34: Drive with statice (*Limonium perezii*), probably Los Angeles (16025)

35: Missing

36: Santa Barbara Mission, Santa Barbara, fountain and entrance facade (16089)

37: Santa Barbara Mission, arcade (16024)

39: Glendessary, Robert Cameron Rogers house, Santa Barbara, walk from terrace to fountain (16007)

40: Glendessary, along the fountain walk (16093)

41: Glendessary, shaded terrace (16031)

42: Piranhurst, Henry Ernest Bothin house, Montecito, birdbath on walkway (16032)

43: Piranhurst, garden seat (16033)

44: Piranhurst, view to outdoor theater stage (16028)

45: Inellan, Walter Douglas house, Montecito, view from pergola overlooking the Pacific Ocean (16029)

47: Senuelo, Edward Ditmars Wetmore house, Montecito, pathway to rose garden (16030)

48: Senuelo, rose arbor (16954)

49: La Chiquita, Frances Townsend Underhill house, Montecito, view to Pacific Ocean (16062)

50: La Chiquita, view from house to live oaks (16061)

51: Inellan, Walter Douglas house, Montecito, garden facade (16060)

52: Inellan, porch (16059)

53: Inellan, service entrance (16104)

54: Inellan, pathway to Pacific Ocean (16057)

55: Glen Oaks, James Hobart Moore house, Montecito, rose garden (16056)

56: Glen Oaks, pyrethrum border (16055)

57: Solana, Frederick Forrest Peabody house, Montecito, terrace (16084)

58: Solana, view to interior courtyard (16054)

59: Solana, courtyard (16053)

60: Solana, service arcade (16052)

61: Arcady, George Owen Knapp house, Montecito, lower garden, pool house (16085)

62: Arcady, lower garden, view from swimming pool (16086)

63: Arcady, lower garden, indoor swimming pool at pool house (16075)

64: Arcady, lower garden, view to Santa Ynez mountains (16097)

65: Arcady, roses along pathway (16050)

66: Arcady, wall relief along pathway (16087)

67: missing

68: Arcady, lower garden, walkway to marble seat (16049)

[Figs. 35a, 35b, 35c] El Fureidis, James Waldron Gillespie House, Montecito, California, Bertram Grosvenor Goodhue, Landscape Architect, 1902–06, Reservoir, Italian Cypress, and Quarry Garden, Spring 1917. Three slides of a California estate as FBJ presented them in her lecture, "California Gardens."

69: Arcady, lower garden, marble seat at terminus (16111)

70: Probably Arcady, statice (*Limonium perezii*) along pathway (16048)

71: Casa de Mariposa, Walter Franklin Cobb house, Montecito, rock garden (16047)

72: Casa de Mariposa, garden gate (16046)

73: El Fureidis, James Waldron Gillespie house, Montecito, water terrace facade (16079)

74: El Fureidis, terrace with Pacific Ocean view (16092)

75: El Fureidis, interior court (16043)

76: El Fureidis, lily pool at terrace with Pacific Ocean view (16110)

77: El Fureidis, circular ornamental pool (16081)

78: El Fureidis, Banksia roses (*Rosa banksiae*) along terrace wall (16045)

79: El Fureidis, roses along wall (16044)

80: missing

81: El Fureidis, view from house to casino (16307)

82: El Fureidis, water terrace on stairs to casino (16042)

83: El Fureidis, stairs at water terrace (16080)

84: missing

85: El Fureidis, pergola and fountain (16040)

86: El Fureidis, reservoir (16039)

87: El Fureidis, Italian cypress (16038)

88: El Fureidis, quarry garden (16083)

89: El Fureidis, quarry garden (16088)

90: missing

91: James Kennedy Moffitt house, Piedmont, view from house arcade to water terrace (16035)

92: James Kennedy Moffitt house, view from house to water terrace (16034)

93: James Kennedy Moffitt house, steps from water terrace (16036)

94: Uplands, Charles Templeton Crocker house, Hillsborough, view to porte cochere terrace with herbaceous border (16106)

95: Uplands, view to porte cochere terrace across reflecting pool (16067)

96: Uplands, view to porte cochere terrace (16063)

97: Uplands, reflecting pool (16095)

98: Newmar, Senator George Almer Newhall house, Hillsborough, view from entrance to garden path (16066)

99: Newmar, view from house terrace (16065)

100: Newmar, house terrace (16073)

101: Newmar, rose garden (16094)

102: Newmar, exedra (16064)

103: Newmar, flower garden (16099)

104: Villa Rose, Joseph Donohoe Grant house, Hillsborough, garden gate (16017)

105: Villa Rose, exedra (16068)

106: Villa Rose, garden wall (16008)

107: Villa Rose, view from house library to swimming pool (16074)

108: Villa Rose, pool house (16018)

109: New Place, William Henry Crocker house, Hillsborough, reflecting pool (16072)

110: New Place, balustrade at end of reflecting pool (16019)

A Garden Book Library

Dear Mrs. Devore,

No doubt you have wondered at the mysterious appearance of Avray Tipping's "English Gardens" on your doorstep two or three weeks ago? I came across the book all wrapped up just as I brought it over from England last year, and I thought "what a shame someone cannot have the enjoyment of that book the weeks I am to be away!"[1]

FBJ posted this note to her soon-to-be patron after visiting Fredericksburg in fall 1926. The photo-illustrated book pictured British gardens that Americans were studying and touring. It was one among dozens of books published annually in the States and in Europe on every subject related to making a garden beautiful. American books were mostly by women for other women, many of whom did not plant their gardens but planned and decorated them with ornaments and furnishings. The garden memoir, the garden how-to manual, the garden color guide, the garden history, and garden poetry were standards of garden literature.[2]

In a period when Americans looked for refinement after what Matthew Arnold (1822–88) famously ridiculed as 19th-century philistinism, books were an assured measure of culture. By the 1920s, book collecting and publishing had so increased that intellectuals debated the difference between the true book collector, who read for content, and the book buyer, who collected for prestige.[3] Frances Benjamin Johnston was both.

Researching card catalogs of horticultural collections and knowing "the garden and flower shelf of every second-hand book store in the country," FBJ acquired several hundred period and contemporary books on garden design and history that informed her garden work.[4] She read the *Bulletin of The Garden Club of America,* particularly for book reviews, writing that "My gardens alas! (or fortunately as one chooses) are white paper gardens, for I am of the rare tribe of bookworms who finds immense satisfaction in reading what other gardeners write about gardens."[5] She strategically loaned her library to the New York Horticultural Society and sold titles to the New York Botanical Garden, prestige alliances she publicized in lectures and magazine interviews. She herself authored and self-published a small booklet on The White House with 36 photographs of its interiors and gardens.[6]

As landscape historian Diane Harris writes, books provided women planting advice and a nexus of community. Garden club members shared illustrated publications and displayed volumes at library exhibitions.[7] FBJ catered to this bibliophile world, speaking about books in her lectures and exhibiting them at the Georgetown Garden Club.[8] She recommended titles in newspaper interviews and exchanged bibliographies with collectors.[9] Noted Pittsburgh botanical book collector and Garden Club of America officer Rachel McMasters Miller Hunt (1882–1963) sent FBJ recommendations. FBJ in turn forwarded a garden catalog from London dealer Bernard Quaritch.[10] Ruth B. Dean, landscape architect and author, supplied FBJ her "List of Books on Landscape Architecture," which included both British and American titles.[11] Johnston befriended authors Amélie Rives Troubetzkoy (1863–1945), living at historic Castle Hill in Virginia, and Kate Doggett Boggs (1881–1950) in Fredericksburg.

The following list of 144 titles and eight catalogs, periodicals, and bulletins is from three sources: (1) the sale by Johnston in 1926 of 108 books to John Hendley Barnhart, bibliographer of the New York Botanical Garden; (2) a sale the same year of 10 books to Massachusetts estate gardener Mrs. Gordon "Katharine" Abbott; and (3) FBJ's catalog of books deposited by her at the Library of Congress in the 1940s, which comprised a portion of her final sale to the University of North Carolina in 1952 of 105 books, pamphlets, and journals that remained in her library.[12] This

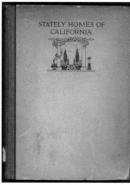

[Figs. 36a, 36b, 36c] Mrs. Leslie Williams, A Garden in the Suburbs *(1901)*, Cover; Porter Garnett, Stately Homes of California *(1915)*, Cover and Inside Cover with Frances Benjamin Johnston Bookplate. FBJ collected garden bulletins, magazines and illustrated volumes, both antiquarian and modern, that informed her garden lectures. She sold these two books to the New York Botanical Garden, Bronx, New York in 1926. They remain there today.

list represents only some of the garden books FBJ owned and does not include the over 100 titles on architecture she collected in the 1930s and 1940s. She gave away volumes, made incidental sales, and through her many moves no doubt lost titles.[13]

In its scope, Frances Benjamin Johnston's collection was the library of an educated amateur in the America garden era.

Adams, Henry Gardiner. *Flowers: Their Moral, Language, and Poetry*. London: H. G. Clarke, 1844. (3)

Agar, Madeline. *Garden Design in Theory & Practice*. Philadelphia: J. B. Lippincott, 1912. (1)

Aiken, James Richmond. *In a City Garden*. London: T. N. Foulis, 1913. (3)

Alcock, Randal Hibbert. *Botanical Names for English Readers*. London: E. Newman, 1876. (3)

Aldrich, Thomas Bailey. *The Shadow of the Flowers: From the Poems of Thomas Bailey Aldrich*. Boston: Houghton Mifflin, 1912. (3)

The American Rose Annual (1916–22). (3)

Angier, Belle Sumner. *The Garden Book of California*. San Francisco: Paul Elder, 1906. (1)

Arber, Agnes Robertson. *Herbals: Their Origin and Evolution: A Chapter in the History of Botany, 1417–1670*. Cambridge: Cambridge University Press, 1912. (1)

Archiv für naturgeschichte. Berlin: Nicolai, 1835–1911. (3)

Averill, Mary. *The Flower Art of Japan*. London: John Lane, 1915. (1)

Bacon, Francis. *Of Gardens: An Essay* (1625). London: John Lane, 1902. (3)

Bassett, Mary E. Stone. *Judith's Garden*. Boston: Lothrop, 1902, 1910. (1)

Beals, Katharine McMillan. *Flower Lore & Legend*. New York: Henry Holt, 1917. (1)

Blanchan, Neltje. *The American Flower Garden*. New York: Doubleday, Page, 1909. (2)

———. *The American Flower Garden*. New York: Doubleday, Page, 1913. (3)

———. *Nature's Garden: An Aid to Knowledge of Our Wild Flowers and the Insect Visitors*. New York: Doubleday, Page, 1905. (3)

Blomfield, Sir Reginald Theodore, and F. Inigo Thomas. *The Formal Garden in England*. London: Macmillan, 1892. (3)

Boggs, Kate Doggett. *Prints and Plants of Old Gardens*. Richmond, Va.: Garrett & Massie, 1932. (3)

Bonnier, Gaston Eugène Bonnier. *Name This Flower: A Simple Way to Find a Name…*. London: J. A. Dent & Sons, 1917, 1936. (3)

Botanique de la Jeunesse, avec trente planches contenant les principes de la botanique et cent deux plantes. Paris: Delaunay, 1812. (1)

Boyle, Eleanor Vere. *A Garden of Pleasure*. Boston: Roberts Brothers, 1895. (3)

———. *Seven Gardens and a Palace*. London: John Lane, 1900. (3)

Bradley, William Aspenwall. *The Garden Muse: Poems for Garden Lovers*. New York: Sturgis & Walton, 1910. (3)

Brewster, Kate L. *The Little Garden for Little Money*. Boston: Atlantic Monthly Press, 1924. (3)

Brown, Stewardson. *Alpine Flora of the Canadian Rocky Mountains*. New York: G. P. Putnam's Sons, 1907. (3)

Brown, Mary Elizabeth. *Joy in Gardens*. New York: Privately printed for Mrs. J. C. Brown by Stercks-Miller Press, 1914. (3)

Buchanan, Emily Handasyde. *The Four Gardens*. London: G. T. Foulis, 1924. (3)

Bulletin of The Garden Club of America (1913–32). (3)

Cable, George Washington. *The Amateur Garden*. New York: Charles Scribner's Sons, 1914. (3)

Carnegie Institute Catalogue, [unidentified]. (3)

Castle, Agnes, and Egerton Castle. *Our Sentimental Garden*. Illustrated by Charles Robinson. Philadelphia: J. B. Lippincott, 1914. (1)

Cecil, Mrs. Evelyn. *Children's Gardens*. London: Macmillan, 1902. (3)

Chappell, Marion. *Gardening Don'ts*. New York: Charles Scribner's Sons, 1913. (1)

———. *More Gardening Don'ts*. New York: Charles Scribner's Sons, 1914. (1)

Clay, John Cecil. *In Love's Garden: A Human Nature Book*. Indianapolis: Bobbs-Merrill, 1904. (3)

Clutton-Brock, Arthur, and Mrs. Francis King. *Studies in Gardening*. New York: Charles Scribner's Sons, 1916. (2 and 3)

Coan, Clarence Arthur. *The Fragrant Notebook: Romance and Legend of the Flower Garden and the Bye-Way*. New York: G. P. Putnam's Sons, 1917. (3)

Coles, Rosemary E. A. *Bible Flowers*. London: Methuen, 1904. (3)

Coley, May, and Charles Alfred Weatherby. *Wild Flower Preservation: A Collector's Guide*. New York: Frederick A. Stokes, 1915. (1)

Coville, Frederick Vernon. *The Formation of Leafmold*. Washington, D.C.: Washington Academy of Sciences, 1913. (3)

Crisp, Sir Frank. *Mediaeval Gardens, "Flowery Medes" and Other Arrangements of Herbs, Flowers, and Shrubs Grown in the Middle Ages: With Some Account of Tudor, Elizabethan, and Stuart Gardens*. London: John Lane, 1924. (3)

Crofton, Helen Rose Anne Milman. *In the Garden of Peace*. London: John Lane, 1896. (3)

Curtis, Charles Henry. *The Book of Topiary*. London: John Lane, 1914. (3)

Curtis, William. *The Botanical Magazine, or, Flower-Garden Displayed*. London: Fry & Couchman, 1787, 1800. (1)

———. *Lectures on Botany, as Delivered to His Pupils*, vol. 3. London: William Phillips, 1803, 1804. (3)

Davidson, K. L. *Gardens Past and Present*. London: T. W. Laurie, 1908. (3)

Downing, Andrew Jackson. *Landscape Gardening: A Treatise on the Theory and Practice of Landscape Gardening* (1844). New York: J. Wiley & Sons, 1921. (1)

Drummond, James Lawson. *First Steps to Botany*. London: Longman, Hurst, Rees, Orme, Brown & Green, 1823. (1)

Du Cane, Florence. *Flowers and Gardens of Madeira*. London: A. & C. Black, 1909. (3)

——— and Ella Du Cane. *The Flowers and Gardens of Japan*. London: A. & C. Black, 1908. (3)

Durand, Herbert. *Taming the Wildings: A Book of Cultural Information for Lovers of Our Wildflowers, Wild Bushes, and Ferns, Who Desire to Grow Them for Landscape and Garden Effects or for Planting … Where They Can Be Protected from Their Foes*. New York: G. P. Putnam's Sons, 1923. (3)

Duryea, Minga Pope. *Gardens in and about Town*. New York: E. P. Dutton, 1923. (3)

Earle, Alice Morse. *Old-Time Gardens*. New York: Macmillan, 1901. (3)

———. *Sun Dials and Roses of Yesterday: Garden Delights Which Are Here Displayed in Very Truth and Are Moreover Regarded as Emblems*. New York: Macmillan, 1902. (3)

Earle, Marie Theresa Villiers. *More Pot-Pourri from a Surrey Garden*. London: Smith, Elder & Company, 1899. (1)

———. *Pot-Pourri from a Surrey Garden*, London: Smith, Elder, 1897. (3)

Edward, Agnes Edwards (Agnes Rothery). *A Garden Rosary*. Boston: Houghton Mifflin, 1917. (1)

Eliot, Charles William. *Charles Eliot, Landscape Architect: A Lover of Nature and of His Kind Who Trained Himself for a New Profession Practised It Happily and Through It Wrought Much Good*. Boston: Houghton Mifflin, 1902. (2,3)

Ellwanger, George Herman. *The Garden's Story, or Pleasures and Trials of an Amateur Gardener*. New York: D. Appleton, 1889. (1)

Ely, Helena Rutherfurd. *A Woman's Hardy Garden, with Illustrations from Photographs Taken in the Author's Garden by Prof. C. F. Chandler*. New York: Macmillan, 1903. (1)

The Famous Parks and Gardens of the World Described and Illustrated. London: T. Nelson & Sons, 1880. (3)

Flowers, Their Language, Poetry, and Sentiment, with Choicest Extracts from Poets, a Dictionary of the Sentiment of Every Flower, Botanical Descriptions, &c. Philadelphia: Porter & Coates, 1870. (1)

Friend, Rev. Hilderic. *Flowers and Flower Lore*. London: W. S. Sonnenschein, 1884. (1)

Garden Club of Virginia. *Descriptive Guide Book of Virginia's Old Gardens*. Richmond, Va.: J. W. Fergusson & Sons, 1929. (3)

Garden Guide: The Amateur Gardener's Handbook. New York: A. T. De La Mare, circa 1920. (1)

Garnett, Porter. *Stately Homes of California*. Boston: Little, Brown, 1915. (1)

Gerard, John. *The Herball, or General Historie of Plants, Gathered by John Girard … Very Much Enlarged and Amended by Thomas Johnson*. London: Printed by Adam Islip, Joice Norton and Richard Whitakers, 1633. Bookplate of George Ghering Marshall. (1)[14]

Gibson, William Hamilton, and Helena Dewey Leeming Jelliffe. *Our Native Orchids: A Series of Drawings from Nature of All the Species Found in the Northeastern United States*. New York: Doubleday, Page, 1905. (3)

Going, Maud. *With the Wild Flowers from Pussy-Willow to Thistledown: A Rural Chronicle of Our Flower Friends and Foes, Describing Them under Their Familiar English Names, by E. M. Hardinge [pseud.]*. New York: Baker & Taylor, 1901. (1)

Gotthilf, Heinrich von Shubert. *Naturgeschichte des pflanzenreichs nach dem Linneschen System*. Stuttgart: J. F. Schreiber, [1887]. (1)

Gray, Asa. *Gray's School and Field Book of Botany*. New York: Ivison, Blakeman, Taylor, 1881. (1)

Haines, Jennie Day. *Ye Gardeyn Boke: A Collection of Quotations Instructive & Sentimental*. San Francisco: Paul Elder, 1906. (3)

Hale, Sarah Josepha Buell. *Flora's Interpreter, and, Fortuna Flora*. Boston: Sanborn, Carter, Bazin, circa 1848. (1)

Harper, William Warner. *Andorra Hand-book of Trees & Shrubs.* Chestnut Hill, Pennsylvania: Andorra Nurseries, 1903.

Hibberd, Shirley. *Familiar Garden Flowers*, vol. 2. London: Cassell, Petter, Galpin, 1883. (1)

Hodge, Clifton Fremont. *Nature Study and Life.* London and Boston: Ginn & Company and the Atheneum Press, 1902. (3)

Hole, Samuel Reynold. *A Book about the Garden and the Gardener.* 2nd ed. London: E. Arnold, 1892. (1)

Hubbard, Henry Vincent, and Theodora Kimball. *An Introduction to the Study of Landscape Design.* New York: Macmillan, 1916. (2,3)

The Illustrated Dictionary of Gardening: A Practical and Scientific Encyclopaedia of Horticulture for Gardeners and Botanists. Edited by George Nicholson, assisted by J. W. H. Trail. 8 vols. London : L. Upcott Gill; New York: Sole agent for the U.S. and Canada, J. Penman, 1887–89. (1)

Jäger, Hermann. *Gartenkunst und Gärten Sonst und Jetzt: Handbüch für Gärten, Architeckten und Liebhaber.* Berlin: P. Parey, 1888. (1)

Jekyll, Gertrude. *Annuals & Biennials: The Best Annual and Biennial Plants and Their Uses in the Garden.* London: Offices of "Country Life," 1916. (1)

———. *Home and Garden: Notes and Thoughts, Practical and Critical, of a Worker in Both.* London: Longmans, Green, 1900 or 1901. (1)

Johnson, George William. *A Dictionary of Modern Gardening.* Philadelphia: Lea & Blanchard, 1847. (1)

Johnson, Louisa. *Every Lady Her Own Flower Gardener.* New Haven, Conn.: S. Babcock, 1842; or New York: C. M. Saxton, 1852. (1)

Journal of the International Garden Club 1, no. 1 (August 1917); 3, no. 2. (June 1919). (3)

Karr, Jean-Baptiste Alphonse. *Tour around My Garden.* London: George Routledge, 1855 or 1865. (1)

Keeler, Harriet Louise. *Our Early Wild Flowers: A Study of the Herbaceous Plants Blooming in Early Spring in the Northern States.* New York: Charles Scribner's Sons, 1916. (1)

———. *Our Garden Flowers: A Popular Study of Their Life Histories, and Their Structural Affiliations.* New York: Charles Scribner's Sons, 1910. (1)

———. *Our Native Trees and How to Identify Them: A Popular Study of Their Habits and Their Peculiarities.* New York: Charles Scribner's Sons, 1929. (1)

Kemp, Edward. *How to Lay Out a Garden: Intended as a General Guide in Choosing, Forming or Improving an Estate.* New York: Wiley & Halsted, 1858. (1)

King, Mrs. Francis. *The Little Garden.* Boston: Atlantic Monthly Press, 1921. (2,3)

———. *Pages from a Garden Notebook.* New York: Charles Scribner's Sons, 1921. (1)

———. *The Well-Considered Garden.* New York: Charles Scribner's Sons, 1915. (2)

The Lady's Book of Flowers and Poetry, to Which Are Added, a Botanical Introduction, a Complete Floral Dictionary; and a Chapter on Plants in Rooms. Edited by Lucy Hooper. New York: J. C. Riker, 1842. (1)

The Language & Poetry of Flowers. London: M. Ward, 1875. (1)

Lomas, Charlotte. *Garden Whimseys.* New York: Macmillan, 1923. (1)

Loudon, Jane. *Gardening for Ladies, and, Companion to the Flower Garden.* New York: John Wiley, 1855. (1)

Loudon, John Claudius. *Encyclopaedia of Gardening Comprising the Theory & Practice of Horticulture, Floriculture, Arboriculture, and Landscape-Gardening.* London: Longman, Hurst, Rees, Orme & Brown, 1830. (1)

Lounsberry, Alice. *A Guide to the Wild Flowers.* New York: Frederick A. Stokes, 1899. (3)

MacCartney, Mervyn E., et al. *English Houses and Gardens in the Seventeenth and Eighteenth Centuries….* London: B. T. Batsford, 1908. (3)

Maeterlinck, Maurice. *Old Fashioned Flowers, and Other Out-of-Door Studies.* New York: Dodd, Mead, 1905. (1)

Marble, Annie Russell. *Nature Pictures by American Poets.* London and New York: Macmillan, 1899. (3)

Matthews, F. Schuyler. *Field Book of American Wildflowers….* New York: G. P. Putnam's Sons, 1902. (3)

Miller, Thomas. *The Poetical Language of Flowers, or, The Pilgrimage of Love.* New York: J. C. Riker, 1848. (1)

Mitchell, Donald Grant. *Wet Days at Edgewood, with Old Farmers, Old Gardeners, and Old Pastorals.* New York: Charles Scribner, 1865. (1)

Moore, Frank Frankfort. *A Garden of Peace.* New York: George H. Doran, 1920. (1)

Moore, N. Hudson. *Flower Fables and Fancies.* New York: Frederick A. Stokes, 1904. (1)

Neuhaus, Karl Eugen. *The San Diego Garden Fair: Personal Impressions of the Architecture, Sculpture, Horticulture, Color Scheme and Other Aesthetic Aspects of the Panama-California Exposition.* San Francisco: Paul Elder, 1916. (1)

Nichols, Rose Standish. *English Pleasure Gardens.* New York: Macmillan, 1902. (3)

———. *Italian Pleasure Gardens.* New York: Dodd, Mead, 1931. (3)

Olmsted, Frederick Law. *Walks and Talks of an American Farmer in England*, vols. 1 and 2. New York: G. P. Putnam, 1852. (1)

O'Neill, George Henry. *Messages of Flowers or Their Floral Code and Dictionary.* Brooklyn, N.Y.: George H. O'Neill, 1917. (1)

Osborn, Charles Francis. *The Family House.* Philadelphia, The Penn Publishing Company, 1910. (3)

Parsons, Frances Theodora. *According to Season: Talks about the Flowers in the Order of Their Appearance In the Woods and Fields by Mrs. William Starr Dana.* New York: Charles Scribner's Sons, 1894. (1)

Perry, Elizabeth Williams. *Studies of a Plant Lover.* Cincinnati: Ebbert & Richardson, 1921. (1)

Phillpotts, Eden. *My Garden.* London: Charles Scribner's Sons, 1906. (2)

Pine, John Buckley. *The Story of Gramercy Park.* New York: Gramercy Park Association, 1921. (1)

Price, Sir Uvedale. *An Essay on the Picturesque, as Compared with the Sublime and the Beautiful,* vols. 1 and 2. London: Printed for J. Robson, 1794; and Herford: Printed by D. Walker for J. Robson, 1798. With the bookplate of William Bennet Martin. (1)

Rehmann, Elsa. *The Small Place: Its Landscape Architecture.* New York: B. P. Putnam's Sons, 1918. (2)

Roberts, Harry. *The Chronicle of a Cornish Garden.* London: John Lane, 1901. (1)

Robinson, William. *The Wild Garden, or Our Groves and Gardens….* London: Garden Office; and New York: Scribner & Welford, 1881. (1)

Rogers, William Snow. *Garden Planning.* Garden City, N.Y.: Doubleday, Page & Company, 1911. (1)

Root, Ralph Rodney. *Design in Landscape Gardening.* New York: Century, 1914. (1)

Saunders, Frederick. *Salad for the Solitary, by an Epicure.* New York: Lamport, Blakeman & Law, 1853. (1)

Sedgwick, Mabel Cabot with Robert Cameron. *The Garden Month by Month; Describing the Appearance, Color, Dates of Bloom and Cultivation of All Desirable, Hardy Plants for the Formal or Wild Garden, with Additional Lists of Aquatics, Vines, etc.* New York: Frederick. A. Stokes, 1907. (2)

Shand, Alexander Innes. *Memories of Gardens: With a Memoir by the Right Hon. Sir Rowland Blennerhassett Bart LL.D.* London: West Strand, 1908. (1)

Shelton, Louise. *Continuous Bloom in America: Where, When, What, to Plant, with Other Gardening Suggestions.* New York: Charles Scribner's Sons, 1915. (1)

———. *The Seasons in a Flower Garden: A Handbook of Information and Instruction.* New York: Charles Scribner's Sons, 1906, 1907, 1926. (1)

Shoberl, Frederic. *The Language of Flowers.* London; Carey, Lea & Blanchard, 1843, 1835, 1839. (1)

Simson, Alfred. *Garden Mosaics, Philosophical, Moral and Horticultural.* New York: D. Appleton and Company, 1903. (1)

Skinner, Charles M. *Little Gardens; How to Beautify City Yards and Small Country Spaces.* New York; D. Appleton and Company, 1904. (1)

———. *Nature in a City Yard: Some Rambling Dissertations Thereupon.* New York: The Century Company, 1897. (1)

Stowe: A Description of the Magnificent House and Gardens of the Right Honourable George Grenville Nugent-Temple, Marquis of Buckingham. London: Printed by J. Seeley, 1797. (1)

Stowe: A Description of the Magnificent House and Gardens of the Right Honourable George Grenville Nugent-Temple, Marquis of Buckingham. London, Calkin and Budd, 1838. (1)

Tabor, Grace. *Making a Bulb Garden.* New York: McBride, Nast & Company, 1912. (1)

———. *Making a Garden to Bloom This Year.* New York: McBride, Nast & Company, 1912. (1)

———. *Making the Grounds Attractive with Shrubbery.* New York: McBride, Nast & Company. 1912. (1)

———. *Suburban Gardens.* New York: Outing Publishing Company, 1913. (1)

Thonger, Charles. *Book of Garden Design.* London: John Lane, 1905. (1)

Van Rensselaer, Mrs. Schuyler. *Art Out-of-Doors: Hints on Good Taste In Gardening.* New York: Charles Scribner's Sons, 1893 or 1925. (2)

Vick, James. *Vick's Flower and Vegetable Garden.* Rochester, N.Y.: E. R. Andrews, n.d. (1)

Wade, Blanche Elizabeth. *A Garden in Pink.* Chicago: A. C. McClurg, 1905. (1)

Warner, Charles Dudley. *My Summer in a Garden.* Boston and New York: Houghton Mifflin & Company, 1871, 1872, or 1898. (1)

Wheeler, Candace. *Content in a Garden.* Boston and New York: Houghton Mifflin & Company, 1901. (1)

Wilder, Louise Beebe. *My Garden.* Garden City, N.Y.: Doubleday, Page & Company, 1916. (2)

Williams, Leslie. *A Garden in the Suburbs.* London: John Lane , 1901. (1)

Wilson, Mary G. W. *Garden Memories.* Edinburgh: T.N. Foulis, 1918. (3) Wirt, Elizabeth Washington. *Flora's Dictionary, by a Lady.* Baltimore: Fielding Lucas, Jr., 1832. (1)

Wright, Mabel Osgood. *Garden of a Commuter's Wife.* New York: The Macmillan Company, 1901. (1)

Wright, Walter Page. *Alpine Flowers and Rock Gardens Illustrated in Color: With Notes on "Alpine Plants at Home" by William Graveson.* New York: Frederick A. Stokes, 1911. (1)

———. *An Illustrated Encyclopaedia of Gardening.* London: J. M. Dent; New York: E. P. Dutton, 1932. (1)

Endnotes

Introduction

Epigraph: "Miss Johnston is a lady…," Theodore Roosevelt, 1899. FBJ, determined to photograph Admiral George Dewey, went to Sagamore Hill, Roosevelt's country house in Oyster Bay, New York, to secure his endorsement. The then governor of New York wrote this message on her calling card. LOCFBJ reel 24.

1. Marion Cran, *Gardens in America* (New York: Macmillan, 1932), 201.

2. For Royal Cortissoz and Mary Rutherford Jay, FBJ press release "Letters from Garden and Women's Clubs" [circa 1925], 5, LOCFBJ reel 32.

3. Letter from FBJ to The Librarian, Library of Congress, January 1, 1930, LOCFBJ reel 11. Though FBJ left most of her photographs at the Library of Congress as she moved from Washington, D.C., to New Orleans in the 1940s, her will was not explicit about the bequest. Consequently, the library purchased most of its Johnston photographs and slides from her estate in 1953.

4. *Ambassadors of Progress*, edited by Bronwyn A. E. Griffith (Washington, D.C.: Musée d'Art Américain Giverny, France, in Association with the Library of Congress, 2001); Maria Elizabeth Ausherman, *The Photographic Legacy of Frances Benjamin Johnston* (Gainesville: University Press of Florida, 2009); and Bettina Berch, *The Woman behind the Lens* (Charlottesville: University of Virginia Press, 2000) are contemporary studies of FBJ providing extensive bibliographies of writings relating to her career. I am indebted to all three for their perspectives.

5. Garden and landscape lantern slides are found throughout American archives. Substantial collections, with slides by Frances Benjamin Johnston and other photographers, are: American Architectural and Landscape Design, 1850–1920, Frances Loeb Library at the Harvard University Graduate School of Design, Cambridge, Massachusetts; Beatrix Jones Farrand and Mary Rutherford Jay collections, Environmental Design Archives, University of California, Berkeley; Martha Brookes Brown Hutcheson Collection, Fosterfields Living Historical Farm, Morris County Park Commission, Morristown, New Jersey; Warren H. Manning Architectural Landscape Lantern-Slide Collection, Digital Collections, Iowa State University, Ames; Frank A. Waugh Papers, Special Collections and University Archives, W. E. B. Du Bois Library, University of Massachusetts, Amherst; Fletcher Steele Lantern-Slide Collection, F. Franklin Moon Library, SUNY College, Environmental Science and Forestry, Syracuse, New York; Bradford Williams Collection, author's collection, Los Angeles. The Smithsonian Institution's extensive Archives of American Gardens collection includes 35mm copies of lantern slides from the Library of Congress' Frances Benjamin Johnston slide collection, donated as part of The Garden Club of America Collection. These copies, made circa 1985, are intended for study purposes only, not reproduction.

6. For this use of "garden" and "landscape," see Robin Karson, *A Genius for Place* (Amherst: University of Massachusetts Press, 2007), x, citing Warren Henry Manning as influential in her definitions.

7. Frances Benjamin Johnston, "Memorandum F.B.J." [circa 1925], LOCFBJ reel 32.

A Garden Photographer

Epigraph: "I know my chief assets…," FBJ, "Notes, February 20, 1936," LOCFBJ reel 21.

1. Nancy Burncoat, "Burncoat's Letter," *Worcester Sunday Telegram*, January 26, 1923, and "Garden Lore and Flower Legend," *Lexington Lender*, May 2, 1920, LOCFBJ reel 29.

2. "Anderson D. Johnston, Dead," *Washington Post*, December 19, 1906.

3. Walter Benjamin, "Paris: Capital of the Nineteenth Century" (1935), in *Reflections, Essays, Aphorisms, Autobiographical Writings*, edited by Peter Demetz (New York: Harcourt, Brace, Jovanovich, 1978).

4. Catherine Fehrer, "A New Light on the Académie Julian and Its Founder (Rodolphe Julian)," *Gazette des Beaux-Arts* 6, no. 103 (1984): 207–16.

5. H. Barbara Weinberg, *The Lure of Paris: Nineteenth-Century American Painters and Their French Teachers* (New York: Abbeville Press, 1991), 221–81.

6. "For Informal Talk by Frances Benjamin Johnston at the Quota Club dinner, February 20th, 1938," LOCFBJ reel 21.

7. Elizabeth Sylvester was the daughter of early *Washington Post* political columnist Major Richard H. Sylvester (1830–95), an editor in the 1880s of *Art in Advertising* and in the 1890s of the illustrated literary magazine *Truth*. "Maj. Sylvester Dead," *Washington Post*, September 2, 1895; "Christmas Issue of Truth," *Washington Post*, December 16, 1859.

8. "Speaking of Pictures…These Are by a U.S. 'Court Photographer,'" *Life* 26, no. 17 (April 25, 1949): 13 and notes from the interview for this profile, "Parker, Research on Frances Benjamin Johnston," March 11, 1949, LOCFBJ reel 16. FBJ varied this story throughout her life, sustaining the basic premise. Another version was, "Send me one of your little shadow boxes." Maud O'Bryan Ronstrom, "60 Years with a 'Shadow Box,'" *The Times-Picayune New Orleans States Magazine*, November 2, 1947.

9. The story of Eastman and Hagan is based on letters kept by George Eastman, now in his archive at Eastman House, Rochester, New York. Elizabeth Brayer, *George Eastman: A Biography* (Baltimore: Johns Hopkins University Press, 1994), 61–66.

10. For a history of the house, see Paul Kelsey Williams, "Scenes from the Past…," *The InTowner* (October 2003): 12.

11. [Leonard Barron], "Garden Photography as a Fine Art," *The Garden Magazine* 38, no. 4 (December 1923): 205.

12. Eben E. Rexford, "Inside of a Score of Gardens," *The Ladies' Home Journal* 16, no. 3 (February 1899): 18.

13. Sidney Allen [Carl Sadakichi Hartmann], "Color and Texture in Photography," *Camera Notes* 4, no. 1 (July 1900): 11. The photograph of Miss Neith Boyce Hapgood is LOCFBJphot Lot 11735, LC-USZ62-85579. Hartmann noted that a kimono photograph by Albert Herter, later a garden client of FBJ, was more poetic.

14. For FBJ and the exposition, see *Ambassadors of Progress: American Women Photographers in Paris*, edited by Bronwyn A. E. Griffith (Giverny: Musée d'Art in association with the Library of Congress, 2001).

15. Ibid., 27.

16. Lewis Mumford, *The City in History: Its Origins, Its Transformations, and Its Prospects* (New York: Harcourt, 1961), 446.

17. For these schools, see Thaïsa Way, *Women and Landscape Architecture in the Early Twentieth Century* (Charlottesville: University of Virginia Press, 2009), 109–26.

18. Anne Fior Scott, *Natural Allies: Women's Associations in American History* (Chicago: University of Illinois Press, 1992), 80.

19. *Country Life in America Index* I (November 1901 to April 1902): title page.

20. Wilhelm Miller, "The Talk of the Office," *The Garden Magazine* 1, no. 1 (January 1901): 5. Liberty Hyde Bailey brought Wilhelm Miller, later a proponent of native Prairie planting, to *Country Life in America* as horticultural editor. Christopher Vernon, "Wilhelm Miller and the Prairie Spirit in Landscape Gardening," in *Regional Garden Design in the United States*, edited by Therese O'Malley and Marc Treib (Washington, D.C.: Dumbarton Oaks Research Library and Collection, 1995), 271–72.

21. In 1901 *Country Life in America* at the newsstand was 35 cents per single copy; in 1915, 50 cents, which it remained until ceasing publication in 1942; *The Garden Magazine* was first 10 cents; from 1915, 15 cents until it was *Garden and Home Builder* in 1924; *The House Beautiful*, founded in 1896, was 25 cents, with a run of 45,000, circulation rising to 100,000 by 1930. *House & Garden*, founded in 1901 by architects Frank Miles Day, Wilson Eyre, and Herbert C. Wise in Philadelphia, was the same price. After Condé Nast purchased the title in 1915, *House & Garden* circulation rose from 10,000 to 100,000 by 1926. Its editor from 1914 until 1950 was Richardson Little Wright, the author of three books on gardening and a judge at flower shows and photography contests. *The Craftsman* magazine in 1915, then at its peak, printed 22,500 copies and charged 25 cents per copy.

In contrast to house magazines, *The Ladies' Home Journal* in 1915 was 15 cents a copy with a circulation of 1.6 million. *The Saturday Evening Post* was 5 cents, with a circulation over 2 million. Cyrus H. Curtis owned both publications.

For garden magazine history, see *The Once & Future Gardener*, edited and with introduction by Virginia Tuttle Clayton (Boston: Richard R. Godine, 2000), xi–xxxi, and Leland M. Roth, "Getting the Houses to the People," *Perspectives in Vernacular Architecture* 4 (1991): 187.

22. Charles F. Lummis, "The Greatest California Patio House," *Country Life in America* 6, no. 6 (October 1904): 533–40.

23. See FBJ diary entries, October 7 and 20, 1903, LOCFBJ reel 1. On October 21, FBJ went with Charles F. Lummis to the Glenwood Mission Inn, Riverside, where she lunched with its founder, Frank Augustus Miller. The photographs of the inn and its gardens from this meeting are in the LOCFBJphot Lot 11729-4.

24. Class in the context of publications was a code for Protestant. Henry J. Whigham, editor of *Town & Country,* for whom Johnston worked in the 1920s, distinguished his magazine as a "class paper." Unlike larger-circulation magazines, it did not have to appeal to "the masses," but to "a small and discriminating circle of readers." H. J. Whigham "XLII: H. J. Whigham, Editor, Town and Country," Doris Ulmann, *A Portrait Gallery of American Editor* (New York: William Edwin Rudge, 1925), 170. Professional journals *The American Architect* and *The Architectural Record* published architectural series by FBJ that included gardens.

25. Alice Boughton worked in both art photography and direct styles. Pictorialist Clara E. Sipprell (1885–1975) photographed gardens, interiors, and landscapes, and had her work reproduced in house and garden magazines. Diana Gaston, "Picturing Domestic Space: Clara E. Sipprell and the American Arts and Crafts Movement," *Image* 38, nos. 3–4 (Fall–Winter 1995): 16–29.

26. Mattie Edwards Hewitt studied at the St. Louis School of Fine Arts before turning to photography. "I never thought in my youth of a professional career … I just lived the usual home and social life till suddenly I found my accustomed world dissolving and a new one rising up in which I had to support myself," she explained to a reporter in 1923. Hewitt divorced her husband Arthur Hewitt in 1909 and moved to New York. "The Camera Has Opened a New Profession for Women—Some of Those Who Have Made Good," *New York Times,* April 20, 1913; "Mrs. Hewitt, Photographer of Homes," *Christian Science Monitor,* December 22, 1923; Leslie Rose Close, *Portrait of an Era in Landscape Architecture: The Photographs of Mattie Edwards Hewitt,* exhibition catalog, New York, Wave Hill, September 15–November 30, 1983. See also notes 45 and 88 below. For FBJ and Mattie Edward's Hewitt relationship, see Bettina Burch, *The Woman behind the Lens* (Charlottesville: University of Virginia Press, 2000), 80–89.

27. Similarly, the garden photographer Ella M. Boult and illustrator Beatrice Stevens (1876–1947) lived together at Brisk-to-High at Pomfret, Connecticut. "Some People You Must Know Write and Picture Garden—and Other Things," *Country Life in America* 33, no. 11 (March 1919): 54–55. For photographing the house of Elsie de Wolfe, Miss Impertinence, "They Photograph the Smart Set," *Vanity Fair* 69, no. 1218 (December 14, 1912): 18.

28. New York City Phone Directories, 1909–17.

29. In a letter to Frederick Law Olmsted Jr., June 5, 1909, FBJ wrote: "There is a possibility that I shall be in Brookline [Massachusetts] a little later on to do some natural color (autochrome) and architectural photography for private individuals and for publication and I am writing back if you have any thing in mind you might care to have me undertake. I have had a deal of success with the autochrome plates and I trust you will recall my work through my connection with the Park Commission plans etc." Johnston had photographed in 1904 Olmsted Brothers' plans for the MacMillan Commission. The Larz Anderson and Charles Sprague Sargent gardens are the only Brookline estates in FBJ lantern-slide and print collections. Newspapers reported that FBJ photographed Faulkner Farm, owned by Charles Franklin Sprague. LOCOA reel 131.

30. Miss Impertinence, "The Photograph," 18. A letter from Thomas W. A. Harper to FBJ, February 4, 1907, recommending houses in Pittsburgh FBJ could photograph suggests a date she decided to "specialize." LOCFBJ reel 1.

31. Thaïsa Way, *Unbounded Practice,* 30–31.

32. *Bulletin of The Garden Club of America* published this mission statement at the introduction to each issue.

33. *Bulletin of The Garden Club of America* 1 [n.d., Summer 1913]: n.p. [1]; "History of The Garden Club of America," *Garden Club of America Almanac* (1930): 78.

34. Helen S. Thorne, "A Perfect Interpretation of the Meaning of The Garden Club of America," n.d. [1931], Archives of The Garden Club of America, New York.

35. Dominique Bauron, "Transition of the Club," August 2003, n.p.; and Barbara H. Lord, *Brief History of the Southampton Garden Club, 1912–1980* (Southampton, N.Y.: Southampton Garden Club, August 28, 2002), both in the Archives of The Garden Club of America, New York. Individual members paid $50 ($1,160 in 2011) annual dues to the Southampton club in 1912. In 1921 the annual dues paid by the club to The Garden Club of America were $80 ($975). Consumer Price Index, Measuringworth.com.

36. The autochrome plate, coated with granules of starch, colored automatically when exposed to light. For FBJ's early garden autochromes, see here note 29 and interview in "Newest Portraits Are Color-Photo Transparencies." *The Evening Sun,* New York, October 28, 1912, LOCFBJ reel 29. FBJ began working with the process by 1905. See invoice, the Lumière Company, 11 West 27th Street, New York, for "Autochrome, Plates and Chemicals," April 14, 1905, and invoice dated May 1, 1908, LOCFBJ reel 21.

37. Letter from Thomas Shields Clarke, June 10, 1915, in *Bulletin of The Garden Club of America* 9 (July 1915). Clarke published his autochromes of his Berkshire and Florida gardens in "Color Studies in My Gardens," *The New Country Life* 36, no. 4 (August 1919): 25–27.

38. "The Garden Lovers," promotional brochure, n.d. [1916 or 1917], LOCFBJ reel 33.

39. FBJ recounted in an interview that after making autochromes for "a number of clubs" she presented them at their request. Given the difficulty of projecting the dense, dark plates, more easily viewed with a diascope or light box, Johnston converted, circa 1915, to hand-painted slides shown with commercial projectors. For this change, see Katherine Cole, "Lecturer-Photographer Discusses Experiences,"

South Bend Tribune, March 18, 1923, LOCFBJ reel 29. Additional considerations may have been that Lumière autochromes were developed in Paris and difficult to reproduce in print, conditions limiting sales.

Landscape architect, photographer, and Garden Club of America lecturer on old New England gardens Loring Underwood (1874–1930) projected autochromes by building a custom projector and requesting that clubs pay for its shipment and a trained projectionist. "Loring Underwood," *Landscape Architecture* 20, no. 3 (April 1930): 232. For his photographs, see *Gentlemen Photographers: The Work of Loring Underwood and Wm. Lyman Underwood*, edited by Robert Lyons (Florence, Mass.: The Solio Foundation, 1987).

40. An advertisement by Johnston-Hewitt in *Bulletin of The Garden Club of America* 17 (November 1916): n.p., states that the partners had "150 slides of many notable estates and gardens shown successfully at Lenox at the annual meeting of The Garden Club of America." The meeting was in June 1916.

Georgina Bonner Boardman was on the national Garden Club of America committee that collected Lumière plates of member gardens for the exhibition. Given her association with Johnston and Hewitt, their autochromes were certainly among those exhibited. *Bulletin of The Garden Club of America* 7 (January 1915): n.p.

41. "The Talk of the Office," *The New Country Life* 31, no. 9 (January 1917): 16-d.

42. The article was by the decorator of the sunroom, Agnes Rowe Fairman, "Furnishing and Decorating the Summer House," *The New Country Life* 32, no. 1 (May 1917): 36, 37, 47.

43. Louise Shelton, *Beautiful Gardens in America* (New York: Charles Scribner's Sons, 1915): frontispiece, flower garden, Thomas J. Emery house, Newport, Rhode Island, and plate 5, Dr. Peter B. Wyckoff flower garden, Southampton, New York. The colored slides from these autochromes are LC-DIG-ppmsca-16801 and 16563.

44. "The Photograph," 18.

45. *Indenture*, dated March 1, 1917, between France Benjamin Johnston and Mattie Edwards Hewitt. By an oral agreement they had formed a partnership about November 1913. Hewitt agreed to pay FBJ $500 ($8,500 in 2011) to dissolve the partnership and delivered to her "the garden lectures in color and all the garden slides; a choice of the autochrome plates remaining in the firms files; a selected set of garden prints for record; The 5 by 7 outfit-camera, lenses, plate holders, kits and tripod used for making lantern slides; And upon the agreement that the said FBJ shall have access to the firm's files at any future time for the use of garden negatives from which to make new slides; And upon further agreement that MEH guarantees FBJ that no garden slides shall be made from the Johnston–Hewitt files for the use of any other person or firm than the said FBJ;" signed March 12, 1917. LOCFBJ reel 22; Consumer Price Index, Measuringworth.com.

Mattie Edwards Hewitt left her archive to her nephew, architecture and garden photographer Richard Averill Smith (1897–1971). When he died, the Nassau County Museum, Roslyn Harbor, New York, received Hewitt's 12,000 prints and negatives. Nassau dispersed the collection to museums and historical societies by city and state, retaining photographs of Long Island and Connecticut houses and gardens.

Institutions receiving Hewitt photographs accessioned them as by Mattie Edwards Hewitt, though some have the Johnston–Hewitt Studio stamp. To catalog the Library of Congress lantern slides, I created an inventory of relevant Hewitt photographs.

46. FBJ listed her profession as "Photographer lecturer writer" in her U.S. federal tax returns. Her income, from photography, an inheritance from 1930, and rental income, was $4,798.00 (1923) ($61,300 in 2011); $3,355.00 (1927) ($42,100); $2,794.00 (1928) ($35,600); $2,973.00 (1929) ($37,800); and $1,948.00 in 1930 ($25,400) due to high expenses at the beginning of her work with the Library of Congress' Pictorial Archives of Early American Architecture project. In 1933, the first year of funding from the Carnegie Survey of the Architecture of the South, her income was $3,196.10 ($53,800). In 1930 inheritance income was about $1,700 ($22,800). Income Taxes, LOCFBJ reel 22 and letter from FBJ to John Jay Edson, Washington Loan and Trust Company, August 12, 1931, LOCFBJ reel 10. Consumer Price Index, Measuringworth.com.

FBJ's photography charges varied depending on commission and user. *Town & Country* editor Henry J. Whigham wrote FBJ, October 4, 1929, LOCFBJ reel 11: "There are no hard and fast rules for costs of photographs, but generally speaking, where a set of photographs has been made either for the architect or for the owners and we have a chance to buy them afterwards, our invariable habit is to pay $5 a print. The best photographers in New York like [Hendrick] Duryea, Mrs. Hewitt, Gottscho, etc., are willing to deal with us on that basis. I have always made rather a special price for you, partly because I like the quality of your work and partly because you are always kind enough to give us first choice." To bulb supplier John Scheepers Inc., April 1926, FBJ charged for six plates, two prints each, $35 ($431 in 2011), LOCFBJ reel 9; the same year she received $75 to $85 ($924 to $1,050) per series, usually four to five print photographs, published by *Town & Country*. FBJ to Augusta Owen Patterson, July 20, 1926, LOCFBJ reel 9. Consumer Price Index, Measuringworth.com.

47. For a humorous account of FBJ's travel necessities, see "Notes Made While Packing to Leave for the U.S.A.," LOCFBJ reel 29.

48. The last recorded date for FBJ photographing in autochrome is 1917, when the process itself was fading in art photography circles. See invoice to Mrs. A. C. James,

Beacon Hill House, Newport, August 25, 1917, for 10 autochromes @ $35 ($595 in 2011) each, LOCFBJ reel 21. Consumer Price Index, Measuringworth.com. See here "Gardens of the Old World," p. 351, note 15.

49. Vera Norwood, *Made from This Earth: American Woman and Nature* (Chapel Hill: University of North Carolina Press, 1993), 119.

50. Lucy Page Stelle, "Frances Benjamin Johnston," *Harper's Bazar* 29, no. 14 (April 4, 1896): 309.

51. Regarding the benefits of her European photographs at the Ferargil Gallery and in *Town & Country*, FBJ wrote, "so gradually I am getting a return on my investment." FBJ to Mrs. Nesbitt, March 30, 1926, LOCFBJ reel 9.

52. Letter from FBJ to Mr. [Leonard] Barron, October 14, 1923, LOCFBJ reel 9.

53. For the complexities of status and photography with the rise of the published photograph, see Michele H. Bogart, *Artists, Advertising and the Borders of Art* (Chicago: University of Chicago Press, 1995), 15–78, 171–77. Architectural photography had critical acceptance by 1900. For this history, see Richard Pare, *Photography and Architecture, 1839–1939* (Montreal: Canadian Centre for Architecture, 1982). The enduring prestige of building photography as allied to architecture is reflected in Helmut Gernsheim, *Focus on Architecture and Sculpture: An Original Approach to the Photography of Architecture and Sculpture* (London: Fountain Press, 1949), and Robert C. Cleveland, *Architectural Photography of Houses* (New York: F. W. Dodge, 1953), both written before FBJ's death in 1952, with no comparable book on garden photography published in the same period.

54. *Careers for Women*, edited by Catherine Filene (Boston: Houghton Mifflin, 1920), ix–x. "Arts and Crafts" included direct color photography [autochrome], wood carving, stage design, sculpture, and miniature painting, a discipline associated with lantern-slide painting. Landscape design as a profession for women fared better, as it was identified with architecture, itself a fine art. Oil painting and music composition, on the other hand, were not professions for women.

55. *American Landscape Architecture*, edited by P. H. Elwood Jr. (New York: Paul Wenzel & Maurice Krakow, 1924), vii. Unidentified FBJ photographs are of the California gardens of Wellington S. Morse (1923), 63, and John L. Severance (1923), 64, and the Arthur C. James Blue Garden long pool (1914), 111.

56. The Thorne photograph was reproduced in the *Official Program, Thirteenth Annual International Flower Show*, March 15–20, 1926, conducted by the Horticultural Society of New York and the New York Florists' Club, 133. The photograph credit, to Frances Benjamin Johnston, notes, "First Prize in a recent competition held by The Garden Club of America for the Best Photograph of a Garden Vista." FBJ supplied three other photographs to the program and likely wrote the captions that included poetry. For the award, see *Bulletin of The Garden Club of America* 4, 3rd series (July 1925): 30 and 33.

57. Review of "Beautiful Gardens in America," *Landscape Architecture* 15, no. 3 (April 1925): 218. Shelton was exceptional for her acknowledgment of photographs in both her 1915 and 1924 editions. Why she credited owners and photographers is not known, though it was common practice for garden club publications to acknowledge garden owners, not landscape architects. Possibly, in exchange for credit, the photographers loaned their pictures without charge. There are no invoices in the LOCFBJ archive for Johnston's contributions to the book.

58. Jeanne M. Gamble, *Surroundings of Inspiration: The Progressive Era through the Lens of Mary H. Northend, 1904–1926*. Unpublished master's thesis, Harvard University, 2008. Northend, an upper-class New Englander, had to make a living to support herself and possibly her single mother and siblings. She employed from one to three photographers in a business that succeeded with the New England Colonial Revival.

59. John Wallace Gillies trained as a civil and electrical engineer at Columbia University. He worked in landscape architecture with photography as a hobby before it was his profession. For Emil Brunel's New York Institute for Photography, founded in 1910, with branches in Brooklyn and Chicago, he wrote *Principles of Pictorial Photography* (New York: Falk, 1923) in line with the art photography movement. Gillies was among the most published first-generation house and garden photographers, competing with Mattie Edwards Hewitt for East Coast assignments. See "John W. Gillies Dead," *New York Times*, February 1, 1927.

60. Pamela Hartford, "Poet behind the Lens," *View*, no. 10 (Summer 2010): 25–27.

61. Gabriel Moulin, from age 12 in 1884, learned to photograph as an apprentice in the San Francisco studio of Isaiah West Tabor (1830–1912). Like Johnston, he found early success with the Lumière process, making prints he sold as official photographer of the 1915 Panama-Pacific International Exposition. Unlike Johnston, he meticulously controlled the printing of his photographs and did not lecture. Donald DeNevi and Thomas Moulin, *Gabriel Moulin's San Francisco Peninsula, Town & Country Homes 1910–1920* (Sausalito, Calif.: Windgate Press, 1985), ix–x.

62. Samuel Henry Gottscho acquired his first camera in 1896 and went on to photograph architecture, houses, and gardens. He wrote *A Pocket Guide to Wild Flowers: How to Identify and Enjoy Them* (New York: Washington Square Press, 1951). Obituary, *Camera* 51 (March 1971): 54.

63. Carla Conrad Freeman, "Visual Media in Education: An Informal History," *Visual Resources* 6 (1990): 327–40. Howard B. Leighton, "The Lantern Slide and Art History," *History of Photography* 8, no. 2 (April–June 1984): 107–19.

64. Fees ranged from $25 ($272 in 2011) for landscape architect Elsa Rehmann (1886–1946), sister of garden photographer Antoinette R. Perrett, to $100 ($1,090 in

2011) for birdsong concerts by Mrs. Edward Avis. For lecture prices by FBJ and her competition, see "The Garden Club of America's List of Lecturers," *Bulletin of The Garden Club of America* 4, new series (May 1920): 60–62; "A Circular Letter," March 22, 1922, LOCFBJ reel 21; letter from FBJ to Mrs. A. D. Taylor, May 15, 1926, LOCFBJ reel 9. Consumer Price Index, Measuringworth.com.

65. "Famous Gardens Are to Be Shown," *Post-Star*, Glen Falls, New York, March 6, 1917, LOCFBJ reel 29.

66. For strata of wealth and class, see Frederic Cople Jahr, *The Urban Establishment: Upper Strata in Boston, New York, Charleston, Chicago, and Los Angeles* (Urbana: University of Illinois Press, 1982).

67. Charles Moore, "Coöperation in All the Arts," *Landscape Architecture* 20, no. 4 (July 1930): 277.

68. "Garden Photography as a Fine Art: Illustrated by Rare Photographs of Beautiful Gardens," *The Touchstone* 2, no. 3 (December 1917): 278.

69. Though John Ruskin's influence was waning among intellectuals by the end of the 19th century, his aesthetic theories and late socialism still appealed to progressives. See Roger B. Stein, *John Ruskin and Aesthetic Thought in America, 1840–1900* (Cambridge, Mass.: Harvard University Press, 1967). The countervailing, emerging definition of beauty was beauty for beauty's sake. Charles Adams Platt was an early leader of "art for art" in garden design. Keith N. Morgan, *Charles A. Platt: The Artist as Architect* (Cambridge, Mass.: MIT Press, 1985), 44–45.

70. John Ruskin, *Modern Painters*, vol. 1 (London: Smith Elder, 1848, 4th edition), 25.

71. Andrew Jackson Downing, "Hints to Rural Improvers," *The Horticulturist and Journal of Rural Art and Rural Taste* 3, no. 1 (July 1848): 11.

72. Charles Eliot, "Landscape Gardening in Its Relations to Architecture," paper delivered to the Boston Society of Architecture, October 2, 1891, in Charles W. Eliot, *Charles Eliot, Landscape Architect* (Amherst: University of Massachusetts Press, 1999, reprint of 1902 edition), 366.

73. As quoted in "Exterior of Home Is Public Property," *St. Joseph Gazette*, Missouri, April 23, 1924, LOCFBJ reel 29.

74. Frances Benjamin Johnston, "The Gardens of a Garden Spot," *Santa Barbara Community Life* 1, no. 9 (September 1923): 4.

75. For lectures, see "A List of Garden Lectures," n.d. [circa 1940], compiled by FBJ from her diaries and archives, LOCFBJ reel 28. FBJ, press release, December 9, 1920, LOCFBJ reel 9.

76. Competing lectures with 50–100 slides included Beatrix J. Farrand, "Problems in Garden Design"; J. Horace McFarland, "American Roses and Other Roses"; Miss Rosalie E. Zimmerman, "On Famous Gardens" and "American Gardens." From "The Garden Club of America's List of Lecturers," 60–62. In the 1920s, Mary H. Northend offered lectures on "The Small House and Garden" and "Famous Gardens of Noted People." Gamble, *Surroundings of Inspiration*, 52.

77. "With a personality of great charm, a thorough grasp of her subject, a memory which permits her to cover all her topics practically without notes, and finally gifted with a saving sense of humor, Miss Johnston's success as a lecturer has been little short of phenomenal." FBJ was a juror on the International Jury of Awards. FBJ, "Miss Frances Benjamin Johnston," press release n.d. [circa 1923], LOCFBJ reel 32; G. A. Lyon, "'They Do Things Better in France,'" *Washington Life* 4, no. 7 (February 18, 1905).

78. Loretta Lorden, "'Small Garden' Is Subject of Illustrated Talk," *South Bend News*, Indiana, March 18, 1923, LOCFBJ reel 29.

79. Burncoat, "Burncoat's Letter."

80. "The Garden Spot," 1.

81. Frances Benjamin Johnston, "Gardens in City Environment," *New York Sun*, December 19, 1922, LOCFBJ reel 29.

82. "Newport, First of Series of Red Cross Benefits Big Success," *Providence Journal*, July 11, 1917. At a program organized by landscape architect Bryant Fleming to bring attention to the "wonderful development of gardens," at the Albright Art Gallery and Guild of Allied Arts in Buffalo, New York, Johnston showed "The Pageantry of Gardens" in slides and a poet and musician presented "The Poetry of Gardens." "Art Gallery to Have Garden Conference," *Buffalo Express*, May 4, 1920, LOCFBJ reel 29.

83. FBJ took the photographs intending to sell them to *Country Life in America*, knowing that its publisher, Doubleday Page & Company, published Rudyard Kipling in America. "Groups of Photographs submitted to Country Life, Shipped prepaid, Am. Railway, Jan. 23, 1926," LOCFBJ reel 28. Five of the Blue Garden series of originally 10 or 11 are in the Library of Congress, LOCFBJ-phot Lot 12641-1. Earlier Johnston had combined poetry and photography for her photo–verse pictorial of Thomas Buchanan Read's popular 1864 "Sheridan's Ride"; see FBJ, "The Country of Sheridan's Ride," *The Ladies' Home Journal* 18, no. 8 (July 1901): 16–17.

84. FBJ to the Friday Morning Club, Los Angeles, reported in Myrna Nye, "Federation of Clubs to Meet," *Los Angeles Times*, April 29, 1923.

85. In 1921 FBJ "had been spending some weeks in the libraries and laboratories of the Department in furthering work in the dissemination of information familiarizing the public, through writings, photographs and lectures with a knowledge of the wild flowers of the United States." Letter from Susan Hunter Walker, U.S. Department of Agriculture Library, to Harlan Smith, Director of Information, June 2, 1921, LOCFBJ reel 8.

Edgar T. Wherry and FBJ shared a program at the New York Botanical Garden in September 1921; he lectured on "How to Grow Wild Flowers," and she spoke about "the most beautiful gardens in this country, among them those of wealthy women belonging to famous gardens clubs." The *New York Times*, August 28, 1921; and *Journal of the New York Botanical Garden* 22, no, 259 (September 1921): 140. Albert C. Burrage exhibited FBJ's garden photographs at the Boston Horticultural Society, Horticulture Hall, December 1929, and she photographed his native flower exhibition at the hall, 1921. See here p. 26, fig. 14, and p. 290.

86. There are no bird slides in the FBJ slide collection. Johnston likely borrowed slides from the Museum of Natural History, New York, where her colorist, Grace S. Anderson, was an ornithological slide colorist and where FBJ lectured. For FBJ considering billboard removal as "propaganda" in her lectures, see letter FBJ to Mrs. W. L. Lawton, March 1930, LOCFBJ reel 9.

87. Jessie C. Glasier, "Women to Hear Talk on Gardens," *Cleveland Plain Dealer*, March 27, 1921, LOCFBJ reel 29.

88. Elizabeth Lounsbery, "The Art in Garden Photography," *The Garden Magazine* 40, no. 1 (September 1924): 50.

89. Barron, "Garden Photography," 205.

90. Smoking was a prerogative of men that Johnston self-consciously used for self-portraits as a New Woman. Dolores Mitchell, "Women as Prometheus: Women Artists Depict Women Smoking," *Women's Art Journal* 12, no. 1 (Spring–Summer 1991): 3–9.

91. For this tradition, see John Tomsich, *A Genteel Endeavor: American Culture and Politics in the Gilded Age* (Stanford, Calif.: Stanford University Press, 1971); Howard Mumford Jones, *The Age of Energy: Varieties of American Experience, 1865–1915* (New York: Viking, 1971).

92. Mark Twain, "Private History of a Manuscript that Came to Grief" (1899), in *Autobiography of Mark Twain*, edited by Harriet Elinor Smith et al., vol. 1 (Berkeley: University of California Press, 2010), 164.

93. In addition to making their portraits, FBJ worked as a photographer with Ida M. Tarbell when she was an editor at *McClure's* in the 1890s and photographed the Theodore Roosevelt family for Jacob A. Riis, "Mrs. Roosevelt and Her Children," *The Ladies' Home Journal* 19, no. 7 (July 1902): 5–6. This article was followed by a photo portfolio, "President Roosevelt's Children," no. 8 (August 1902): 18–19. For FBJ's account of this assignment and Theodore Roosevelt's permission, see Burncoat, "Burncoat's Letter."

94. In her garden brochure "Miss Frances Benjamin Announces . . ." [1921], FBJ introduced herself as "a charter member of Mary Washington Chapter, D.A.R.," LOCFBJ reel 33.

95. FBJ, "In Yesterday's Gardens," Introduction, [1926], LOCFBJ reel 21.

96. Ibid.

97. Ronstrom, "60 Years with a 'Shadow Box.'"

The Garden Photograph

Epigraph: "There is more to photography…," FBJ, "Memorandum F.B.J.," 1922, LOCFBJ reel 32.

1. Charles A. Platt was at the academy from 1884 through the fall of 1885. Erika E. Hirshler, "The Paintings of Charles A. Platt," Keith Morgan, *Shaping an American Landscape: The Art and Architecture of Charles A. Platt* (Hanover, N.H.: University Press of New England, 1995), 61, 63.

2. Charles Percier and Pierre Fontaine, *Choix des plus célèbres maisons de plaisance de Rome et de ses environs* (Paris: Didot, 1809). Platt's illustrated essays on Italian gardens first appeared in *Harper's New Monthly Magazine*, July 1893 and August 1893.

3. Charles Adams Platt, *Italian Gardens*, with an overview by Keith Morgan (Portland, Ore.: Sagapress/Timber Press, 1993 reprint of 1894 edition), 15. For Platt's photography sources, including Fratelli Alinari and Edizoni Brogi, see 104–11.

4. FBJ knew Charles Dudley Arnold (1844–1927), the official photographer of the Chicago World's Fair. His high-view, utopian visions of the exposition's buildings and waterways clearly influenced Johnston's own photographs of the fair. Precedents for Arnold and Johnston's work date to 1840s city documentary photography. For this history and the fair photography, see Peter Bacon Hales, *Silver Cities: Photographing American Urbanization* (Albuquerque: University of New Mexico Press, 2005).

5. For Charles A. Platt and his varied uses and understanding of the photograph, see Morgan, *Shaping an American Landscape*, 5-6, 31–49, and passim. In France, from the 1890s, Jean-Eugène-Auguste Atget (1857–1927) documented French parks and palaces in an artistic, on-the-ground style similar to Platt's. Photographer Berenice Abbott (1898–1991) brought these photographs to the attention of American viewers after his death.

6. FBJ photographed Mount Vernon in 1894 with the support of Phoebe A. Hearst, the first regent from California to the Mount Vernon Ladies' Association. See letter from Hearst to FBJ, March 9, 1894, LOCFBJ reel 1. For the South Lawn photographs, see lantern slides LC-DIG-ppmsca-21852 and 21855. For related views, see Hon. Benjamin Harrison, "The Domestic Side of the White House," *The Ladies' Home Journal* 15, no. 6 (May 1897): 7, and FBJ, "The New Tenants of

the White House," *The Ladies' Home Journal* 14, no. 11 (October 1897): 3, photo essay with photographs "Taken by Frances Benjamin Johnston Especially for the Journal." Captions are not credited but were likely written by FBJ. A view from a second-floor bedroom to the north garden, characteristic of the elevated city view, notes that it was the first "taken from this point of observation." For this view, see digital image "White House garden," cph 3c27422 or print LC-USZ62-127422.

7. Letter from Henry J. Whigham to FBJ, October 20, 1928, LOCFBJ reel 9.

8. "I like you [Fred Holland Day] as a juror—but Miss Johnston! And even Troth." Letter from Stieglitz to Day, March 31, 1899, quoted in Estelle Jussim, *Slave to Beauty: The Eccentric Life and Controversial Career of F. Holland Day, Photographer, Publisher, Aesthete* (Boston: David R. Godine 1981), 137.

9. Joseph T. Keiley, "The Philadelphia Salon—Its Origin and Influence," *Camera Notes* 2 (January 1899): 130.

10. For Troth's photographs, see "Harvesting," *Country Life in America* 1, no. 2 (December 1901): 50–51. Two amateur women photographers won second and fourth prizes, for a road through woods and a duck farm; see p. 59. For McFarland, see "Country Life Photographs," 53. To professionalize submissions, the magazine turned to big-game photographer Arthur Radclyffe Dugmore (1870–1955). In eight columns on how to photograph out-of-doors, he followed established genres, "Landscape and Marine," "Flowers," "Clouds," and the general subject of "Illustrating by photography." See "The Amateur Photographer," *Country Life in America* 7, no. 3 (March 1907): 568.

11. For the struggle of photographers to be both artists and commercial professionals, see Sarah Greenough, "'Of Charming Glens, Graceful Glades, and Frowning Cliff': The Economic Incentives, Social Inducements, and Aesthetic Issues of American Pictorial Photography, 1880–1902," *Photography in Nineteenth-Century America*, edited by Martha A. Sandweiss (New York: Harry Abrams, 1991), 258–81.

12. P. H. Emerson, *Naturalist Photography for the Student of Art* (New York: Scovill & Adams, 1899), 12.

13. For landscape photography and nature, see Christian A. Peterson, *Peter Henry Emerson and American Naturalistic Photography* (Minneapolis: Minneapolis Art Institute, 2008).

14. Jessie Tarbox Beals, "The Garden Photographer," *Careers for Women*, edited by Catherine Filene (Boston: Houghton Mifflin, 1920), 63–66. Similarly, "Home and Garden Portraiture," *The Photo Miniature* 15, no. 174 (May 1919), provided instruction for photographing house owners and their children in houses and gardens.

15. Lucy Page Steele, "Frances Benjamin Johnston, Expert Photographer," *Harper's Bazar* 29, no. 14 (April 4, 1896): 309.

16. The autochrome, a version of the print, was reproduced in black and white in "Newest Portraits Are Color-Photo Transparencies," *Evening Sun*, New York, October 28, 1912. FBJ took the black-and-white print photograph with a Kodak fitted with a Zeiss Protar lens stopped to f/32 slow shutter. See Eva Vom Baur, "Frances Benjamin Johnston, Mattie Edwards Hewitt," *Wilson's Photographic Magazine* 50, no. 6 (June 1913): 252. I thank Candace Vanderlip for searching for the Vanderlip autochrome in family archives, regrettably with no success.

17. John C. Van Dyke, *How to Judge of a Picture: Familiar Talks in the Gallery with Uncritical Lovers of Art* (New York: Chautauqua Press, 1889), 95.

18. Sadakichi Hartmann, *Landscape and Figure Composition* (New York: Baker Taylor, 1912), 29. John Wallace Gillies, "The Significance of Design in Picture Making," *The Photo-Miniature* 15, no. 176 (September 1919): 330–52. Though he practiced in a direct style when photographing houses and gardens for magazines, John Wallace Gillies used Pictorialist photographs, definably artistic, to illustrate his instructional manuals.

19. Maud O'Bryan Ronstrom, "60 Years with a 'Shadow Box,'" *Times-Picayune New Orleans States Magazine*, November 2, 1947.

20. "Garden Photography as a Fine Art: Illustrated by Rare Photographs of Beautiful Gardens," *The Touchstone* 2, no. 3 (December 1917): 278–80. A print of the Hill photograph is in LOCFBJphot Lot 12637-6, and the equivalent slide is LC-DIG-ppmsca-16858. For further commentary on garden photography, see "A Garden of Everlasting Beauty," *The Touchstone* 1, no. 4 (August 1917): 359–63, with photographs by Carole Greiger of the Farquhar Ferguson estate in Huntington, New York.

Photographers and editors agreed on what made a professional garden photograph. When Elizabeth Lounsbery profiled Mattie Edwards Hewitt, she wrote: "The most interesting phase of garden photography, Mrs. Hewitt finds, is composition … and that because photographs were only black and white and the beauty of the garden is color, the spirit of the garden must be introduced as a substitute and the photograph be made to tell a story, if it's it to be a really beautiful garden picture." Elizabeth Lounsbery, "The Art in Garden Photography," *The Garden Magazine and Home Builder* 50, no. 1 (September 1924): 30.

21. For the history of the pictorial view of nature and its influence in landscape design, see Gina Crandell, *Nature Pictorialized: "The View" in Landscape History* (Baltimore: Johns Hopkins University Press, 1993), and the review of this book by Marc Treib in *Journal of Garden History* 13, no. 1 (Spring 1995): 55–57, noting that composition, rather than pictorial convention, is the determinant in two- and three-dimensional form. In contrast to her citing literary sources, FBJ did not compare her photographs to known paintings, speaking about them in compositional terms only.

22. FBJ produced slides of 11 landscape plans from *Monograph of the Work of Charles*

Adams Platt (New York: Architectural Book Publishing, 1913), the greatest number by an architect in her slide collection. The only slides of Platt's garden work are of the Larz Anderson house, Brookline, Massachusetts. For Platt, pictures, and garden design, see Rebecca Warren Davidson, "Charles A. Platt and the Fine Art of Landscape Design," in Morgan, *Shaping an American Landscape*, 75–76. Also, see here "A Garden Photographer," p. 339, note 29.

23. Liberty Hyde Bailey, "What Are the Fundamental Concepts in Landscape Gardening?" *Park and Cemetery* 7, no. 10 (December 1897): 226.

24. In 1908 and 1909, Waugh curated shows of "Landscape Photographs" at the Wilder Hall of the Massachusetts Agricultural Hall for the Department of Landscape Gardening, including works by Charles Vandervelde, C. F. Clarke, William T. Knox, J. Horace McFarland Co., Miss Fedora E. D. Brown, and Waugh himself. These photographs have not been identified, but their titles suggest they incorporated both artistic landscape photographs and instructional images, including "Spirea Walk, Brookline, Mass." and "Avenue of White Pines, Wellesley, Mass." by McFarland (1908). See "Salon" programs in the Frank A. Waugh Papers, Ms. FS 88, Special Collections and University Archives, University of Massachusetts, Amherst.

Waugh's advocacy and presentation of photographs in his program was exceptional. The registers for Harvard's landscape architecture program, from its founding in 1900 through 1915, when Johnston established her practice, make no reference to photography as a medium of representation or as a course offering. Similarly, the landscape architecture program at Cornell University, founded in 1904, did not offer photography courses in its first two decades. Programs in both schools used lantern slides.

The photograph as a mechanical tool—and not art—limited its academic reception. An English educator wrote: "As to the camera *v.* sketching, the student might easily be led to devote too much time to the camera and too little to the pencil." Photography was too facile when the general principle in education was "la nécessité de rendre l'étude difficile" ("the necessity to make study difficult"). Francis R. Taylor, "Photography for Architects," *The Builder* 85, no. 2176 (December 12, 1903): 599–602. Similarly, at Harvard, this Beaux-Arts approach prevailed, with students receiving instruction in drawing from the university's fine-arts and museum departments through the 1920s.

Waugh wrote FBJ about acquiring work after seeing her photographs at the 1926 International Flower Show Thirteenth Annual International Flower Show, March 15–20, 1926. Today no photographs by FBJ have been identified in the Frank A. Waugh papers.

Letter from Waugh to John Young, International Flower Show, March 30, 1926.

"In the official catalogue of the recent New York flower show there were some very excellent photographs made by Mrs. Francis B. Johnston…. I would like to get copies of these pictures for our use here [Amherst];" letter from FBJ to Frank Waugh, April 6, 1926, LOCFBJ reel 9. For the photographs, see "Official Program, Thirteenth Annual International Flower Show," March 15–20, 1926, conducted by the Horticultural Society of New York and the New York Florists' Club.

25. Frank A. Waugh, *Book of Landscape Gardening* (Amherst: University of Massachusetts Press, 2007, reprint of 1926 edition), 3.

26. Frank A. Waugh, "Photographic Diversions of a Landscape Architect," *Photo-Era Magazine* 47, no. 1 (July–December 1921): 27. Landscape photographs by the author illustrated this article.

27. Ibid., 26–27.

28. Henry Vincent Hubbard and Theodora Kimball, *An Introduction to the Study of Landscape Design* (New York: Macmillan, 1917), vii.

29. Ibid., 128.

30. Similarly, "Of course we prefer to have photographs of complete estates rather than simply the gardens where the estates are worth doing but you can use your own judgment in every instance." Letter from Augusta Owen Patterson, *Town & Country*, July 17, 1926, to FBJ. See also letter from Fletcher Steele to FBJ, September 24, 1924, re. photography of John H. Towne garden, Mount Kisco, New York, LOCFBJ reel 9. Small landscaped the Franklin A. Delano house, Washington, D.C., designed by Waddy B. Wood, that FBJ photographed in 1927. Letter from John S. Small to FBJ, April 18, 1928, LOCFBJ reel 10.

31. Advances in lens design at the turn of the century made possible undistorted, wide-view garden photographs. In 1866 German lens maker Carl Zeiss hired Ernst Abbe to manufacture instruments to scientific standards. In 1880 he hired Otto Schott to develop glass. They established Jena Glassworks in Jena, Germany, and by 1886 had 44 types of glass. In 1890 Paul Rudolf at Carl Zeiss Jena produced the Protar series, made with high-index crown lenses. Emil van Höegh at Goerz from 1892 produced the Dagor. These new lenses permitted extended and flat-field images without the astigmatism of earlier glass. Johnston used throughout her career 8- by 10–inch, 11- by 14–inch, and 5- by 7–inch (for lantern slides) view cameras. Her changeable lenses were Zeiss Protar series V and Goerz Dagor series III for wide-angle shots and Zeiss Protar Series VIIA for long focus. For specific f-stop settings, length of exposure, and lenses used by FBJ in garden and architecture photographs, see Eva Vom Baur, "Frances Benjamin Johnston," 241–54. For FBJ's recommendation of lens and camera outfit, see FBJ, "What a Woman Can Do with a Camera," *The Ladies' Home Journal* 14, no. 10 (September 1897): 6. For lens development, see Gregory Hallock Smith, *Camera Lens: From Box Camera*

to Digital (Bellingham, Wash.: SPIE Press, 2006), 128–34, 139–47. For the anastigmatic lens as necessary for lantern slides, see Frank A. Waugh, "Photographing for Lantern Slides," [unidentified journal], Frank A. Waugh Papers, 190–93.

32. Letter from Beatrix J. Farrand to FBJ, April 14, 1920, LOCFBJ reel 9.

33. Hildegarde Hawthorne, "Color in California," *The Touchstone* 8, no. 4 (January 1921): 287.

34. Rose Greely, "What Is a Garden?" *The House Beautiful* 62, no. 4 (October 1927): 389.

35. Eloise Roorbach, "Creating Atmosphere in the Gardens: Illustrated by a Japanese Half-Acre in California," *The Craftsman* 24, no. 6 (September 1913): 568.

36. Unpublished essay by Frances Benjamin Johnston, "In Yesterday's Garden," 17, LOCFBJ reel 23.

37. Letter from Cornelia J. Hagan to FBJ about relative Mabel Fishback's visit, undated [December 1917], LOCFBJ reel 2.

38. FBJ applied stars and dots in different colors to slide borders, sometimes together, to indicate multiple uses for images. There is no lexicon for slide groupings in the LOCFBJ.

39. For critical implications of the multiplicity of the camera view in altering the picture aesthetic that dominated garden discussions at the time, see *Landscape Design and the Experience of Motion*, edited by Michel Conan (Washington, D.C.: Dumbarton Oaks Research Library and Collections, 2003).

40. Though likely unknown to FBJ, who is not documented to have studied lantern-slide history or presentation, already in the 1890s Charles-Émile Reynaud (1844–1918) in Paris was exploring the potential of lantern slides to produce sequential action with hand-painted and hand-drawn sequences on film strips shown with lantern projectors. See Laurent Manoni and Donata Presenti Campagnoni, *Lanterne magique et film peint* (Paris: Editions de la Martinère, 2009), 245–68.

41. Louise Shelton, *Beautiful Gardens in America* (New York: Charles Scribner's Sons, 1915), xv. For the garden photograph and book design, see Mark Treib, "Frame, Moment and Sequence: The Photographic Book and the Designed Landscape," *Journal of Garden History* 15, no. 2 (Summer 1995): 126–34.

42. Lary May, *Screening Out the Past: The Birth of Mass Culture and the Motion Picture Industry* (Chicago: University of Chicago Press, 1983), 163–66. "Garden Movies" launched in January 1919. For the evolved version with film sprocket design, see "Garden Movies No. 5," *The Garden Magazine* 16, no. 1 (January 1920): 181.

43. FBJ, "Moving Pictures in Color," LOCFBJ reel 32. See also letter from Herbert T. Kalmis, President Technicolor Motion Picture Company, to FBJ, July 6, 1924, LOCFBJ reel 9.

44. Helen S. Thorne, "A Flower Show Garden," *Bulletin of The Garden Club of America* 13 (January 1927): 37.

45. After seeing autochromes of her house Munstead Wood, likely by Herbert Wood, gardening editor of the English *Country Life*, published by the magazine in 1912, Gertrude Jekyll thought color photography had not reached "a degree of precision and accuracy as can do justice to a careful scheme of colour groupings." "A Border of Irises and Lupines," *The Garden* 76 (December 21, 1912): 639, as quoted in Judith B. Tankard and Martin A. Wood, *Gertrude Jekyll at Munstead Wood* (Sagaponack, N.Y.: Sagapress, 1996), 56. See also Judith B. Tankard and Michael R. Van Valkenburgh, *Gertrude Jekyll: A Vision of Garden and Wood* (New York: Harry N. Abrams/Sagapress, 1988).

46. Louise Beebe Wilder, *Colour in My Garden* (Garden City, N.Y.: Doubleday, Page, 1918), title page.

47. [Leonard Barron], "Garden Photography as a Fine Art," *The Garden Magazine* 38, no. 4 (December 1923): 205.

48. Marion Bowen, "Pioneer Camera Expert Selects Residence Here," *Hollywood Daily Citizen*, June 1923, LOCFBJ reel 29.

49. Until 1923, when she began to sell books and collections in storage, FBJ had complete sets of *Camera Work* and *Camera Notes*. LOCFBJ reel 28 and reel 8.

50. This reformulation of *Ut pictura poesis* by critic and author Louis Viardot (1800–83) in 1859 was commonplace in French art and music circles by the 1870s. Andrew Kagan, "Ut Pictura Musica, I: to 1860," *Arts Magazine* 60 (May 1986): 86–91. See also Kermit Swiler Champa, "Painted Responses to Music: The Landscapes of Corot and Monet," *The Arts Entwined: Music and Painting in the Nineteenth Century*, edited by Marsha L. Morton and Peter L. Schmunk, 101–18 (New York: Garland, 2000).

51. Letter from FBJ to [Frances A. Johnston and Cornelia J. Hagan], July 30, 1910, LOCFBJ reel 3; Henri Matisse, "The Role of Modalities in Color," 1945, as quoted in Charles A. Riley II, *Color Codes: Modern Theories of Color in Philosophy, Painting and Architecture, Literature, Music and Philosophy* (Lebanon, N.H.: University of New England Press, 1995), 135.

52. The *Post-Star*, Glen Falls, New York, reported on Johnston's "Famous American Garden" talk: "The slides are hand-colored, with beautiful tinting by Mrs. Grace Smith Anderson of Philadelphia, formerly of Dayton, Ohio. Mrs. Anderson's work has become very well known through the displays of garden pictures which have been shown everywhere by the National Cash Register Company for whom Mrs. Anderson worked for a number of years." The only records of Smith's employment at the National Cash Register Company are her pay, recorded in the American Factory Lecture ledger, January–June 1907. Letters between FBJ and Anderson date from 1919 until 1928. *Post-Star*, "Garden Exhibition by Miss Johnston," n.d. [March 8, 1917], LOCFBJ reel 29; ledger, Archives of the National Cash Register

Company, Dayton History, Dayton, Ohio; letters from Grace S. Anderson to FBJ, March 24, 1920, September 8, 1926, and May 19, 1928, LOCFBJ reels 9 and 10.

53. For this early history of Grace Smith Anderson, see Museum of Natural History, New York, Archives and Special Collections Folders 51b, 225, 262, 409. Though its card catalog records Grace Smith's résumé on file, the museum purged employee records in the 1960s. For Chapman, see letter from Dr. George H. Sherwood to Aldred M. Collins, October 9, 1916, folder 262. No bird slides remain in the museum's collection. For FBJ's black-and-white photograph of Anderson's Philadelphia house, see slide LC-DIG-ppmsca-16986.

54. There were two methods of printing images to plates. One was the exposure of a 4- by 5–inch negative to a plate coated with emulsion; the other, the exposure of a 3¼- by 4–inch plate to a larger negative, both placed in camera bellows, adjusted for transference, and exposed to light. FBJ used both methods. Dwight Lathrop Elmendorf, *Lantern Slides: How to Make Them* (New York: E. & H. T. Anthony, 1895). FBJ's Washington, D.C., studio and New York studios with Mattie Edwards Hewitt had darkrooms. It is not known if the partners produced their own glass plates for painting. After 1917, Johnston contracted her processing and from time to time had an assistant who developed photographs.

55. An undated [circa 1917] promotional card for FBJ's lecture advertises "Stereopticon Lecture on Famous Eastern Gardens 100 Views Colored from Autochromes by Miss Frances Johnston of New York City." LOCFBJ reel 33. These slides were of the American gardens in the Northeast circa 1913 until 1915 that Johnston first photographed as autochromes.

56. No invoices for finished work by Grace S. Anderson are in the FBJ ms. archive. FBJ noted on the back of a print photograph of Charles Templeton Crocker's Uplands estate entrance, slides of which are in the FBJ slide collection, that three lantern slides, at her price to the garden owner, for "best coloring," were six for $35 ($595 in 2011). LOCFBJphot Lot 11729-7. Consumer Price Index, Measuringworth.com. For slide prices, see here "Gardens of the Old World," p. 351, note 17.

57. For FBJ and photographing, see Ronstrom, "60 Years," 8.

58. The Library of Congress photography conservator is developing a plan to determine whether watercolor or transparent oils were used for tinting by artists working for FBJ. The initial visual examination was inconclusive.

59. "Leicester Bodine Holland, *The Garden Blue Book* (Garden City, N.Y.: Doubleday, Page, 1915), 2–3. For color slides in relation to color charts, see Robin Veder, "Color Gardens before Color Photography," *Cabinet* 6 (Spring 2002): 72–75. The Garden Club of America carefully cataloged and quantified color and formed a color chart committee, headed by member-at-large Fletcher Steele. See "Sample Color Chart Cards," *Bulletin of The Garden Club of America* 7 (September 1922): 55, and "Officers of The Garden Club of America," no. 8 (January 1923): 3. Steele recommended both the *Répertoire des Couleurs* published by the Société Française des Chrysanthémistes (1905) and American ornithologist Robert Ridgeway's *Color Standards and Color Nomenclature* (1912). He criticized the latter for its placement of a color's most intense hue at the middle of the spectrum, urging instead a graduated scale. "Color Charts for Gardeners," *The Garden Magazine* 33, no. 3 (March 1921): 186.

60. At the same time that garden painters and designers were advocating for gradual, subtle color, so were photographers working in autochrome. Sally Stein, "Autochromes without Apologies: Heinrich Kühn's Experiments with the Mechanical Palette." *History of Photography* 18, no. 2 (Summer 1994): 132.

61. For lupine and poppies, see LC-DIG-ppmsca-16185; for Lob's Wood and Kies gardens, see here plates 97 and 180–82.

62. Belinda Gertz, "The Garden Colorist," *The Architectural Record* 52, no. 1 (July 1922): 44–45.

63. "Miss Frances Benjamin Johnston Announces a New Series of Garden Lectures," brochure, LOCFBJ reel 33.

64. Arthur G. Eldredge, "Photographing the Garden," *Photo-Era* 33, no. 1 (July 1914): 4.

65. McFarland, "Country Life Photographs," 53. McFarland's position was commonly held. See Peterson, *Peter Henry Emerson*, 45.

66. "Exterior of Homes Is Public Property," *St. Joseph Gazette,* April 23, 1924, LOCFBJ reel 29.

67. Frank A. Waugh, "Photographing for Lantern Slides," 190–93.

68. Theorists debate the role of the caption in viewing a photograph, citing Walter Benjamin, who wrote in 1931 that text diminished the association experienced when viewing a painting or a Pictorialist, manipulated photograph; finer print reproduction and technical advances brought increased specificity, further distancing the photograph from the time and space disruption of fine-art images. See essay first published in *Literarische Welt,* 1931, Walter Benjamin, "A Short History of Photography," *Classic Essays on Photography*, edited by Alan Trachtenberg (New Haven, Conn.: Lette's Island Books, 1980), 199–216.

69. See the "House in Good Taste" feature of architect Edward Clarence Dean's Greenwich, Connecticut, cottage and garden photographed by FBJ, *House & Garden* 63, no. 7 (June 1928): 753–57. For letters relating to this project, see LOCFBJ reel 10. For another approach to the artistic presentation, see "The Garden of Maxfield Parrish in Cornish, New Hampshire," with photographs by Clara E. Sipprell reproduced with their original, gray-toned matting. *The House Beautiful* 53, no. 5 (June 1923): 617–19.

70. "Spring Is Just around the Corner," *Country Life in America* 61, no. 4 (February 1927): 60–61. FBJ likely supplied the biblical verse.

71. *Our Garden Journal* 1, no. 1 (September 1917), n.p. Elinore Harde published this letterpress journal quarterly from 1917 until 1921; subscription was $6 a year by invitation. Amateur authors wrote on flower gardening. Mattie Edwards Hewitt advertised as the "Official Photographer of Our Garden Journal" in issue 1, no. 4 (March 1919): n.p.. Grace S. Anderson likely tinted FBJ's print photographs. No confirming records are in the Johnston archive at the Library of Congress.

72. FBJ, "The Old World Gardens" press release, n.d. [1925 or 1926]: 2.

73. For a Pictorialist print, see Turtle Bay Gardens Willow Fountain [Fall 1920] lot 12637-4. This photograph and straight photographs of the gardens illustrated, without credit, Arthur Willis Colton, "Turtle Bay Gardens, New York City, *The Architectural Record* 48, no. 6 (December 1920): 466–93. Soft-focus images were unsuited to lantern slides, which required pale half tones for projection. Waugh, "Photographing for Lantern Slides," 192.

74. Ruth B. Dean, "The Spring Exhibit of Landscape Architecture at the Arden Studios," *Bulletin of The Garden Club of America* 17 (September 1927): 83.

75. Frances Benjamin Johnston, "Memorandum F.B.J.," undated [circa 1925], LOCFBJ reel 32.

76. Anna Gilman Hill, *Forty Years of Gardening* (New York: Frederick A. Stokes, 1938), 13. When Hill was preparing this book, she wrote FBJ requesting her photographs of Gray Gardens. "Do you remember me and [the] good times we had at Easthampton [*sic*] along about 1914–17? I need three glacé prints for reproduction … I am writing a book about gardening & my little gardens … I am always on the lookout for your wonderful work." Letter from Mrs. Robert Carmer Hill to FBJ, November 7 [1937], LOCFBJ reel 13. Hill published photographs of the gardens credited to Mattie E. Hewitt and Frances Benjamin Johnston individually. This is likely because Hewitt supplied prints from negatives left with her in 1917.

77. Letter from [J]. P. Stewart to FBJ, July 7, 1923, LOCFBJ reel 8.

78. Gretchen Smith, "Memories Perpetuated in Inclosed Garden," *The Star*, Washington, D.C., June 22, 1941. See letters from Virginia D. Lightfoot to FBJ, September 6 and November 28, 1937, and April 25, 1938, LOCFBJ reel 13. FBJ sent Lightfoot willow slips and photographs of southern gardens.

Gardens of the East

Epigraph: "The exterior of your home…," "Exterior of Home Is Public Property," *St. Joseph Gazette*, Missouri, April 23, 1924. LOCFBJ reel 29.

1. Ralph Adams Cram, "Preface," *American Country Houses of Today* (New York: Architectural Book Publishing, 1913), 1.

2. Letter from C. H. Thomas to FBJ, February 18, 1921, LOCFBJ reel 9. Hoffman was a founder of the Newport Garden Club, incorporated August 4, 1914, and affiliated with the Royal Horticultural Society of Great Britain and International Garden Club of New York. *Annuaire of the Newport Garden Club*, issued November 1914, printed January 1915. This volume and the *Annuaire* for 1915–16 include Johnston–Hewitt photographs of the Alfred G. Vanderbilt, Thomas J. Emery, Frederick S. Hoffman, Edward J. Berwind, and Cornelius Vanderbilt II gardens, all photographed in 1914. Dating for these early photographs is from photo prints in the Mattie Edwards Hewitt Collection, Lot 97, Rhode Island Historical Society, Providence.

3. "The International Garden Association is affiliated with the Royal Horticultural Society of England," *Evening Sun*, New York, May 25, 1914. Also Mrs. Charles F. Hoffman, "The Establishment of the International Garden Club," *Journal of the International Garden Club* 1, no. 1 (August 1917): 257–62.

4. FBJ's first ad was for "Photographs in Color of Gardens" by Miss Frances Benjamin Johnston and Mrs. Mattie Edwards Hewitt, *Bulletin of The Garden Club of America* 13 (March 1916), n.p. Though early to advertise in the *Bulletin*, the partners were not exceptional. Reflecting the enduring low status of garden photography and the primacy of Europe, Boston-based house and garden photographer Paul Julius Weber (1881–1958) advertised as a "Photographer of Architecture," with a photograph of a fountain at the Villa d'Este. *Studies in Landscape Architecture* (Boston: Bruce Humphries, [1935]), n.p.

5. Letter from FBJ to Helen Fogg, January 13, 1927, LOCFBJ reel 10.

6. Letter from Beatrix J. Farrand to FBJ, April 14, 1920, LOCFBJ reel 9.

7. FBJ wrote this in response to a lawsuit threatened by Fitz Eugene Dixon after FBJ published in *Country Life in America* her 1926 photographs of his bulb gardens, taken and paid for by supplier John Scheepers. Letter from FBJ to Helen Comstock at the *Studio* magazine, February 27, 1929, LOCFBJ reel 10. See also here "The Garden Photograph," p. 43, and "The Garden Photograph," p. 348, note 70. Though no permission letters exist in the FBJ archive, there are references to owners' authorization. FBJ wrote Helen Devore that she would not use any pictures of Chatham house "without your full approval." Letter from FBJ to Mrs. Devore, November 6, 1926, LOCFBJ reel 9.

8. Telegram from FBJ to C. H. Thomas, April 23, 1921, and subsequent telegrams confirming arrangements, LOCFBJ reel 9.

9. For the Pratt gardens, see Cynthia Zaitzevsky, *Long Island Landscapes and the Women Who Designed Them* (New York: Society for the Preservation of Long Island Antiquities in association with W. W. Norton & Company, 2009), 40–42,

65–70. Greenleaf may have used Martha B. Hutcheson's 1911 design of a circular sunken terrace at Welwyn for his circa-1913 terrace at Killenworth. Slides of these gardens are LC-DIG-ppmsca-16568, 21801, and 16868.

10. John Dixon Hunt, *Gardens and the Picturesque: Studies in the History of Landscape Architecture* (Cambridge, Mass.: MIT Press, 1992), 291.

11. "Annual Meeting and Conference," *Women's National Farm and Garden Association Bulletin* 7, no. 1 (July 1919): 4.

12. Michael C. Kathrens, *American Splendor: The Residential Architecture of Horace Trumbauer* (New York: Acanthus Press, 2002), 232–48.

13. FBJ to Horace Trumbauer, February 21, 1926, LOCFBJ reel 9. For photographs of Whitemarsh Hall and a Stotesbury bound photograph album, see LOCFBJphot Lot 12647.

14. Letter from Mary Fanton Roberts to FBJ, April 8, 1926, LOCFBJ reel 10.

Gardens of the West

Epigraph:" No matter how well…," FBJ, "Gardens of the Pacific," *Bulletin of The Garden Club of America* 14, new series (November 1923): 17.

1. William Deverell, "Convalescence and California: The Civil War Comes West," *Southern California Quarterly* 90, no. 1 (Spring 2008): 1–26. Also, *To Bind Up the Nation's Wounds: The American West after the Civil War* (New York: Bloomsbury Press, forthcoming).

2. Letter from Louise Shelton to FBJ, February 28, 1917, LOCFBJ reel 9. Shelton suggested that Johnston be in Chicago by June 15, 1917, in time for the annual meeting of The Garden Club of America held that year in Lake Forest. There is no record that FBJ attended the meeting.

3. FBJ diary for April 1917, LOCFBJ reel 1.

4. "Merry Go Round," *Morning Press*, Santa Barbara, May 1, 1917, LOCFBJ reel 29.

5. Invitation by Paul Elder & Company, undated [lecture was May, 22, 1917], LOCFBJ reel 28. Elder published books of poetry and on beauty, and an early photo-illustrated portrait of California gardens, Belle Summer Angier, *The Garden Book of California*, 1906.

6. For photographs in this exhibition that included East and West Coast gardens, see "Miss Johnston," exhibition catalog that also announced her new "The Intimate Garden," "Formal Gardens," and "California Gardens," LOCFBJ reel 33.

7. Letter from FBJ to Mr. [Leonard] Barron, October 14, 1923, LOCFBJ reel 9.

8. Hildegarde Hawthorne, "Color in California," *The Touchstone* 8, no. 4 (January 1921): 276. Mary Fanton Roberts began as associate editor for *The Craftsman*, which published the photographs of FBJ and other women garden photographers, sometimes with credit, but profiled art photographers Arnold Genthe, Baron Adolph de Meyer (1868–1949), and Gertrude Käsebier. She addressed this bias in 1917 after assuming management of the magazine which she renamed *The Touchstone*. For Mary Fanton Roberts and the preferential treatment of men artists, see Madlyn Millner Kahr, "Women as Artists and 'Women's Art,'" *Woman's Art Journal* 3, no. 2 (Autumn 1982–Winter 1983): 28–31.

9. Aaron A. Sargent, "Address Delivered before the State Agricultural Society," fall 1870, as quoted in W. McPherson, *Los Angeles and Description Thereof, with Sketches of the Four Adjacent Counties: Being an Answer to Inquiries Concerning Their Progress, Attractions and Resources* (Los Angeles: Mirror Book and Job Printing Establishment, 1873), 69. Sargent became a U.S. senator from California in 1873.

10. FBJ, "Garden Pools of California," *Harper's Bazaar* 53, no. 1 (January 1918): 30.

11. See "Outline of Proposed Contract with Douglas Fairbanks Studio for Display Prints. Pictorial Stills." [August 1923] LOCFBJ reel 22.

12. Letter from Page Eaton to FBJ, June 6, 1923, LOCFBJ reel 9.

13. Joseph Duveen was advisor to both Henry E. Huntington and Edward T. Stotesbury, whose Whitemarsh Hall Johnston photographed in 1922 and 1923. For the recommendation, see letter from FBJ to Mr. Morgan, January 12, 1923, LOCFBJ reel 9. Because of the disintegration of nitrate negatives, only two slides of a recorded 11 negatives of the Huntington gardens remain, with no prints to date identified. See here plate 123 and LC-DIG-ppmsca-16929.

14. For this sale, see Jennifer A. Watts, "Frances Benjamin Johnston: The Huntington Portrait Collection," *History of Photography* 19, no. 3 (Fall 1995): 252–62.

15. *Bulletin of the Architectural Club of Los Angeles*, no. 4 (April 9, 1943): 1; letter from FBJ to Frederick Law Olmsted, August 7, 1926, LOCFBJ reel 9; FBJ, "Frances Benjamin Johnston and Her Gardening Photography," [circa 1922], LOCFBJ reel 33.

16. FBJ, "In Yesterday's Gardens," introduction, LOCFBJ reel 21.

17. Alexander Alland Sr., *Jessie Tarbox Beals: First Woman Photographer* (New York: Camera Graphic Press, 1978), 87–89.

18. See Myron Hunt garden, plates 188 and 191, and Francis L. Loring garden, designed by Hunt, plate 155; also plate 59, Arthur G. Reynolds garden by Charles Gibbs Adams. Winifred Starr Dobyns, *California Gardens* (New York: Macmillan, 1931).

19. Frank A. Waugh, "A Personal View of California Gardens," *The Garden Magazine and Home Builder* 60, no. 4 (December 1924): 233.

20. Ernest H. Wilson, *If I Were to Make a Garden* (Boston: Stratford, 1931), 124–30.

21. Mrs. Francis King, *Chronicles of the Garden* (New York: Charles Scribner's Sons, 1925), 165.

22. Mrs. Philip Martineau, *Gardening in Sunny Lands*, introduction by Edith Wharton (New York: D. Appleton, 1924), 189.

23. FBJ, "Gardens of the Pacific," 17, 19.

24. Marion Bowen, "Frances Benjamin Johnston Has Led Eventful Career Seeking Photographs in Far Places of World: Has Smithsonian Institute Exhibits," *Hollywood Daily Citizen*, June 9, 1923, LOCFBJ reel 29.

25. Letter from E. W. Ziegler to FBJ, March 10, 1946, LOCFBJ reel 16.

Gardens for City and Suburb

Epigraph: FBJ, "What must be the sensations…," *New York Sun*, December 19, 1922.

1. Edith Wharton, *A Backward Glance* (New York: Charles Scribner's Sons, 1933), 54.

2. Jacob A. Riis, *How the Other Half Lives: Studies among the Tenements of New York.* (New York: Charles Scribner's Sons, 1890), 9.

3. "What You May See in City War Garden," *New York Times*, August 17, 1919.

4. Anne Fior Scott, *Natural Allies: Women's Associations in American History* (Chicago: University of Illinois Press, 1992), 140.

5. Frances Benjamin Johnston, "Flower Gardens as Usual in 1918," *The Gardeners' Chronicle of America* 22, no. 1 (January 1918): 56.

6. Mary Cadwalader Jones, *Lantern Slides* (privately printed [Beatrix Jones and Max Farrand], 1937), 1.

7. Bertha A. Clark, "The Society of Little Gardens," *The House Beautiful* 41, no. 2 (January 1917): 72, and "The Society of Little Gardens," *Bulletin of The Garden Club of America* 2, new series (January 1920): 44–45.

8. Bertha Clark, *The House Beautiful*, 72.

9. For the club history, see Emily Legutko, *The First 85 Years: A History of the City Gardens Club of New York City, 1918 to 2003* (New York: The City Gardens Club of New York City, 1923). Also Jeannette B. Hodgdon, "Back Yard or Garden?" *The House Beautiful* 79, no. 3 (March 1931): 248–51, 308, 311. For activities at the Museum of Natural History, see the museum's Archives and Special Collections Folders 1268A, 130AJ A–D, 130 B–C.

10. Frances Benjamin Johnston, "Notice for City Gardens Club of New York," *The Gardeners' Chronicle of America* 26, no. 2 (February 1922): 245–46. For the exhibition solicitation, see *New York City Gardens Club Bulletin*, n.d. [Spring 1922], LOCFBJ reel 33.

11. First prize, Ruth B. Dean for backyard garden; second prize, Clarence Fowler for Dr. Henry Alexander garden; third prize, terrace [roof] garden by Edward Shepard

Hewitt for Mrs. Cornelius Poillon, a manufacturer of Arts & Crafts pottery. For others and notable mentions, including the janitor garden, see *The City Gardens Club Bulletin* 1, no. 3 (Fall and Winter 1922): 3–4, LOCFBJ reel 33. For 1921 correspondence between FBJ and Frances Peters, see reel 18.

12. Frances Benjamin Johnston, "Gardens in City Environment," *New York Sun*, December 19, 1922.

13. For photographs of these Sutton Place projects, see LOCFBJphot Lot 12637-4.

14. "A House of Personality and Its Successor," *Vogue* 57, no. 6 (March 15, 1921): 59. For Sutton Place, Turtle Bay, and Jones Wood, see Andrew Scott Dolkart, *The Row House Reborn: Architecture and Neighborhoods in New York City, 1908–1929* (Baltimore: Johns Hopkins University Press, 2009), 87–108.

15. FBJ spoke at the National Cash Register Company, January 17, 1917, on "American Gardens in Color," May 18, 1920, and again circa 1937. See "A List of Garden Lectures," and letter from Eugene Lee Ferguson to FBJ, March 18, 1938, LOCFBJ reels 28, 12.

16. Untitled press release, LOCFBJ reel 37. For the study of nature in schools, in backyards, and in community nature centers, see Sally Gregory Kohlstedt, "'A Better Crop of Boys and Girls': The School Garden Movement," *History of Higher Education Quarterly* 48, no. 1 (February 2008): 58–93.

Gardens of the Old World

Epigraph: "We have, to be sure, much…," FBJ, "In Yesterday's Garden," [1926], 1, LOCFBJ reel 21.

1. Martha Brookes Hutcheson, *The Spirit of the Garden*, introduction by Ernest Peixotto (Boston: Little, Brown, 1923), n.p.

2. George Burnap, "Style Gardens," *The Architectural Record* 54, no. 2 (August 1923): 121.

3. FBJ, "In Yesterday's Gardens," 21.

4. Letter from FBJ to Helen Fogg, January 13, 1927, LOCFBJ reel 8.

5. Letter from FBJ to Captain Peter Beeman, July 29. 1925, LOCFBJ reel 9.

6. Mary Fanton Roberts, "Mrs. Burnett's Rose Garden in Kent: Evolved from Centuries-Old Orchard," *The Craftsman* 12, no. 5 (August 1907): 537–47.

7. The Garden Club of America led a tour through French gardens the same summer. FBJ wrote the secretary of the Bienvenue Française that she wanted to know what gardens members were visiting, but that she could not travel with them because "it would be much too hurried for my work." Letter from FBJ to Madame Rose de Jouvenal, May 16, 1925, LOCFBJ reel 8.

8. FBJ, "In Yesterday's Garden," 7 and 2.

9. FBJ, "The Old World Gardens," undated press release [circa January 1926], 1, LOCFBJ reel 21.

10. For correspondence relating to this trip, see LOCFBJ reel 9.

11. For books, FBJ, "In Yesterday's Gardens," 2.

12. *Bulletin of The Garden Club of America* 15, new series (January 1924): 56. The photographer of the Pratt sculpture, reproduced in the *Bulletin*, is unidentified. FBJ's slide of this sundial, circa 1918, is here plate 59.

13. For prints from this exhibition and its four-page catalog, "In Old World Gardens," February 15 to March 1, 1926, LOCFBJphot Lot 11731 (Box 1), LC-USZ62-137843.

14. FBJ, "The Old World Gardens," undated press release [circa January 1926], 1, LOCFBJ reel 21.

15. The *Christian Science Monitor* wrote of FBJ's Boston show: "Miss Johnston divides [by geographic location] her collection of photographs, which will be on view at Horticultural Hall for another 10 days…. Many of the photographs are beautifully colored, some by direct color photography, others in which color has been applied by a Dayton artist, Grace Smith Anderson." What FBJ showed at this exhibition is not known. This review suggests that FBJ still had autochromes, possibly of Long Island and East Coast gardens. The only record of autochrome photography after FBJ's break with Mattie Edwards Hewitt is an invoice to Mrs. A. C. James, Beacon Hill House, Newport, August 25, 1917: 10 "autochromes @ $35.00 each," LOCFBJ reel 21. *Christian Science Monitor*, December 13, 1927; for James see here "The Garden Photographer," p. 341, note 48.

16. Ada Rainey, "69 Photographs," *Washington Post*, February 6, 1927, p. f5.

17. Edward Cornelius van Altena was born in Milwaukee, Wisconsin. He trained as a photographer and was in business with his father Henry van Altena, born in Holland. By 1894, they were producing lantern slides. In 1906 Edward was still in business with H. van Altena & Son at 786 Jefferson Avenue, Brooklyn, New York, working for the Museum of Natural History in Manhattan. John Duer Scott (b. Canada, 1876), a colorist, became Altena's partner and in 1904 they formed Scott & van Altena at 59 Pearl Street, New York. The firm dissolved circa 1919, with the partners continuing individually. The firm Edward van Altena, with slide label addresses of 71–79 West 45th Street and 29 West 38 Street, New York, tinted the majority of Johnston's European slides. After the period when he worked for FBJ, Edward van Altena developed an additive process. He layered three positive negatives in primary colors to produce color plates.

Archives and Special Collections, File 63, Museum of Natural History, New York, New York; *Encyclopedia of the Magic Lantern*, edited by David Robinson, Stephen Herbert and Richard Crangle (London: The Magic Lantern Society, 2001),

315; Harriet Jackson Phelps, *Newport in Flower* (Newport, R.I.: The Preservation Society of Newport County), 22–24; Charlotte Tancin, librarian, Hunt Institute for Botanical Documentation, "Edward van Altena Garden Slides, "http://lists.nidhog.com/pipermail/cbhl/2006-January/000570.html; "Colored Slides of Gardens Here to Be Shown Nov. 4," *Newport Daily News*, October 24, 1966.

Altena charged for a standard 3- by 4¼-inch slide from a print or photograph 50 cents, from a negative, 25 cents. The coloring cost from 25 cents to 90 cents per slide. *Bulletin of The Garden Club of America* 11, new series (January 1920): 43.

18. "In Yesterday's Garden," 17. FBJ intended this essay, illustrated with her photographs and written without a commitment, to be published as a series of six articles. See letter from FBJ to George Horace Lorimer, April 24, 1926, LOCFBJ reel 21.

Gardens of the South

Epigraph: "It was during my travels…," Ross Well, "She Saves Virginia's Charm for Future," *Richmond Times-Dispatch*, December 15, 1935.

1. For the interrelationship of the Italian Renaissance and Colonial revivals, see the 1983 essay by Richard Guy Wilson, "Architecture and the Reinterpretation of the Past in the American Renaissance," *American Architectural History: A Contemporary Reader*, edited by Keith L. Eggener (London: Routledge, 2004), 227–46.

2. For a history of these volumes, published in 1930 (vol. 1) and 1934 (vol. 2), see "Introduction" by Mac Griswold to reprint of vol. 1, Alice G. B. Lockwood, *Gardens of Colony and State: Gardens and Gardeners of the American Colonies and of the Republic before 1840* (New York: The Garden Club of America, 2000), n.p.

3. The Daughters of the American Revolution was founded in October 1890, endorsed by an early Johnston supporter, First Lady Caroline Scott Harrison. Johnston's D.A.R. member number is 1,140. Per author communication with Steve Davidson, assistant library director, National Society of the Daughters of the American Revolution, Washington, D.C., July 2011.

4. Letter from FBJ to Mrs. Fairfax Harrison, February 28, 1933, LOCFBJ reel 11.

5. Today the Water Garden is known as the Italian Garden. Identification as by Pierre S. du Pont, per author correspondence with Colvin Randall, Longwood Gardens, June 2011. For FBJ's trip through Delaware, where she was unable to photograph the Rodney Sharp garden, then being replanted, and Winterthur, owned by Henry Francis du Pont, where she could only "get permission to visit" because the owner was away, see FBJ to Franklin Coe, publisher of *Town & Country*, September 1, 1926, LOCFBJ reel 21.

Not surprisingly, H. F. du Pont became interested in FBJ's photographs of southern buildings. In September 1934 she returned to Winterthur at his invitation to show him the "complete records of the Virginia survey." Letter from FBJ to du Pont, September 3, 1934, Winterthur Archives, AD Box 32, quoted courtesy the Winterthur Library.

6. Letter from Augusta Owen Patterson to FBJ, July 23, 1926, LOCFBJ reel 21.

7. FBJ to Patterson, October 31, 1926, LOCFBJ reel 21.

8. Davyd Foard Hood, "The Renaissance of Southern Gardening in the Early Twentieth Century," *Journal of Garden History* 16, no. 2 (Summer 1996): 129–52.

9. Letter from FBJ to Mrs. Jarman, February 27, 1927, LOCFBJ reel 10. FBJ writes about her move and states that she has an "elaborate plan for photographing the old gardens and houses of the south particularly in Virginia and Maryland."

10. Lecture to Mary Washington Chapter, Washington, D.C., May 2, 1929, LOCFBJ reel 33.

11. For membership, see undated [circa 1930] Washington, D.C. Arts Club notice, LOCFBJ reel 33; see "Dummy Garden Booklet, Sept. 1935," LOCFBJphot Lot 11748.

12. From the 1910 U.S. Census, William O. Hazard was a photographer working for the federal government; by 1930 he was an artist with the U.S. Geological Survey, living in Takoma Park, Maryland. Johnston produced slides of southern buildings in sepia. For its flower-gardening members, the Garden Club of Virginia continued to order colored plates. See letter from Mrs. Stanhope S. Johnson, chairman of the club, to FBJ, May 1936, and bills from William O. Hazard in the 1930s, LOCFBJ reels 12, 13. The label of a colored slide of Wellington house near Mount Vernon is: "Alexandria Garden Club, no. 157." See LC-DIG-ppmsca-16340.

13. Taylor Scott Hardon to FBJ, January 7, 1929, LOCFBJ reel 10.

14. Davyd Foard Hood, "'Gathering Up the Fragments that Remain': Southern Garden Clubs and the Publication of Southern Garden History, 1923–1939," *The Influence of Women in the Southern Landscape: Proceedings of the Tenth Conference on Restoring Southern Gardens and Landscapes*, October 5–7, 1995 (Winston-Salem, N.C.: Old Salem, 1995), 172–95.

15. Letter from Ethel B. Powers to FBJ, July 6, 1920, and letter from FBJ to Mrs. William Wilson Sale, Kingway Court, Route 2, Richmond, Virginia, April 15, 1928, LOCFBJ reel 10.

16. Edith Tunis Sale, "Brandon-on-the-James," *The House Beautiful* 64, no. 6 (December 1928): 740–41.

17. Letter from Ellen Shipman, Landscape Architect, 19 Beekman Place, to FBJ, February 24, 1928, LOCFBJ reel 10.

18. LOCFBJphot Lot 2501. A slide of the image in this notice is of the Rappahannock River, LC-DIG-ppmsca-16591.

19. Charles E. Peterson to the Director, United States Department of the Interior, Office of National Parks, Buildings, and Reservations, Washington, D.C., November 13, 1933. Reprinted in the *Journal of the Society of Architectural Historians* 16, no. 3 (October 1957): 29–31.

20. FBJ advertised her "The Tales Old Houses Tell" lecture as having 100 slides. In an inventory, November 10, 1940, she listed 45 slides in the collection. There are 62 sepia-toned slides of old southern buildings in the Library of Congress FBJ lantern-slide collection. Johnston likely exaggerated the number or included slides now lost.

Except for several images, FBJ's slides of the historic South overlap with images in the Carnegie Survey of the Architecture of the South because Johnston added to that survey prints of photographs she had taken in the late 1920s. Notice for lecture at the Arts Club in Washington, D.C., March 23, 1942, LOCFBJ reel 33; 1940 inventory, reel 20.

21. The books, all published by the University of North Carolina Press and written by restoration historian Thomas Tileston Waterman (1900–51) with photographs by FBJ, were *The Mansions of Virginia* (1946); *The Early Architecture of North Carolina: A Pictorial Survey* (1941 and 1947), with introductions by Leicester B. Holland; and *Dwellings of Colonial America* (1950). A reviewer of the first edition of North Carolina architecture observed that "the photographs, unsurpassed in artistic beauty and selective taste," were nonetheless diminished by "the gloss of shiny paper." This volume followed the *Homes and Gardens of North Carolina* (1939) by Archibald Henderson with photographs by Bayard Wooten, also published by the university, under the auspices of the Garden Club of North Carolina. *The American Historical Review* 48, no. 2 (January 1943): 429.

22. Harnett T. Kane, "New Orleans Architecture Is Being Saved in Pictures," *Sunday Item-Tribune*, New Orleans, May 22, 1938, LOCFBJ reel 29.

23. "Leicester Bodine Holland," *Journal of the Society of Architectural Historians* 11, no. 2 (May 1952): 24. Letter from Holland to FBJ, November 1, 1929, LOCFBJ reel 10.

"Our American Gardens" Slides

1. Letter from Mrs. Walter Jennings to Olmsted Brothers, August 24, 1937, LOCOP reel 296, job 6287.

"California Gardens" Slides

1. "Put California to Shame Miss Johnston Tells City," *Youngstown Telegram*, March 18, 1921.

A Garden Book Library

1. Letter from FBJ to Mrs. [Helen Stewart] Devore, November 6, 1926, LOCFBJ reel 9.
2. Beverly Seaton, "Gardening Books for the Commuter's Wife, 1900—1937," *Landscape Journal* 13, no. 2 (1994): 113–23. Also Susan E. Schnare, "Woman Garden Writers: Gardening, Reading about Gardening, and Writing about Gardening Are All One," *Influence of Women on the Southern Landscape: Proceedings of the Tenth Conference on Restoring Southern Gardens and Landscapes*. Old Salem, Winston-Salem, N.C., October 5–7, 1995. (Winston-Salem: Old Salem, 1995), 83–99.
3. Megan Benton, "'Too Many Books': Book Ownership and Cultural Identify in the 1920s," *American Quarterly* 49, no. 2 (June 1997): 268–97.
4. Letter from FBJ to Dr. John H. Barnhart, January 23, 1926, and letter from FBJ to Mr. [Leonard] Barron, October 14, 1923, LOCFBJ reel 9.
5. Letter from FBJ to Mrs. F., n.d., LOCFBJ reel 18.
6. Frances Benjamin Johnston, *The White House Illustrated* (Washington, D.C.: Gibson Brothers, 1893).
7. Diane Harris, "Cultivating Power: The Language of Feminism in Garden Literature, 1870–1920," *Landscape Journal* 13, no. 2 (1994): 113–23.
8. For her Georgetown exhibit, FBJ augmented her collection with titles from the U.S. Department of Agriculture. See letters from Louise Ihlder, chair of the Program Committee, Georgetown Garden Club, to FBJ, January 22, 1925, LOCFBJ reel 9; and Claribel R. Barnett to FBJ, February 7, 1928, and FBJ to Barnett, February 8, 1928, reel 10.
9. For books recommended, see "Best Books on Gardening to Be Had at the Public Library," *The Youngstown Vindelator*, Youngstown, Ohio, March 29, 1920, LOCFBJ reel 29.
10. Letter from FBJ to Mrs. [Rachel M.] Hunt, n.d. [February 1927], and response to letter by Hunt to FBJ, February 13, 1927, reels 28 and 10.
11. For lists, see LOCFBJ reel 32.
12. See letter from Mrs. Gordon "Katharine" Abbott to FBJ, July 24, 1926, and letter from FBJ to Abbott, LOCFBJ reel 9. Abbott, owner of Glass Head in Manchester, Mass., photographed by Johnston in 1924, needed books for the Massachusetts Horticultural Society library. See letter from FBJ to Dr. John H. Barnhart, January 23, 1926, and invoice and letter January 26, 1926, 108 books for $165, reel 9. This sale represented approximately half of FBJ's library. See "For Sale, Books on Flower and Landscape Gardening," reel 9.

    For North Carolina, see letter from Rosen, Kammer, Hopkins, Burke & LaPeyre, executors of FBJ estate to O. [Olan] V. Cook, July 24, 1952, reel 31, and letter from Cook, assistant librarian at the university, to Felix H. LaPeyre, July 31, 1952, answering that the Library of Congress had shipped the books in 1951 and the university had paid FBJ $500, Box 1:10 of the Records of the Office of the University Librarian, Davis Reference Library, University of North Carolina, Chapel Hill. Titles from the sale to Barnhart remain in the LuEsther T. Mertz Library of the New York Botanical Garden, Bronx, N.Y., some with FBJ's bookplate, a typed label: "Frances Benjamin Johnston, 629 Lexington Avenue." The books FBJ sold to the University of North Carolina Library, Chapel Hill, have not been identified. I thank Marie Long, reference librarian; Donald Wheeler, collection development librarian; Emma Antobam at the New York Botanical Garden; and Carol M. Tobin, head, Davis Library Reference, for their pursuit of these sales.
13. Because FBJ lists do not indicate edition, alternate dates are provided in this assembled bibliography. Unidentified is "Camden," (1).
14. George G. Marshall was an eminent collector of herbals. How FBJ acquired the book is not known, but she noted its importance when she tried to sell her library to the New York Horticultural Society in 1925. See letter from FBJ to Elizabeth Peterson, December 12, 1925, LOCFBJ reel 9, regarding the sale of 109 books.

Selected Bibliography

ARCHIVES AND PRIMARY RESOURCES

Archives of American Gardens, Smithsonian Institution, Washington, D.C.

The Athenaeum, Newport, R.I.

Botany-Horticultural Library, National Museum of Natural History, Washington, D.C.

East Hampton Library, East Hampton, N.Y.

Environmental Design Archives and Library, University of California, Berkeley, Calif.

Frances Benjamin Johnston Papers, Manuscript Division, Library of Congress, Washington, D.C.

Frances Benjamin Johnston Photograph Collection, Prints & Photographs Division, Library of Congress, Washington, D.C.

The City Gardens Club of New York City, New York, N.Y.

The Garden Club of America, New York, N.Y.

Grosse Pointe Historical Society, Grosse Pointe, Mich.

Huntington Library, Art Collections and Botanical Gardens, San Marino, Calif.

Lyndhurst, Tarrytown, N.Y.

Massachusetts Historical Society, Mattie Edwards Hewitt Collection, Boston, Mass.

Nassau County Museum, Mattie Edwards Hewitt Collection, Roslyn Harbor, N.Y.

The NCR Archive, Dayton History, Dayton, Ohio

New England Preservation Society, Boston, Mass.

New York Botanical Garden, LuEsther T. Mertz Library, Bronx, N.Y.

New York Historical Society, Mattie Edwards Hewitt Collection, New York, N.Y.

New York Horticultural Society, New York, N.Y.

New York Public Library, New York, N.Y.

New York State Historical Association, Cooperstown, N.Y.

Ohio Historical Society, Columbus, Ohio

Olmsted Associates Records, Manuscript Division, Library of Congress, Washington, D.C.

Rhode Island Historical Society, Providence, R.I.

Santa Barbara Botanic Garden, Blakesley Library, Santa Barbara, Calif.

Southampton Historical Museum, Southampton, N.Y.

PERIODICALS AND JOURNALS

Annuaire of the Newport Garden Club
The American Architect
The American City
The Architectural Record
Arts & Decoration
Bulletin of The Garden Club of America
Camera Work
Country Life in America
The Craftsman
Demorest's Family Magazine
The Garden Magazine
The Gardeners' Chronicle
The Gardeners' Chronicle of America

Harper's Bazar; Harper's Bazaar from 1929

The Horticulturist and Journal of Rural Art and Rural Taste

The House Beautiful

House & Garden

The International Studio

Journal of Garden History

Journal of the International Garden Club

Journal of the New England Garden History Society

The Ladies' Home Journal

Our Garden Journal

The Touchstone

Town & Country

Vanity Fair

Vogue

Women's National Farm and Garden Association Bulletin

BOOKS AND CATALOGS

Alland, Alexander, Sr. *Jessie Tarbox Beals: First Woman News Photographer*. New York: Camera/Graphic Press, c. 1978.

Ambassadors of Progress. Edited by Bronwyn A. E. Griffith. Washington, D.C.: Musée d'Art Américain Giverny, France, with the Library of Congress, 2001.

American Gardens, 1890–1930. Edited and with introduction by Sam Watters. New York: Acanthus Press, 2006.

American Impressionists in the Garden. Introduction by May Brawley Hill. Nashville, Tenn.: Cheekwood Botanical Garden & Museum of Art, 2010.

"Arcady" Montecito, Santa Barbara, California. Privately printed [by George Owen Knapp], 1926.

Ausherman, Maria Elizabeth. *The Photographic Legacy of Frances Benjamin Johnston*. Gainesville: University Press of Florida, 2009.

Bemiss, Margaret Page. *Historic Virginia Gardens: Preservation Work of the Garden Club of Virginia, 1975–2007*. Charlottesville: University of Virginia Press, 2009.

Berch, Bettina. *The Woman behind the Lens*. Charlottesville: University of Virginia Press, 2000.

Bissell, Ervanna Bowen. *Glimpses of Santa Barbara and Montecito Gardens*. Santa Barbara, Calif.: Schauer Printing Studio, 1926.

Bogart, Michele H. *Artists, Advertising, and the Borders of Art*. Chicago: University of Chicago Press, 1995.

Campbell, Katie. *Paradise of Exiles: The Anglo-American Gardens of Florence*. London: Frances Lincoln, 2009.

Close, Leslie Rose. *Portrait of an Era in Landscape Architecture: The Photography of Mattie Edwards Hewitt*. New York: Wave Hill, 1983.

Cothran, James R. *Gardens of Historic Charleston*. Columbia: University of South Carolina Press, 1995.

Cran, Marion. *Gardens in America*. New York: Macmillan, 1932.

Daniel, Pete, and Raymond Spock. *A Talent for Detail*. New York: Harmony Books, 1974. [Frances Benjamin Johnston]

Dean, Ruth. *The Livable House: Its Garden*. New York: Moffat, Yard, 1917.

DeNevi, Donald, and Thomas Moulin. *Gabriel Moulin's San Francisco Peninsula: Town & Country Homes, 1910–1920*. Sausalito, Calif.: Windgate Press, 1985.

Desmond, Harry W., and Herbert Croly. *Stately Homes in America from Colonial Times*. New York: D. Appleton, 1903.

Dobyns, Winifred Starr. *California Gardens*. Foreword by Myron Hunt. New York: Macmillan, 1931.

Dolkart, Andrew. *The Row House Reborn: Architecture and Neighborhoods in New York City, 1908–1929*. Baltimore: Johns Hopkins University Press, 2009.

Edwards, Rebecca. *New Spirits: Americans in the Gilded Age, 1865–1905*. New York: Oxford University Press, 2005.

Eliot, Charles N. *Charles Eliot, Landscape Architect*. Amherst: University of Massachusetts Press, 1999.

Elmendorf, Dwight Lathrop. *Lantern Slides: How to Make and Color Them*. New York: E. & H. T. Anthony, 1895.

Emerson, Peter H. *Naturalist Photography for the Student of Art*. New York: Scovill & Adams, 1899.

Gamble, Jeanne M. *Surroundings of Inspiration: The Progressive Era through the Lens of Mary H. Northend, 1904–1926*. Unpublished master's thesis, Harvard University, 2008.

Garnett, Porter. *Stately Homes of California*. Boston: Little, Brown, 1915.

Gentlemen Photographers: The Work of Loring Underwood and Wm. Lyman Underwood. Edited by Robert Lyons. Boston: The Solio Foundation, 1987.

Goodman, Ernestine Abercrombie. *The Garden Club of America: History, 1913–1938*. New York: The Garden Club of America, 1938.

Griswold, Mac, and Eleanor Weller. *The Golden Age of American Gardens*. New York: Harry N. Abrams, 1992.

Hales, Peter Bacon. *Silver Cities: Photographing American Urbanization*. Albuquerque: University of New Mexico Press, 2005.

Hewitt, Mark Alan. *The Architect & the American Country House.* New Haven, Conn.: Yale University Press, 1990.

Hill, Anna Gilman. *Forty Years of Gardening.* New York: Frederick A. Stokes, 1938.

Hill, May Brawley. *Grandmother's Garden: The Old Fashioned American Garden, 1865–1915.* New York: Harry N. Abrams, 1995.

Historic Gardens of Virginia. Edited by Edith Tunis Sale. Richmond, Va.: The James River Garden Club, 1924.

Homes and Gardens in Old Virginia. Edited by Susanne Williams Massie and Frances Archer Christian. Richmond: Garrett & Massie, 1932.

Hubbard, Henry Vincent, and Theodora Kimball. *An Introduction to the Study of Landscape Design.* New York: Macmillan, 1917.

Hunt, John Dixon. *The Afterlife of Gardens.* London: Reaktion Books, 2004.

———. *Gardens and the Picturesque: Studies in the History of Landscape Architecture.* Cambridge, Mass.: MIT Press, 1992.

Johnston, Frances Benjamin. *The White House.* Washington, D.C.: Gibson, 1893.

Jones, Howard Mumford. *The Age of Energy: Varieties of American Experience, 1865–1915.* New York: Viking, 1971.

Jones, Mary Cadwalader. *Lantern Slides.* Privately printed [by Max and Beatrix Jones Farrand], 1937.

Karson, Robin. *A Genius for Place: American Landscapes of the Country Place Era.* Amherst: University of Massachusetts Press, 2007.

King, Mrs. Francis. *Chronicles of the Garden.* New York: Charles Scribner's Sons, 1925.

Klein, William M., Jr. *Gardens of Philadelphia and the Delaware Valley.* Philadelphia: Temple University Press, 1995.

Landscape Design and the Experience of Motion. Edited by Michel Conan. Washington, D.C.: Dumbarton Oaks Research Library and Collections, 2003.

Lawrance, Gary, and Anne Surchin. *Houses of the Hamptons.* New York: Acanthus Press, 2007.

Lazarro, Claudio. *The Italian Renaissance Garden: From the Conventions of Planting, Design and Ornament to the Grand Gardens of Central Italy.* New Haven, Conn.: Yale University Press, 1990.

Lears, Jackson. *Rebirth of a Nation: The Making of Modern America, 1877–1920.* New York: Harper, 2009.

———. *No Place of Grace: Antimodernism and the Transformation of American Culture, 1880–1920.* Chicago: University of Chicago Press, 1994.

Le style Duchêne: Architectes paysagistes, 1841–1947. Edited by Claire Frange et al. Paris: Editions du Labyrinthe, 1998.

Legutko, Emily. *The First 85 Years: A History of the City Gardens Club of New York City, 1918 to 2003.* New York: City Gardens Club of New York City, 2003.

Liberty Hyde Bailey: Essential Agrarian and Environmental Writings. Edited by Zachary Michael Jack. Ithaca, N.Y.: Cornell University Press, 2008.

Liserre, Francesca Romana. *Giardini anglo-fiorentini: Il Rinascimento all'inglese di Cecil Pinsent.* Florence: Angelo Pontecorboli, 2008.

Long Island Country Houses and Their Architects. Edited by Robert B. MacKay, Anthony Baker, and Carol A. Traymor. New York: Society for the Preservation of Long Island Antiquities in association with W. W. Norton, 2009.

Manoni, Laurent and Donata Presenti Campagnoni. *Lanterne magique et film peint.* Paris: Editions de la Martinère, 2009,

Martineau, Mrs. Philip [Alice]. *Gardening in Sunny Lands.* Introduction by Edith Wharton. New York: D. Appleton, 1924.

———. *The Herbaceous Garden.* London: Williams & Norgate, 1917.

May, Lary. *Screening Out the Past.* Chicago: University of Chicago Press, 1983.

Morgan, Keith. *Shaping an American Landscape: The Art and Architecture of Charles A. Platt.* Hanover, N.H.: University Press of New England, 1995.

Morrison, Ernest. *J. Horace McFarland: A Thorn for Beauty.* Harrisburg: Pennsylvania Historical and Museum Commission, 1995.

Myrick, David F. *Montecito and Santa Barbara—Volume I, From Farms to Estates.* Glendale, Calif.: Trans-Anglo Books, 1987.

———. *Montecito and Santa Barbara—Volume II, The Days of the Great Estates.* Glendale, Calif.: Trans-Anglo Books, 1991.

Norwood, Vera. *Made from This Earth: American Women and Nature.* Chapel Hill: University of North Carolina Press, 1993.

The Once & Future Gardener: Garden Writing from the Golden Age of Magazines, 1900–1940. Edited and with an introduction by Virginia Tuttle Clayton. Boston: David R. Godine, 2000.

Panzer, Mary. *In My Studio: Rudolf Eickemeyer, Jr. and the Art of the Camera, 1885–1930.* Yonkers, N.Y.: The Hudson River Museum, 1986.

Pare, Richard. *Photography and Architecture, 1839–1939.* Toronto: Canadian Centre for Architecture, 1982.

Pauly, Philip J. *Fruits and Plains: The Horticultural Transformations of America.* Cambridge, Mass.: Harvard University Press, 2007.

Pereire, Anita, and Gabrielle van Zuylen. *Jardins Privés en France.* Paris: Arthaud, 1984.

Phelps, Harriet Jackson. *Newport in Flower.* Newport, R.I.: The Preservation Society of Newport County, 1979.

Platt, Charles Adams. *Italian Gardens.* With an overview by Keith N. Morgan. Portland, Ore.: Sagapress/Timber Press, 1993.

Pollution and Reform in American Cities, 1870–1930. Edited by Martin V. Melosi. Austin: University of Texas Press, 1980.

Rainey, Sue. *Creating Picturesque America*. Nashville, Tenn.: Vanderbilt University Press, 1994.

Riis, Jacob A. *How the Other Half Lives: Studies among the Tenements of New York* (1890). New York: Hill and Wang, 1957.

Riley, Charles A., II. *Color Codes: Modern Theories of Color in Philosophy, Painting and Architecture, Literature, Music, and Philosophy*. Lebanon, N.H.: University of New England Press, 1995.

Scott, Anne Firor. *Natural Allies: Women's Associations in American History*. Urbana: University of Illinois Press, Illini Books edition, 1993.

Shelton, Louise. *Beautiful Gardens in America*. New York: Charles Scribner's Sons, 1915, and revised edition, 1924.

Streatfield, David C. *California Gardens: Creating a New Eden*. New York: Abbeville Press, 1994.

Stein, Roger. *John Ruskin and Aesthetic Thought in America, 1840–1900*. Cambridge, Mass.: Harvard University Press, 1967.

Tankard, Judith. *Beatrix Farrand: Private Gardens, Public Spaces*. New York: Monacelli Press, 2010.

———— and Martin Wood. *Gertrude Jekyll at Munstead Wood: Writing, Horticulture, Photography, Homebuilding*. Sagaponack, N.Y.: Sagapress, 1996.

Tomsich, John. *A Genteel Endeavor: American Culture and Politics in the Gilded Age*. Stanford, Calif.: Stanford University Press, 1974.

Ulmann, Doris. *A Portrait Gallery of American Editors*. New York: William Edwin Rudge, 1925.

Veblen, Thorstein. *The Theory of the Leisure Class: An Economic Study of Institutions*. New York: Macmillan, 1899.

Watters, Sam. *The Houses of Los Angeles*, vol. 1, *1885–1919*, and vol. 2, *1920–1935*. New York: Acanthus Press, 2007.

Waugh, Frank A. *Book of Landscape Gardening*. Amherst: University of Massachusetts Press, 2007. Reprint of 1926 edition.

Way, Thaïsa. *Unbounded Practice: Women and Landscape Architecture in the Early Twentieth Century*. Richmond: University of Virginia Press, 2009.

Weiss, Elaine F. *Fruits of Victory: The Woman's Land Army of America in the Great War*. Washington, D.C.: Potomac Books, 2008.

Wexler, Laura. *Tender Violence: Domestic Visions in an Age of U.S. Imperialism*. Chapel Hill: University of North Carolina Press, 2000.

Wharton, Edith. *Italian Gardens and Their Villas*. New York: The Century Co., 1904.

Wiebe, Robert H. *The Search for Order, 1877–1920*. New York: Hill and Wang, 1967.

Wood, John. *The Art of the Autochrome: The Birth of Color Photography*. Iowa City: University of Iowa Press, 1993.

Zaitzevsky, Cynthia. *Long Island Landscapes and the Women Who Designed Them*. New York: Society for the Preservation of Long Island Antiquities in association with W. W. Norton, 2009.

ARTICLES AND BOOK CHAPTERS

Beals, Jessie Tarbox. "The Garden Photographer." In *Careers for Women*, edited by Catherine Filene, 63-66. Boston: Houghton Mifflin, 1920.

Benjamin, Walter. "A Short History of Photography" (1931). In *Classic Essays on Photography*, edited by Alan Trachtenberg, 199–216. New Haven, Conn.: Lette's Island Books, 1980.

Benton, Megan. "'Too Many Books': Book Ownership and Cultural Identify in the 1920s." *American Quarterly* 49, no. 2 (June 1997): 268–97.

Bushong, William B. "Frances Benjamin Johnston's White House." In *The White House: Actors and Observers*, edited by William Seale, 97–103. Boston: Northwestern University Press, 2002.

"The Camera Has Opened a New Profession for Women—Some of Those Who Have Made Good." *The New York Times*, April 20, 1913, p. 12.

Champa, Kermit Swiller. "Painted Responses to Music: The Landscapes of Corot and Manet." In *The Arts Entwined: Music and Painting in the Nineteenth Century*, edited by Marsha L. Morton and Peter L. Schmunk, 101–18. New York: Garland, 2000

Clark, Bertha A. "The Society of Little Gardens." *Bulletin of The Garden Club of America*, no. 2, new series (January 1920), 44–45.

————. "The Society of Little Gardens." *The House Beautiful* 41, no. 2 (January 1917): 72–75; 102.

Davidson, Rebecca Warren. "The Spirit of the American Garden: Landscape and Cultural Expression in the Work of Martha Brookes Hutcheson." *Journal of the New England Garden History Society* 4 (Spring 1996): 22–29

Deverell, William. "Convalescence and California: The Civil War Comes West." *Southern California Quarterly* 90, no. 1 (Spring 2008): 1–26.

Doherty, Ann S. "Frances Benjamin Johnston, 1864–1952." *History of Photography* 4, no. 2 (April 1980): 97–111.

"Garden Photography as a Fine Art: Illustrated by Rare Photographs of Beautiful Gardens." *The Touchstone* 2, no. 3 (December 1917): 278–87.

Eldredge, Arthur G. "Photographing the Garden." *Photo-Era* 33, no. 1 (July 1914): 3–8.

Gaston, Diana. "Picturing Domestic Space: Clara E. Sipprell and the American Arts and Crafts Movement." *Image* 38, no. 3–4 (Fall–Winter 1995): 16–29.

Gebhard, David. "The Myth and Power of Place." In *Modern Regionalism, Referential Regionalism,* edited by Vincent B. Canizaro, 194–203. New York: Princeton Architectural Press, 2007.

Gerdts, William H. "The Artist's Garden: American Floral Painting. 1850–1915." *Portfolio* 4, no. 4 (July-August 1982): 44-51.

———. "The Teaching of Painting Out-of-Doors in America in the Late Nineteenth Century." *In Nature's Ways: American Landscape Painting of the Late Nineteenth Century.* Edited by William H. Gerdts and Bruce Weber, 25-40. Exhibition catalog. Norton Gallery of Art: West Palm Beach, Fla., 1987.

Gertz, Belinda. "The Garden Colorist." *The Architectural Record* 52, no. 1 (July 1922): 44–45.

Hannum, Gillian Greenhill. "Frances Benjamin Johnston: Promoting Women Photographers in *The Ladies' Home Journal.*" *Nineteenth Century* 24, no. 2 (Fall 2004): 22–29.

Harris, Diane. "Cultivating Power: The Language of Feminism in Garden Literature, 1870–1920." *Landscape Journal* 13, no. 2 (1994): 113–23.

Hartford, Pamela. "Poet behind the Lens," *View,* no. 10 (Summer 2010): 25–27. [Arthur G. Eldredge]

Hawthorne, Hildegarde. "Color in California." *The Touchstone and The American Student Magazine* 8, no. 4 (January 1921): 276–79.

Helder, Arthur H., "What a City Garden Club May Do." *The American City* 16, no. 3 (January–June 1916): 264–65.

Hill, May Brawley. "The Art of Gardens: Visions of the Garden by Women Painters, Photographers, and Garden Writers in the South, 1865–1915." *Influence of Women on the Southern Landscape: Proceedings of the Tenth Conference on Restoring Southern Gardens and Landscapes.* Old Salem, Winston-Salem, October 5–7, 1995. Winston-Salem, N.C.: Old Salem, 100–118.

Hodgdon, Jeannette B. "Back Yard or Garden?" *The House Beautiful* 79, no. 3 (March 1931): 248–51, 308, 311.

Hood, Davyd Foard. "'To Gather Up the Fragments That Remain:' Southern Garden Clubs and the Publication of Southern Garden History, 1923–1939." *The Influence of Women on the Southern Landscape: Proceedings of the Tenth Conference on Restoring Southern Gardens and Landscapes.* October 5–7, 1995. Winston–Salem, N.C., 1995, 172–95.

———. "The Renaissance of Southern Gardening in the Early Twentieth Century." *Journal of Garden History* 16, no. 2 (Summer 1996): 129–52.

Impertinence, Miss. "They Photograph the Smart Set." *Vanity Fair* 69, no. 1218 (December 14, 1912): 18. [Frances Benjamin Johnston and Mattie Edwards Hewitt]

Isler-de-Jongh, Ariane. "The Origins of Colour Photography." *History of Photography* 18, no. 2 (Summer 1994): 111–19.

Johnston, Frances Benjamin. "A'Dobe Trophy House." *Country Life in America* 36, no. 4 (August 1919): 54–55. [John Henry Fisher]

———. "Château de Bréau, Dammarie-lès-Lys." *Town & Country* 82, no. 3958 (April 1, 1927): 74–77.

———. "Château d'Ussé, Near Tours." "*Town & Country* 81, no. 3942 (August 15, 1926): 56–59.

———. "Les Colombières at Menton-Garvan." *Town & Country* 82, no. 3966 (August 15, 1927): 56–59.

——— "The Country of Sheridan's Ride." *The Ladies' Home Journal* 18, no. 8 (July 1901): 16–17.

———. "The Country Seat of Moses Taylor Pyne." *Town & Country* 66, no. 3409 (September 16, 1911): 26.

———. "Flower Gardens as Usual in 1918." *Gardeners' Chronicle of America* 22, no. 1 (January 1918): 56.

———. "Garden of Mrs. William. S. Kies at Scarborough, New York." *The Garden Magazine* 37, no. 4 (June 1923): 262–63.

———. "Garden Pools of California." *Harper's Bazar* 53, no. 1 (January 1918): 20–21.

———. "A Garden Set by the Sea: The Estate of John S. Kennedy." *Vogue* 58, no. 1 (July 1, 1921): 65, 98.

———. "Gardens in a City Environment." *New York Sun,* December 19, 1922.

———. "The Gardens of a Garden Spot." *Santa Barbara Community Life* 1, no. 9 (September 1923): 3–6.

———. "Gardens of the Pacific." *Bulletin of The Garden Club of America* 14, new series (November 1923): 17–20.

———. "Hammersmith Farm." *Town & County* 54, no. 7 (July 1919): 64.

———. "The Mellow Charm of an Old-Fashioned Garden." *Vogue* 58, no. 7 (October 1, 1921): 73, 100. [Charles W. Moseley]

———. "Mrs. Käsebier, Professional Photographer." *Camera Work,* 1, no. 1 (1903): 10.

———. "The New Tenants of the White House." *The Ladies' Home Journal* 14, no. 11 (October 1897): 3.

———. "Notice for City Gardens Club of New York." *Gardeners' Chronicle of America,* 26, no. 2 (February 1922): 245–46.

———. "Painting the Rainbow in a Tulip Garden." *Vogue* 57, no. 6 (April 15, 1921): 63, 96. [Ogden Mills]

———. "Pavilion Colombe at Saint-Brice-Sous-Forêt." *Town & Country* 82, no. 3963 (July 1, 1927): 34–37.

———. "Rose Gardens of America." *Art and Life* 10, no. 6 (June 1919): 303–7.

———. "Some Homes under the Administration: Sen. Hearst of California." *Demorest's Family Magazine* 26, no. 12 (October 1890): 713–20.

———. "Some White House Orchids." *Demorest's Family Magazine* 31, no. 8 (June 1895): 432–38.

———. "Thornedale, the Country Estate of Mr. Oakleigh Thorne." *Harper's Bazar* 55, no. 6 (June 1920): 6–7.

———. "Vaux-le-Vicomte, Near Melun." *Town & Country* 82, no. 3974 (December 15, 1927): 74–77.

———. "What a Woman Can Do with a Camera." *The Ladies' Home Journal* 14, no. 10 (September 1897): 6–7.

Kagan, Andrew. "Ut Pictura Musica, 1: To 1860." *Arts Magazine* 60 (May 1986): 86–91.

Leighton, Howard B. "The Lantern Slide and Art History." *History of Photography* 8, no. 2 (April–June 1984): 107–19.

Libby, Valencia. "The Pennsylvania School of Horticulture for Women." *Journal of the New England Garden History Society* 10 (Fall 2002): 44–52.

Linn, Eva. "Comfortable Haven: The Garden Writing of Ruth B. Dean." *Journal of the New England Garden History Society* 3 (Fall 1993): 34–38.

Lummis, Charles F. "The Greatest California Patio House." Photographs by Frances Benjamin Johnston. *Country Life in America* 6, no. 6 (October 1904): 533–40. [Phoebe A. Hearst, California]

McFarland, J. Horace. "Country Life Photographs," *Country Life in America* 1, no. 2 (December 1901): 53.

———. "The Passing of a Great Rosarian." In *The American Rose Annual*, 53–58. Harrisburg, Pa.: American Rose Society, 1919. [Rear Admiral Aaron Ward]

Moore, Dorethea. "The Work of the Women's Clubs in California." *Annals of the American Academy of Political and Social Science* 28 (September 1906): 59–62.

Moore, William J. *Fun with Fritz: Adventures in Early Redlands, Big Bear and Hollywood, with John H. "Fritz" Fisher.* Redlands, Calif.: Moore Historical Foundation, 1986.

"Mrs. Hewitt, Photographer of Homes." *Christian Science Monitor*, December 22, 1923.

Nevins, Deborah. "The Triumph of Flora: Women and American Landscape, 1890–1935." *Antiques* 127 (April 1985): 904–22.

Rogers, George C. "Gardens and Landscapes in Eighteenth-Century South Carolina," *British and American Gardens in the Eighteenth Century*, edited by Robert MacCubbin. Williamsburg: The Colonial Williamsburg Foundation, 1984.

Ronstrom, Maud O'Brien. "60 Years with a 'Shadow-Box.'" *The Times-Picayune New Orleans States Magazine*, November 2, 1947, pp. 8–9. [Frances Benjamin Johnston interview]

Roorbach, Eloise J. "Making a City Backyard Garden: Experiences of the Touchstone Garden Editor." *The Touchstone* 3, no. 6 (September 1918): 480–88.

Schnare, Susan E. "Woman Garden Writers: 'Gardening, Reading about Gardening, and Writing about Gardening Are All One.'" *Proceedings of the Tenth Conference on Restoring Southern Gardens and Landscapes.* Old Salem, Winston-Salem, October 5–7, 1995. Winston-Salem, N.C.: Old Salem, 83–99.

Seaton, Beverly. "Gardening Books for the Commuter's Wife, 1900–1937." *Landscape Journal* 13, no. 2 (1994): 113–23.

"Speaking of Pictures … These Are by a U.S. 'Court Photographer.'" *Life* 26, no. 17 (April 25, 1949): 13–15. [Frances Benjamin Johnston]

Steele, Fletcher. "Color Charts for Gardeners." *The Garden Magazine* 33, no. 3 (March 1921): 185–86.———. "The Secrets of Garden Furnishings." *Vogue* 45, no. 9 (May 1, 1915): 47–48, 68.

Stein, Sally. "Autochromes without Apologies: Heinrich Kühn's Experiments with the Mechanical Palette." *History of Photography* 18, no. 2 (Summer 1994): 129–33.

Tankard, Judith B. "Ellen Biddle Shipman's Colonial Revival Style." In *Recreating the American Past: Essays on the Colonial Revival*, edited by Richard Guy Wilson, Shaun Eyring, and Kenny Marotta, 67-82. Richmond: University of Virginia Press, 2006. [Chatham house, Virginia]

Tuggle, Catherine T. "Edward Steichen and the Autochrome, 1907–1909." *History of Photography* 18, no. 2 (Summer 1994): 145–47.

Vanderbilt, Paul. "Frances Benjamin Johnston, 1864–1952," June 6, 1952, Photographic Archives Report, Manuscript Division, Library of Congress.

Veder, Robin. "Color Gardens before Color Photography." *Cabinet*, no. 6 (Spring 2002): 72–75.

Vom Baur, Eva. "Frances Benjamin Johnston, Mattie Edwards Hewitt." *Wilson's Photographic Magazine* 50, no. 6 (June 1913): 241–53.

Watts, Jennifer A. "Frances Benjamin Johnston: The Huntington Portrait Collection." *History of Photography* 19, no. 3 (Fall 1995): 252–62.

Waugh, Frank A. "The Camera as an Art Accessory." *American Photography* 30, no. 10 (October 1936): 648–55.

———. "Photographic Diversions of a Landscape Architect." *Photo-Era Magazine* 47, no 1. (July–December 1921): 26–27.

Wilson, Richard Guy. "Architecture and the Reinterpretation of the Past in the American Renaissance." In *American Architectural History: A Contemporary Reader*, edited by Keith L. Eggener, 227–46. London: Routledge, 2004.

Acknowledgments

Frances Benjamin Johnston's confidence in the Library of Congress as the final repository of her archive was well founded. Throughout this challenging project, experts generously shared their collective history of the Johnston collections and supported with patience the challenges at hand: Beverly W. Brennan, Karen Chittenden, Mary Christ, Gay Colyer, Verna Posever Curtis, Ralph Eubanks, Jeffrey M. Flannery, Janice Grenci, Marilyn Ibach, Charls Jenkins, Carol Johnson, Phil Michel, Barbara Orbach Natanson, C. Ford Peatross, and the guiding spirit Helena Zinkham made the online catalog and this book possible.

Just as FBJ owed her success to the support of The Garden Club of America and its associated members, so do I owe my understanding of the club's founding years to Edith Loening, the national club's archivist who with unfailing patience and knowledge researched club records to answer inquiries that emerged slowly over years. I am indebted to club member and author Arete S. Warren for her warm encouragement the day I first stepped presumptuously into the club's New York office.

Gary Hammond and George Fisher at the Nassau County Museum of Art, Roslyn Harbor, New York, have supported this FBJ project since 2008 as I recreated, as possible, the Mattie Edwards Hewitt archive to date and identify early Johnston photographs. Their scanning and cataloging of the Hewitt and, as it turns out, Johnston–Hewitt photographs in their museum's collection will answer old questions and pose new ones.

For research on Grace Adele Smith Anderson and related issues, I thank Jeff Opt and his colleague Curt Dalton, at the NCR Archive, Dayton History, Dayton, Ohio.

The identification of photographs and lantern slides came with support from archivists, librarians, curators, and scholars in the 15 states and four countries where Johnston photographed. I am grateful to all of them for pursuing minute clues and hunches to identify images and resolve quandaries in a project that by necessity will be ongoing. In particular, Catherine M. Anders, Lyndhurst, Tarrytown, New York; Edward R. Bosley, Gamble House, Pasadena, California; Joseph C. Bright; Leslie Buhler and Wendy Kail, Tudor Place Historic House & Garden, Washington, D.C.; C. Thomas Chapman, James Madison's Montpelier, Orange, Virgina; Erin Chase, Jennifer Goldman, and Melanie Thorpe, Huntington Library, Art Collections and Botanical Gardens, San Marino, California; Laurie Collins and Mary Cummings, Southampton Historical Museum, Southampton, New

York; Laura Condon, Society for the Preservation of New England Antiquities, Boston, Massachusetts: Joyce Connolly and Kelly Crawford, Archives of American Gardens, Smithsonian Institution, Washington, D.C.; Douglas Cordell, Los Angeles County Museum of Art, Los Angeles, California; Cesare M. Cunaccia; Mary F. Daniels, Frances Loeb Library, Harvard University Graduate School of Design, Cambridge, Massachusetts; Steve Davidson, National Society Daughters of the American Revolution, Washington, D.C.; Casimir de Blacas; Paul D. Dolinsky, the Historic American Landscapes Survey, Washington, D.C.; Dr. Michael S. Dosmann, Arnold Arboretum, Brookline, Massachusetts; Brad Emerson; Robin A. Everly, Botany-Horticultural Library, National Museum of Natural History, Washington, D.C.; Jeanne M. Gamble; James B. Garrison; Jordon Goffin, Rhode Island Historical Society, Providence, Rhode Island; Elena Grant; Dr. Alain Gruber; Miranda Hambro and Jason Miller, Environmental College of Design, University of California, Berkeley, California; Ward Hill; Carol F. Humstone, The City Gardens Club of New York City; Jack Judson; Michael Kathrens; Danielle Kovacs, W. E. B. Du Bois Library, University of Massachusetts, Amherst, Massachusetts; Dan Wayne Krall, Cornell University, Ithaca, New York; Gary M. Lawrance; Zach Lemle; Adina Lerner, Santa Monica Public Library, Santa Monica, California; Jim Lewis; Maggie Lidz, Winterthur, Wilmington, Delaware; Marie Long and Donald Wheeler, LuEsther T. Mertz Library, New York Botanical Garden, Bronx, New York; Barbara Mathé and Gregory August Raml, Museum of Natural History, New York, New York; Kelly McAnnaney, the New York Historical Society, New York, New

York; William Morrison; Jenny Namsiriwan, Maryland Historical Society, Baltimore, Maryland; Maureen O'Rourke, New Jersey Historical Society, Newark, New Jersey; William Peniston; Tracy Potter, Massachusetts Historical Society, Boston, Massachusetts; Katherine Powis and Joan Nichols, New York Horticultural Society, New York, New York; Colvin Randall, Longwood Gardens, Kennett Square, Delaware; Jamie Kingman Rice, Maine Historical Society, Portland, Maine; Susan Rissover; Tom Roll; Ian Schlesinger; Earle Shettleworth; Chris Sonne, Tuxedo Historical Society, Tuxedo Park, New York; Charlotte Tancin and Angela Todd, Hunt Institute for Botanical Documentation, Pittsburgh, Pennsylvania; Carol M. Tobin, University Library, University of North Carolina, Chapel Hill; Candace Vanderlip; and Anne Young, Greenwich Historical Society, Greenwich, Connecticut.

Angela Wesley Hardin, Nancy Sherman, and Dalia Stoniene at Acanthus Press, contributed to the publishing of this book.

Frances Benjamin Johnston's life was enriched by the East, West, and Europe. And so is mine, by Gary Cowles, Rebecca Gale, Patrice Marandel, Ruth Sachs, John Willenbecher, and Montague Yudelman.

To Erika Esau, for her unfailing encouragement and knowledge; to Joyce Ashley, William Deverell, Ulysses Grant Dietz, Richard and Susan Levine, Silvia Gaspardo Moro and Charles Ray, Charlotte Mayerson, Jessica and Derick Snare, and Jennifer A. Watts, thank you for seeing me through in your unique ways. To Barry Cenower, words are indeed never enough; to Jane I. Trimble, Paul Micio and David, Alice and Dino Bob Eidenberg, you all make home more beautiful.

Index

Page numbers in *italics* refer to illustrations

Frances Benjamin Johnston advanced her garden photograph career by sustaining contacts with cultural and financial leaders of her time, and by visiting, with seemingly boundless energy, gardens across two continents. Alphabetically ordered in three sections, this index reflects the breath of Johnston's professional social world, the geographic range of her work, and the diversity of subjects she addressed in photographs and lectures.

GARDENS, EXPOSITIONS, AND LOCATIONS

Institute of Classical Architecture & Art

The Classical America Series
1982–2012